First Marathons

First Marathons

Personal Encounters
with the
26.2-Mile Monster

Edited by Gail Waesche Kislevitz

BREAKAWAY BOOKS
NEW YORK CITY
1998

First Marathons: Personal Encounters with the 26.2-Mile Monster
Compilation and introduction copyrights © 1998 by Gail Waesch Kislevitz

ISBN: 1-55821-673-1
Library of Congress Catalog Card Number: 98-70674

Published by BREAKAWAY BOOKS
P.O. Box 1109
Ansonia Station
New York, NY 10023

(212) 595-2216
(800) 548-4348

FIRST EDITION

CONTENTS

This book is dedicated to Beatrice Maleady Waesche,
whose wisdom and love still guide me to this day.
She is always by my side.

ACKNOWLEDGMENTS

IT'S DIFFICULT TO KNOW WHERE TO BEGIN when thanking others who have been part of a process that germinated so long ago. Certainly, a big thanks goes to my family and friends who gave me much-needed support in terms of reading rough drafts, making suggestions, networking for prospective interviewees, and knowing just when I needed an emotional lift with the simple words, "Hey, how's the book coming?" I'm still not sure whether it was a good idea to ask my dad to edit some of the original stories, as the glaring red pencil marks brought me back to the agonizing days of high school when he would check my homework and refuse to understand that a three-hundred-word composition needed lots of adjectives.

I'd also be remiss if I didn't mention Peggy Schmidt, who gave me my first break in writing and also encouraged me to enter my first Central Park road race. Adam Bean, senior editor at *Runner's World,* is another person I'd like to credit with giving me a break and believing in my book. E.B. also deserves a heartfelt thanks for getting me to run my first marathon and has been my running partner ever since. I never told Garth Battista, my editor and publisher, that I don't like Chinese food when he suggested that we meet in a Chinese restaurant for our first meeting to discuss the book. It didn't matter. I was too nervous anyway. He believed in this project from the start and I am forever grateful to him. He has an abundance of patience and probably a strained eardrum from all my phone calls asking if everything was moving along as expected.

The most important people to thank are the inspirational people who make up this book and who shared a part of their lives with me. They entrusted me with their stories, and I hope I have lived up to that trust. I spent many anxious moments waiting for their comments and ultimate approval of the interviews. My biggest fear was not in meeting deadlines, but in representing them in the best light possible. They all took on a challenge, sometimes against great odds, that not only changed their lives, but perhaps can help others change theirs as well. We laughed together, cried together, and whenever possible, met in bars, restaurants, homes, and parks to share running stories. I will never forget meeting Sandy Zanchi at the twenty-mile mark of the East Lyme Marathon. I was just thinking how I would like to interview someone from Kentucky, when she appeared by my side and asked, in that distinctive accent, what the last six miles of the course was like. And then there was the midnight call from Roger Jones asking if I was the writer collecting first marathon stories, because he had one he wanted to share in the hope that others with a smoking habit would realize that running could save their lives.

I'd also like to acknowledge the openness, warmth, and genuine congeniality I experienced with my elite runners. It was somewhat intimidating at first making cold calls to legends. I thought I'd have to run the gauntlet of red tape, screening agents, months between inquiries, and outright rejection. Each one of them returned my phone call in person, and they were all accessible, accommodating, and fun people to be with. They are true ambassadors of their sport, and have sacrificed many years and many more miles then I will ever run in a lifetime to bring the marathon to its world-class status as a spectator and participatory event. Allan Steinfeld, Amelia Hill, and Dick Traum also offered invaluable support and help and were a great source of encouragement.

I also want to acknowledge Androc, Elijah, and Anna, for being my daily source of inspiration. They fill my life with humor, love, and passion, and I am blessed with their presence. Hey guys, it doesn't get better than this!

INTRODUCTION

GAIL WAESCHE KISLEVITZ

"If you have the passion, you have the power."

I HAD ALREADY BEEN POUNDING PAVEMENT for twenty-four years when I made the decision to run my first marathon. Growing up in the late sixties when women's sports was called cheerleading, I had no formal training in running techniques. I just ran, pure and simple. I ran for the joy of it, the thrill of it, the escape of it. During college, I played lacrosse because there wasn't a women's track team and it seemed like the next best thing to do. But I still remained faithful to my daily run. I ran through the bitter-cold winters of Michigan during graduate school, through two pregnancies and countless other miles that seem to blend into one long life's run.

I don't know when I made the transformation from running as a sport to running as part of my life. I can't separate the two. When I run, my mind and body fuse together, creating an energy source that empowers me. It is my private time, my therapy, my religion.

Ultimately I had to test myself, to see just how far I could go. I wanted to train correctly, so I bought running books filled with important information: training routines, nutrition guides, stretching techniques, injury prevention, speed work, pace and performance guidelines. Everything I needed to know about the technical aspects of running a marathon, except the most important thing to me—its soul. No book took on the task of describing the feeling, the heart, the core of a marathon. What would it be like? What would I feel out there? Would I hit the mythical wall? Could the last six miles be so difficult? This was the information I craved.

I spoke with friends (and strangers) who had run marathons. They answered my questions with such passion, such fever and excitement for the event that I was mesmerized. I inhaled their stories as they captured every moment of the race: the lows of utter despair and pain, the highs of inner strength. They became my role models.

That was the beginning of this book. I am going to let runners speak for themselves—famous runners, unknowns, fast and slow, old and young. Through their experiences, you will feel the pain and the glory of running the marathon. Their lives have been changed forever.

When the late Fred Lebow, founding father of the New York City Marathon, was asked why people run marathons, he responded: "I think the real reasons are very personal. I think it is because we need to test our physical, emotional and creative abilities." All of that and more goes into the decision to tackle the marathon. Why do people put themselves through incredible physical and mental trauma, risk their health, endure subliminal allegations of insanity from family and friends, crawl out of a warm bed at five in the morning to run in the dark, the cold, the rain, the sleet, the snow, the scorching hot sun? Why do topics such as interval training, toenails, hamstrings, and fluid intake creep into our vernacular and eventually consume our conversations—and no one else cares?

The people you are about to meet can shed some light on this mystery. After reading their stories, you will understand why they run. Some of these people I've known for years, others for hours. But, one of the beautiful intangibles about runners is the bond we share. Like pregnant women, first-time dads, cancer patients, or recovering alcoholics, we share a deep-rooted commonality. We've been there. We've suffered the pain, felt the glory, and, when all the sweat is spent, we have the faith to reach deep inside to find that ounce of energy left in our heels, our heart, our soul, to carry us across the finish line stiff legged and fatigue racked, but with a smile of victory.

We are not ordinary people; we are extraordinary people. We are believers. George Sheehan, the philosopher-king of runners, summed it up best: "We are here to be heroes. The marathon is the one way we prove it to ourselves. . . . The marathon is a theater for heroism, the common man and an uncommon challenge. [It shows] the extraordinary powers of ordinary people." When you come to understand the mind and soul of a runner, you'll realize it's not about the miles logged, the races won or lost. It's the passion that drives us. Passion is running and running is passion. They are inseparable. And if you have that passion, whether it's to run around the block or around the town, you have the power to go the distance.

I interviewed dozens of people for this book and these are their own words, recorded, transcribed, and edited into flowing narratives.

There are hundreds of thousands of such stories just waiting to be told by proud first-timers (and marathon veterans). When I traveled to Connecticut to conduct one of my interviews, the man who answered the door greeted me with a huge hug and said, "I've been waiting for someone to tell my story to for three years and now I've found you." We talked for hours and by the end of the day we were no longer strangers.

Share your story with everyone. And if your friends and family get tired of hearing it, write to me!

Marathon Stories
c/o Breakaway Books
Box 1109 Ansonia Station
New York, NY 10023

SISTER ACT

KIM AHRENS
RESIDENCE: BIRMINGHAM, ALABAMA
OCCUPATION: DISTRICT REPRESENTATIVE, NATURE'S WAY
FIRST MARATHON: 1994 ST. GEORGE (UT) MARATHON
DATE OF BIRTH: 3-3-70
AGE AT FIRST MARATHON: 24

Kim grew up in a "family comes first" environment, so it seemed a natural decision to want her sister by her side when she ran her first marathon. In fact, the entire family became part of the experience. However, with Kim living in Salt Lake City and her sister in Minnesota, they needed to devise a creative way to train together. They worked out a plan that carried them across the finish line in a photo finish.

I WAS RAISED IN A VERY ACTIVE FAMILY, always on the go. Being physically fit was one of the values my parents imparted to us early in life. I can remember back to grade school always playing a sport, always being on a team. I signed up for track in high school as it was the easiest team to join; no cuts and everyone is guaranteed a position. My first event was the javelin and shot put, but at 5'8" and 120 pounds, I just wasn't strong enough. I tried lifting weights but it was obvious I couldn't compete against girls weighing in at two-hundred-plus pounds who were throwing twice as hard as me. My coach suggested I try running instead and it was the best advice I ever got. I started doing the eight-hundred-meter run and was pretty good at it. Then I tried cross country and fell in love with running. I liked going the distance (three miles) instead of looping around a track all afternoon, and the team support was incredible. It was a great group of girls and guys. We'd run through golf courses, around lakes, all over town. It was fun! There wasn't as much pressure as the field events. The only downside to the team was the coach. He did not like women. It was obvious in every aspect of his coaching. Basically, I think he was a misogynist. The guys were definitely his favorite and he referred to the girls as "candy asses." If a girl complained of an injury he would say she was trying to avoid running and give her a guilt trip. But if a guy was injured he'd be sent to the trainer. By the time I finished high school, I was burned out and stopped running for two years. The other thing I noticed about running in high school is that no one ever promoted it as a lifelong pursuit, something to do as enjoyment, not just a competitive sport. I had no idea people ran after their school years were over. I definitely think the high school coaches should take the opportunity to educate runners that this is a sport that will take them through life.

After high school, I went to Montana State University and tried to get back to running, but I had let myself get out of shape and it's really hard to get over that hump, to get back the endurance and mental habit of getting out the door. I really missed running, but just couldn't pull myself back into a routine. Finally, I joined the cross-country team my senior year and realized how much I had missed it. I had been addicted to running, then stopped cold turkey. Maybe it was the competitive nature of high school sports, or maybe it was the memory of that horrible coach yelling, "Get out there and run or else," but as much as it was a relief to stop it was also a relief to start again.

The other reason I resumed running again was my sister. She was one grade below me at Montana State and when she started running that was the incentive I needed. We shared an apartment at school and we're very close. Running with her brought back all the fun, the reason I fell in love with it in the first place. After college I got married and moved to Salt Lake City. I wanted to continue running but didn't know anyone or any place to run. My husband doesn't run, we were new to the city, had no family or friends as yet, and I really needed to be around runners, other people who understood the addiction to running. Out of desperation, I went into a running store and asked where I could hook up with like-minded runners. At the time I didn't know anything about running clubs or organizations, but it was suggested I join the Salt Lake City Track Club. It was the best thing I ever did. I met a group of people that I am still close with today. The Salt Lake City group tended to be very laid back and relaxed. I liked that. I felt like I found my home away from home. My coworkers and nonrunning friends, even my husband, tend to think I am weird for running. I get tired of defending myself, of trying to make them understand what it means to me. With my running friends, I don't have to go through all that. It's a commonality we all share, a bond I don't have with anyone else. We also share the same compulsive personality: We don't let any grass grow under our feet, we're too busy running! I tried to share this passion with my husband, to bring him along, but at 7 A.M. on a Saturday morning he'd rather be in bed than join me at a local 5K event. Sometimes I'd be at a race, running my heart out and thinking, "What am I doing here? My husband is home in bed and I could be lying next to him. Am I crazy?" Then I'd see my running buddies and I knew I was doing the right thing. The camaraderie is wonderful. We share training tips, correct each others' form, watch out for each other, cheer for each other. And the closer we got, training tips turned into tips for life in general.

We concentrated on road races, mostly 5Ks and 10Ks. Road racing was a big deal out there and I really enjoyed that aspect of running. It brought back my high school days. Some of the members had run marathons and whenever they spoke about it, I'd get interested. They encouraged me to try one, in fact they were training for one coming up in six months. I was very tempted, but first I had to discuss it with my sister. Distance hadn't put a dent in our relationship and I spoke with her often. When I started to talk about running a marathon, she reminded me that back in high school I kept a Franklin Planner with a list of my goals, my ambitions, my dreams. And on that list was to run a marathon. I don't even think I knew what a marathon was, but it sounded good. It was right there, lodged between my expectation of a first-year salary and going on a safari. I also classified my entries into categories of Reality, Far-Fetched, Dreams, and Fantasies. The marathon was somewhere between Reality and Fantasy and beside the entry I wrote, "If I could do that, it would be incredible!" My sister also reminded me that I mentioned it to her in college. So the desire was in my sub-conscious for quite a while. We spoke about it in length and made the decision to run the St. George Marathon in Utah, the same one my club was training for.

I started training with six months to go and a 5K base. No problem. The decision to run a marathon was based on the desire to go for the ultimate challenge. Realistically I didn't know whether I could do it so I was up for the competition. And after my sister decided to run with me, the thought of seeing her in St. George, Utah, was great. I really missed her and I knew that to do this incredible challenge with her by my side would be something I would remember forever. And I also knew that we wouldn't let each other down, that we could count on each other to get through it. It was a strange concept to train together but far apart. We'd set our goals for the week and then call each other to check on the progress. Our parents were also very supportive, immediately jumping into the excitement and promising to be at the finish for us. This was turning into a family affair.

I decided to run a 5K really fast to test myself. However, it was so painful I wondered how I would ever get through a marathon. This was going to be a long road ahead. I was constantly having doubts. When I told my club members about my doubts, they suggested not to set goals based on time, but just to enjoy it and finish. That was one of the best tips I received.

The training changed my running career forever. I went from thinking a 5K was really long, a 10K too long, and whoever ran marathons was crazy. Now a nice ten-miler makes my day.

The coordinator of our track club, Jency Brown, took me under his wing and became my unofficial coach. He has run at least twenty marathons and introduced me to concepts such as building mileage gradually, taking one long run a week, and having some easy days as well. Our first long run together was a thirteen-miler. When we got to mile eight, I was getting tired but hung in. By mile ten I was starving and getting weak. I hadn't eaten any breakfast because that wasn't my usual routine. I forgot to factor in the amount of energy required to run the thirteen miles. By mile eleven I crashed. I started to walk, and ended up walking the last two miles. By the time I got back to the car I had the shakes. Jency had his doubts about my ability to finish a marathon, but I was too busy eating to hear him. And I was still hungry. My body had never had these types of demands put on it and I couldn't stop eating. Prior to this training, I would get through the day on a thousand calories. But when I started training, I needed to eat every few hours. I started grazing through the day, eating a banana, other types of fruits, some toast, anything quick, nourishing, and fueling. It was a huge learning process for me. Another thing I had to relearn was fluid intake. I never hydrated for short races. The water would just swirl around my stomach. Now I had to drink constantly. And I had to learn how to drink while running. That sounds easy, but it's like rubbing your stomach and patting your head at the same time. It takes practice.

The next month we were finally able to do a twenty-miler. In the meantime, I was talking with my sister about her progress. Since we hadn't run together in a while, I didn't know what her pace was like or anything about her training routines except what we went over on the phone. I worried about holding her up. What if she was faster, or slower? What if one of us couldn't finish? She was training in Minnesota with a totally different type of terrain and altitude. It was stressful wondering if we could in fact run this thing together.

As far as injuries, I was being very careful. One of the benefits of going through a structured high school sports program is learning the basic fundamentals early in your career. I knew the importance of stretching, warm-ups, and cool-downs. I knew how to avoid injuries, although that's not always a guarantee. In high school I did suffer through iliotibial (I.T.) band injuries so I was no stranger to injuries stemming from overtraining. And after the twenty-miler I was stiff and tired and couldn't walk the next day. I didn't plan to run a full twenty-six so the last six miles would remain somewhat of a mystery.

I did another twenty miles a few weeks later, then started to taper my training. I read an article about the three Cs of long distance running: chow, chill, and I can't remember the other C, but I followed it and it really worked. I was eating much better by now, the first C, and after the twenty miler or any long run I would cool down, or "chill" with a garden hose. I know that is a strange mental image, just standing in the yard hosing down my legs, but it did work. I also followed another tip about eating something as soon as I came in from a run and not waiting till I felt hungry. It really helped my recovery.

Three days before the marathon we started making travel arrangements. I was driving to St. George with my parents and sister, who flew into Salt Lake City from Minnesota. It took me so long to pack, because I knew there was no going back for something forgotten. The first thing I packed was my socks. I am fanatical about my socks. This particular marathon was tough to dress for because it starts in the desert at forty degrees and ends up in the town of St. George at usually eighty degrees. I packed one of everything, every possible layer of clothing for any possible weather condition. I even had a pile of old clothes for discards in case I wanted to get rid of a few layers along the way. Because so many runners discard layers during this race, the volunteers actually collect all the discards for the first five miles and bring them to the finish line just in case someone wants a particular T-shirt or whatever back. I also packed my special sports mix that I kept in a bottle in a fanny pack. My husband, who wasn't too supportive of my training efforts at first and never attended any of my races, finally mentioned he would like to come to Utah. I was shocked and pleased. For months I had been sleeping, eating, and dreaming of this marathon and I know it took away from our time together, but it meant so much to me. I never seemed to be able to communicate that to him. Sometimes there would be angry words, and I finally had to tell him this aspect of my life was off limits. Running was keeping me sane through a difficult year and I was not going to give it up. I finally took the tack of telling him how much worse it would be if I didn't run, and he stopped complaining. It was not a topic up for negotiation or options. I was touched by his sudden support. He and my father ended up driving separately, which left my mom, my sister, and I plenty of time to catch up and gab for five hours. We talked the entire way. The car must have been glowing with the wattage created from our volts of nervous energy.

The St. George Marathon is supposed to be the fastest qualifying course for Boston, so it gets a lot of participants. It's a point-to-point, mostly downhill course. But people who had run it previously were saying, "Downhill my ass. Where there's a downhill there's an uphill." My sister and I finally got a chance to discuss the race for the first time face to face. We made a pact that we would run our own pace and not hold each other back. If one wanted to go faster we would just meet at the finish line. It took a lot of pressure off to get that out in the open. Our goal was just to finish and try to run the entire course. It sounds so corny but I love my sister and I didn't want something like a race to get in the way of our relationship. We look to each other for support and we have the trust and faith that we'll always be there for each other. It was important that we felt comfortable with each other's personal goals and expectations.

Chris and I even had matching outfits for the race, purple and pink striped T-shirts.

The night before the race we couldn't sleep. I was drinking so much water I had to pee all night long so when the alarm went off at four-thirty I felt like I hadn't slept at all. My parents got up with us and drove us to the bus (my husband stayed in bed) at 5 A.M. It was pitch black out. Chris and I were a little groggy at first, somewhere between semiconscious and awake. When we got to the bus loading area, all of a sudden there were thousands of runners all milling around, laughing, talking, running in place, just being weird and wacky. It caught us off guard and it was a real wake-up call. We fell right in step. As we rode to the start, it was still dark so we couldn't see much of the course but I remember thinking, "Wow, we've been driving a long time!" Then I looked around at all the people who were sharing this adventure together and I nudged Chris and said, "Look at all these people who are as crazy as we are!" It was so cool to be in the presence of others who shared the same passion, the same drive. For the last six months we'd been trying to explain to friends or coworkers why we wanted to run a marathon. Now we were in a crowd of people who understood why. There was no need to explain. I loved being a part of them, of their energy. I felt like I belonged here.

It was still dark when we got to the start. We were in the middle of a desert, not a town or a house in sight. Huge bonfires were burning in big drum kettles. Music was blaring from portable radios. Port-o-Johns were placed all around. Festive lights were strung up. It was forty degrees and everyone huddled around the bonfires trying to keep warm. It was an incredibly eerie sight, like something out of a runners' sci-fi comic book. Some people were taking warm-up laps. Chris and I looked at each other and agreed there was no way we were leaving the warmth of the fire to do a few laps. We stayed by the fire until the last minute, did one more Port-o-John trip, and headed to the start. Everyone was hooting and hollering, pacing in place, and expending energy. I was so nervous my heart rate was up to 150 and I hadn't taken a step yet. When the gun went off, we slowly jogged until we could get a pace going. We ran a few miles and then saw the most incredible sight—the sun coming up over the desert, a bright orange sun rising up creating amazing shadows and bringing the desert flowers to life. The light was beautiful. The air was crisp and chilly. We shed our outer layer and just got into the groove running through the desert in our purple and pink stripes.

We started out with the mind-set that we were just on a nice and easy run, no stress, no pressure. It was so peaceful. At about ten miles the course goes through a very small town and the people come out in their bathrobes and pajamas at seven in the morning to cheer. One woman in a housecoat saw our matching outfits and big smiles, obviously having fun, and said, "Let's hear it for the smiley girls!" That was about it for the fans. Soon after, we encountered our first hill. Actually it's a volcano that loops up and down for a mile. We started running up the hill, knowing we had to save energy, so we took it nice and easy. At the top, we started running down, but you can see it just loops up again. We passed a man who then passed us on the way down. We passed him again on the way up. This became a game for us, but for him it was a challenge. Obviously, he did not want to be passed by two females. Eventually he exhausted himself trying to beat us. We just kept going and waved good-bye.

At the halfway mark we were still cruising. We had been talking the entire time, but now we started to conserve energy. At mile sixteen we just enjoyed taking in the scenery. The course slowly rolls downward the entire race, starting at an elevation of seven thousand feet down to about three thousand. It was getting warm. In fact we were hot and poured water on our heads at the drinking stations. This was quite a change from the frigid conditions at the top of the mountain. Throughout the race we did a ritual that we referred to as "The Body Check." Every few miles we'd shake our arms up and down, shake out the legs, change stride, do a few leg kicks, wiggle our toes, anything to keep us limber and moving. It was also fun and broke the monotony of just running.

At mile eighteen, there was another hill and we were both dragging. I'd keep asking Chris, "How are you feeling?" And a few yards more she'd say, "I'm okay, how are you?" This became routine, our minimal form of conversation. At mile twenty we were running downhill and when I saw the mile marker I got excited. I knew I was going to finish. I remember thinking, "Thank God for downhills." We could see the town of St. George and the realization it would be over in six miles was pretty awesome. Neither of us had run farther than twenty miles so we knew we were in for some unexpected events. At mile twenty-three we were beginning to hurt, but the euphoria of running the distance kept us going. We did another Body Check, but a lot slower. At mile twenty-four things were definitely hurting and we started to swear. At twenty-five miles I wanted to quit, I couldn't go on. I was dying. We had been maintaining eight-minute miles the entire race and I was wiped. There was nothing left inside. I told Chris to go on without me. She said, "I was just going to tell you to go ahead without me." We laughed over that, and agreed to just slow down and still finish together.

By now my knee was on fire and I was getting shooting pains. But when we rounded a bend and saw the finish line, we forgot all the pain, all the miles, all the doubts. We held hands and crossed the finish line together. My dad was there with the video camera and got it all on tape: the hands held high, the medals draped across our chests, the tears, the ear-to-ear smiles, the high-fives and the big huge hug we gave each other.

This was definitely the best thing I ever did in my life. I didn't even feel as if I ran twenty-six miles. When we regrouped with our parents and my husband, I tried to sit down but couldn't. Our time was 3:33 and someone was yelling, "Hey, you qualified for Boston." Well, that was the farthest thing from my mind at that particular moment. Then my mom came over and she was crying and telling us how proud she was, but she took us both by surprise when she said, "Now I want to run a marathon. You girls had so much fun I want to do one." She was fifty at the time and I was somewhat concerned that she really meant it.

We went back to the hotel to shower and I remember that I couldn't bend over to wash my feet. And I'd lost a toenail. I was totally exhausted and starving, so we went out to eat and then went back to the awards ceremony. Our feet were too swollen to wear normal shoes. Chris had packed a pair of sandals so she shared her sandals with me. I wore one on the right foot and she wore the other on her left foot and we each wore a regular running shoe on the foot without blisters. It was quite a sight. The next morning, we made the mistake of going shopping. The stores were up a hill and my mom had to pull us the entire way because we couldn't bend our legs. When we got back to the car, I couldn't step down the curb. I actually had to think about how I was going to negotiate this curb. I grabbed hold of the car in front of us and ever-so-slowly edged my way off the curb. I didn't realize there was someone sitting in that car but after I got settled he rolled down his window, looked right at me, and said, "I know exactly how you feel." He had also run the marathon.

After the five-hour drive home, I couldn't walk. It took about half an hour to get into the house. I spent two days walking like a cripple, another two days hobbling, and finally by the fifth day I could walk seminormal. Then I started thinking of Boston. I had qualified and thought it would be cool to run the Boston One Hundred. I discussed it with Chris. We called Mom to see if she was serious about a marathon and she was definitely into it, so we decided to all run St. George the following year, Chris and I and my dad and mom. But that's another story. Now every member of my family has completed at least two marathons.

After running a few marathons I can explain to people why I run. It calms me. I can't imagine not having it in my life. It helps me to sort through things. It's like stepping outside myself and getting a better perspective of who I am. Running helps me focus better, helps me take my life in the direction it needs to go. It's not like I concentrate on these topics while I'm in the process of running, but running opens my mind to all kinds of possibilities and perhaps the solution is out there waiting for me to find it. Running takes me to that place.

BUSINESS AS USUAL

RICK BACHMANN
RESIDENCE: NEW ORLEANS, LOUISIANA
OCCUPATION: PRESIDENT AND CEO, ENERGY PARTNERS, LLC
FIRST MARATHON: 1987 NEW YORK CITY MARATHON
D.O.B.: 12-6-44
AGE AT FIRST MARATHON: 43

Forget all the excuses you've ever come up with not to run a marathon. Rick Bachmann could probably use any one of them, but doesn't. No time? Get up at four-thirty in the morning. Too hot? Run indoors on a treadmill. Business travel takes you away too much? Plan a marathon around a business trip. Out of shape? Start slowly and work your way up. It's just business as usual. No big deal. He's a man who seems to spend more time on a plane than on the ground, but he has managed to run seven marathons since he took up running at the age of forty-two. His most memorable run, though, was not a marathon—in fact it was less than a mile. For all the community service he performs, Rick was chosen to carry the 1996 Summer Olympic Torch down historic St. Charles Avenue in New Orleans.

PEOPLE DESCRIBE ME AS A SERIOUS BUSINESSMAN, very focused and goal oriented. Whether I am tackling a new business venture, taking the midnight watch during the Newport-to-Bermuda sailboat race, or running a marathon, I am totally focused on that task. I wouldn't know how to operate any other way. In fact, that's how my swimming career started. As a youth, most of my waking hours were spent in a pool. My dad was a competitive swimmer and taught me how to swim, coaching me through my early years. He was a member of the Elks Club in Wisconsin where I spent my childhood and from the time I was four years old, every Sunday morning we would go down to the club and swim.

For more years than I would like to remember, my dad drove me to the pool at four-thirty in the morning to swim laps. Then it was off to school, return to the gym in the afternoon for weight training, go home to study and finish homework, then back in the pool at night to concentrate on my specific event, the individual medley.

I received a swimming scholarship to the University of Wisconsin at Whitewater and swam competitively my freshman year, but by then I was burned out. The time commitment was taking away from my studies, which I took very seriously. I was on the business track and looking for that first corporate opening. Something had to go and swimming was it. Afterward, I attended the University of Wisconsin at Madison to get my graduate degree in business. This was 1967, a very tumultuous time on college campuses, and the University of Wisconsin was a hotbed of violent antiwar activism. Students blew up the Mathematics Building because the math and science departments had some kind of contract with the army. A few people were killed in the bombing. I was more the button-down-shirt-and-tie type of student, very serious and studious. I tried to avoid all the protesting and hysteria and just concentrate on my studies. Since most of my classes were in the Commerce Building, I thought I was safe from being blown up. However, while attending a lecture being given by Dow Chemical, obviously a real focal point of the protest due to their manufacturing of napalm, the activist branch of the student body decided to take over the building. The campus police summoned the city police, who summoned the National Guard. The building was surrounded by all kinds of military police in full riot gear. As we were listening to the lecture, taking notes and minding our own business, tear gas bombs went off. Students and guards clashed all around us. The kid sitting next to me had his head split open, but I managed to get out unharmed. It was just a crazy time, but I didn't let it veer me off course.

After graduate school, I joined Exxon and started traveling, being transferred around the globe from New York, to Florida, to Central America, to El Salvador. I was married with three children and had no time for anything but work. Athletically, I did nothing. Sports faded into the background. In 1982 I was transferred to New Orleans, a thirty-eight-year-old, out-of-shape senior executive, entertaining clients almost every night, working too late and too hard. My company entered a local Corporate Challenge Cup 5K race and our comptroller bet me that I couldn't do it. I wasn't really interested in it, but the guy who ran our executive gym was trying to recruit employees and he eventually talked me into it. It was a team event and one person on the team had to be forty or over, one had to be female, and the other two spots were open to anyone. The rest of the out-of-shape guys in the gym started a wager not to see who would win, but to see who would finish!

Once I committed to the race, I was obsessed with comporting myself in a respectable manner, and the thought of winning was definitely taking shape somewhere in the recesses of my mind. I didn't want to make an ass out of myself, so I started running on the treadmill. Along the way, I unearthed the competitive spirit buried long ago when I stopped swimming.

Running that race regenerated my desire to stay in shape and see just how good I could be. I started to look forward to the next race and the next one and the next one. Could I do it better? Could I do it faster? I kept running. But this is New Orleans, hot as hell and humid as a rain forest. My track was the treadmill in the company gym. I felt like a hamster running the wheel in its cage, but it beat running outside in the stifling heat.

This newfound sport was definitely taking time out of my hide as I'd be in the gym by five-thirty, putting in six to eight miles on the treadmill, and get to the first business meeting of the day usually by seven-thirty. I was driven, dedicated, and I loved it. My second race was the Crescent City Classic 10K, which starts in the French Quarter, goes through the garden district, and winds its way up into Audubon Park. It's got to be one of the most beautiful courses anywhere and attracts about twenty-six thousand runners.

I decided that running was good for me. First, I was losing weight, already down forty pounds, and my body started to look reasonable again. There was also the aspect of using my time more productively, becoming more mentally tough. While running the treadmill, I would plan out my day, working out professional or personal problems. I was also back to doing something competitive, enjoying the challenge, the "I can do this" attitude. I guess I tend to choose individual sports like

swimming, running, or ocean sailing because I have to rely on myself.
When I got interested in ocean racing, I had my own boat built, trans-
ported it to Westport, Connecticut, picked my crew, and started racing.
And even with a crew of nine, it can get pretty lonely out in the middle
of the ocean with no land in sight for days. A 2 A.M. watch with no one
to keep you company but the stars and a stale cup of coffee can be pretty lonely. There is definitely a relationship between sitting on a cold
deck late at night with a bitter wind cutting through your face and
being at the eighteen-mile marker at a marathon. Both instances beg
the question, "What am I doing here?"

There is an answer, although not always so obvious.

The exercise coordinator at our gym encouraged me to run a marathon, feeling it would be the next logical step. I entered a few triathlons,
did really well in the swimming event, pretty good in the running
event, and not so good in the biking event. But I enjoyed it and it
helped to turn my brewing desire to run a marathon into a reality.
The next decision was where and when. I wanted a marathon with
crowd appeal as I knew I'd be running alone and thought I'd need the
support of a large crowd. I read that the New York Marathon had the
best crowds and since I traveled to that city quite frequently, I decided
to run it that November, which would give me about six months to
train. Although New Orleans features the Mardi Gras Marathon, it
doesn't draw a big crowd and it can also get too hot despite the fact
that it's in January. I don't know many locals who attempt it. They
know too well how the heat can reduce any runner to a puddle of
sweat in mere minutes.

So it was back to the treadmill for more training. I increased my
miles in the morning to eight or ten. On weekends, I'd get up at 4:30
A.M. and meet a group of guys at Audubon Park for long runs. We
started out with ten miles and every weekend increased the distance by
two miles. We had to start early because by 7:30 A.M. it could already
be up to ninety degrees with 90 percent humidity. It wasn't easy. We
would place water bottles along our route so we could drink plenty of
liquids. Sometimes our course would take us along the levee and we
would pray for a breeze. But then we'd get the bugs that lived along
the river and waited very patiently for a salty, sweaty body to feast on.
Besides the heat, humidity, and bugs, the other downside to training in
New Orleans was a lack of hills. New Orleans is completely flat. The

only hill we encountered was running up a ramp to a bridge or boat. This type of training took a lot out of our hides. Getting up at four-thirty on a Saturday morning means you don't go out on a Friday night. And by 8:00 P.M. Saturday night, we're ready for bed. Sunday was a normal day, but then it's early to bed in order to get up for work at five on Monday morning.

I enjoyed the camaraderie of running with the guys on weekends. We would talk about nonsensical things to pass the time: restaurants, sports, bars. Everyone was married so there weren't any hot topics. I avoided discussing work because most of the guys worked for me. In fact, they started out calling me Mr. Bachmann, but I put a stop to that. I couldn't ignore the fact that as a group, we were hierarchies apart. Most of the things I was working on were very senior level and confidential and they weren't part of the communications link. I had to work hard at making them feel comfortable with me and it paid off. We all reached a very comfortable level of friendship.

By November, I was definitely ready for the marathon. I went to New York a few days early for my business meeting. Marathon morning I took a cab to the New York Public Library, where buses were transporting runners to the starting line. I wasn't feeling particularly nervous, to me it was just another day. But as I stood in line at the library to get on the bus, I realized this was something different, this was something special. I have to admit, a spark of enthusiasm started to burn a hole in my "business as usual" attitude. I was getting caught up in the elaborate spectacle that is the New York Marathon. The one piece of advice I received was to stay away from the railings while crossing the Verrazano Narrows Bridge. I didn't want to get sprayed by the "yellow rain" falling from the level above.

The noise from the thousands of runners, the helicopters, the fire-boats, the sound of feet pounding across the bridge all contributed to a most amazing beginning.

As anticipated, the crowds were tremendous, everything I expected. For just about every mile along the course there was something to look at, listen to, laugh at, be encouraged by, eat, drink, and be merry. At mile eighteen I was feeling on top of the world. I was flying, didn't even feel as if I had run any distance at all. I attribute this to lots of good luck and proper training. I didn't get my first cramp until mile twenty. I did drink a lot of liquids but I didn't eat anything. I never felt hungry although the crowds were always offering something to boost our energy level: a candy bar, orange slices, a banana. I got the feeling they would give me the shirt off their back if I needed it.

I kept thinking, this isn't as hard as I thought it'd be. I was on an absolute high. I was running better than I expected. The bands, the fire engine companies, the large crowds, sirens blowing, people standing four deep on the sides of the roads yelling support and encouragement, it was everything I wanted it to be and more.

But as the crowds dwindled, the aches and pains become more noticeable. I don't know if there is a scientific corollary to that, but I really looked to the crowds to keep me mentally alert. Once they started to disperse, I realized just how much I was relying on them to get me through. At first I thought this is where I would break down, without the loud cheers and hundreds of fans yelling. But although the crowds were not four deep, they were just as warm and caring, offering us all kinds of fruit, food, and drinks, and it lifted my spirits again.

At about mile twenty-three, the course enters the park and I encountered my first hill, which looked like the Rocky Mountains. My body went into shock and shut down. For the first time I had to stop and knead out a cramp in my thigh. I alternated a walk-run pattern for the next two miles. To my relief, the crowds in the park were back in full force. Their support was overwhelming and it gave me the courage to gut it out and go for all the glory I could muster. I started running again, full throttle—well, at least it seemed like I was going fast, even though it was just sheer adrenaline, willpower, and the emotional charge generated from the voices of the crowds. As I crossed the finish line, one thought kept echoing throughout my head—"It's finally all over." I felt a huge sense of relief and a great deal of pain.

Walking the mile back to the Great Lawn to pick up my gear seemed like an eternity. I didn't think I'd make it. I could hardly walk. Everything shut down, cramped out, gave out. But I made it back to the hotel, took a shower, and went to the airport to catch a plane home. I just sat there, feeling a great sense of pride. But as soon as the plane landed, it was business as usual. I actually did a lot of work on the plane, preparing for the next day's agenda. Surprisingly, all the pain and soreness was gone in two days and I was back to running the treadmill in three days.

Preparing for the marathon took a lot out of my hide. I had real doubts about doing another one. However, by the end of the week I was already thinking how I could improve my time for the next one. I wanted to do better, to improve on what I had already accomplished. I wanted to run New York again in 1988, but there were too many complex corporate issues to attend to so I skipped it and ran again in 1989 and 1991. I kept going back to New York. That was my race.

I have since been divorced and remarried. My current wife is supportive and very encouraging. She'll bike alongside me in the park and has started to run herself. I also ran the Walt Disney Marathon as a qualifier for my first Boston, and then a subsequent Boston. Disney is my favorite course, probably because it was my fastest time, 3:25.

At fifty-two years old, I feel as if I am beginning a second life. I run seven miles a day, I'm starting a new organization, and running helps to put some sense of discipline and structure in my life. I travel too much of the time, but even when overseas I will still get in my daily run. Zurich has to be my favorite foreign city to run in as my course takes me around the lake, looking up at the snowcapped mountains, breathing in the freshest air I have ever inhaled in my life. It truly is a magnificent city for runners. On the other hand, Paris has to be the worst. It is not runner friendly. One memorable Parisian moment was the time I was staying downtown at the Bristol Hotel on the Rue du Faubourg St.-Honoré and planned to run the boulevard to the Champs Elysées. I wasn't aware that I would be passing the Palais de l'Elysée, the French president's residence, but as I ran by I guess I surprised the guard because he turned on me with his Uzi pointing right in my face. I quickly came to a complete stop and tried to use my broken French to say, "Hi, I'm a friend," or something of that nature. He wasn't buying it. He stood there grim faced with the gun still pointing directly at me until his commander came over to check out the situation. Thank God he realized I was just another crazy American jogger and waved me on.

No matter how busy my day gets, I just find a way to fit in my run. And if that means four-thirty in the morning, so be it. Running is a very positive part of my life and I don't feel good mentally or physically if I can't get my daily run in. It would be like missing a friend. I have also found that as I get older I require less sleep, which is a good thing for me. I have more hours in the day so I don't feel as if I make sacrifices to fit in my run. I've been known to hit a hotel treadmill at midnight if I can't sleep, if a time zone keeps me up at night. It is part of my day, like brushing my teeth.

THE MARATHON AS METAPHOR

TORY BAUCUM
RESIDENCE: KANSAS CITY, MISSOURI
OCCUPATION: EPISCOPAL MINISTER
FIRST MARATHON: 1992 MARINE CORPS MARATHON, WASHINGTON, D.C.
D.O.B.: 2-29-60
AGE AT FIRST MARATHON: 32

Suffering through the childhood traumas of divorced parents and a move to a new state, Tory just wanted to fit in with the crowd. To make matters worse, he couldn't participate in sports, one of the easiest ways to meet new friends, due to severe asthma. Beginning a lifelong pattern of gutting it out, Tory worked hard at being one of the guys, and even ran through pain in gym class so as not to divulge his affliction. Later in life, divine intervention sent him on a journey to Little Rock, Arkansas, where he met a parishioner who took him on another journey, Tory's first marathon. And similar to the trials and tribulations of poor Job, Tory endured all the training, the pain, and the mental stress only to come down with the flu the night before the race. He gutted it out and ran anyway, turning his fever into frenzied exhilaration. Nowadays when Tory is preparing his Sunday sermons, he often reflects back on his first marathon experience.

BEING DIAGNOSED WITH ASTHMA AT NINE years old was pretty devastating to me, mostly because it meant I couldn't participate in sports on any level that would be considered competitive. When I moved to Texas at age twelve, I couldn't rely on sports to help break through with the new kids, to join a team or play a pick-up game in the neighborhood. I just wanted to fit in, to be like everyone else, but it was difficult. The peer pressure to be physical, to do something as simple as run in gym class, was intense for me. And because I wanted to fit in so badly, not be viewed as different, I gutted it out and ran anyway, ran through the wheezing, the shortness of breath, the pain. I sucked it all in and endured it. Then one day while running in class, there was an incredible breakthrough and I could breathe. It was amazing; there was no more pain. The doctors attributed it to becoming acclimated to a less-polli- nated climate, but whatever the reason, I remember that day like it just happened. The feeling of being able to breathe without pain was so refreshing.

I threw myself into sports, competing in swimming and basketball. I ran three or four miles as a conditioning exercise, but didn't participate on the track team. I wouldn't consider myself a real jock, but I did like competing. I also studied martial arts, which taught me how to use my lungs more efficiently and breathe more effectively.

After high school, I attended a small Baptist college in Texas. There was no sports program at the school, so I developed a workout routine on my own just to keep in shape. After college, I hitchhiked though Israel and Egypt, studying archaeology, living on a kibbutz, and experi- encing all those great things a college graduate does before starting down the more career-oriented path of life.

After my exploring was over, I came back to the states and took graduate courses in linguistics at the University of North Dakota. During this time I was examining my religious beliefs and becoming less of a Baptist and more of an Episcopalian. After some soulsearching, I entered an Episcopal seminary in Pittsburgh. At twenty-five years old, I chose my life's career and vowed to dedicate myself to helping others on their own unique journey back home to God.

At the seminary, I played basketball and ran to keep fit. And since Pittsburgh has cold, sloppy winters, I skipped the cold, sleet, and snow drenched months in favor of fairer weather. When I finished the semi- nary, I was fortunate to be recommended for an assistant position to the dean of the cathedral in Little Rock, Arkansas, a place more conducive to year-round running.

Home for the next five years was Little Rock, a small southern city that is very insular, very much the "born, bred and never left" mentality. The power and wealth are in the hands of a few. It was a culture clash for me. The cathedral was one block from the governor's mansion, where Bill and Hillary Clinton resided at the time. The connection between my boss, the dean, and the Clintons was very close and I was introduced into a very political circle, which was an interesting education.

During my last year at the cathedral, I met a new parishioner, John Brineman, and we became good friends. We had similar interests, and running was one of them. He is a pathologist and his wife, Sandy, is also a doctor, a pertinent point for later on in my story. John had run a couple of marathons and one night while socializing at a Greek food festival, he mentioned he was planning to run the next Marine Corps Marathon and was I interested in training with him. It may seem that I was not the greatest choice of a partner, having never run distance, but I was healthy, a sometimes-steady runner, and over a great piece of baklava, any idea has merit. Besides, I believed I could do it and the challenge of a marathon appealed to me. *Chariots of Fire,* which is one of my favorite movies, has as its main character a young seminarian who is a runner, and the training scenes along the beaches in England captured my imagination and have stayed with me.

Also, on a subconscious level, I was going through a particularly intense year. There were some toxic-level conflicts occurring in the parish and I thought running would be a much better release for me than wringing my hands or the necks of the pugnacious parishioners. I also rationalized that John was a good friend and this would be a great way to get in even better shape, and I was single, had the time—so why not?

The marathon was scheduled for November and we started training in June. However, the summers in Little Rock are brutally hot and humid, so we couldn't do much distance. John's routine was based on building stamina. We started off with one-mile runs, increasing a mile every couple of weeks. Our slow start was attributed to the heat and also the fact that John didn't want me to injure myself by building distance too fast. One-hundred-degree weather was not conducive to long, hard runs.

As much as I was really into the idea of it all, it wasn't easy. It was tough, didn't feel good. This was not my normal way of running; I was now in training, a different breed. I learned to do things such as speed training, pacing, intervals, and drink tons of fluids, which was one of the factors that saved me in the end.

Come September, we increased our mileage and got in some twenty milers. Our goal was to do three twenties prior to the race, then take a week off, do some fives, and then taper to race day. The closer we got to the marathon, the more I enjoyed the training. It was an escalator effect; I felt like I was being taken to the top of an exciting ride.

The best part of training was becoming close with John. Running was the vehicle that cemented our friendship. We'd discuss religion, and we both felt our faith coming alive. John had lots of questions for me, so we constantly challenged each other's assumptions. And there were other common grounds we discovered, such as the blues and jazz. There are some great blues festivals in Arkansas, such as the famous King Biscuit Blues Festival in Helena.

And to make our runs just a little more interesting, it was Clinton's campaign year for the presidency and all of Little Rock was buzzing. There was lots of juicy gossip.

In essence, our training and time together became a collaboration. I can't think of the marathon without thinking of John. It's a time when our friendship flourished, and even after I moved, our friendship continued to grow. Running, more than any other sport, allows the intensity of a relationship to come through. Sweating and pounding pavement side by side for hours is more time spent with a friend than, say, skiing or tennis or even golf.

My goal for the marathon was just to finish, although John wanted to better his last time, bring it closer to four hours. We had an understanding that if one of us got into a faster rhythm it was kosher to take off. Heck, if one of us was running faster, then by all means go for it.

The race was on a Sunday, and as I was preparing to leave Little Rock, some of my parishioners were concerned whether I would attend church that day. I told them I'd try to fit it all in. I guess I should have been flattered that after four years they were still trying to improve me.

We stayed in Virginia the night before the marathon and gorged on pasta. Then it hit me. I started to feel sick and knew I was coming down with something. I had all the symptoms of a flu: sore throat, congested head, all-over achy feeling. I went into instant denial. I drank wine to drown out the symptoms, but it didn't help. That night I was truly sick and took whatever drugs John gave me. Marathon morning I woke up feverish, sore, and definitely had a case of the flu. More than any of my body aches, I was disgusted, and I was determined to run.

There was no way I wasn't going to run. At least I had to attempt it.

John gave me some more drugs, encouraged me to drink gallons of water, and got me out of bed. I had the shivers, and even though the temperature was mild and pleasant, I wore a long-sleeved shirt and a warm-up suit to the start. I didn't think I could finish, but I had to start. I compromised with myself that I would only run half the race. While waiting at the start, my body temperature warmed up enough for me to forgo the warm-up suit, and I ran in my shorts and long sleeved shirt. John stayed with me and ensured I drank plenty of water at each stop. I felt like crap for the first five miles but by mile thirteen I actually began to feel better; it was as if the germs decided not to go along on the marathon. I continued to feel stronger as I ran and the middle of the race was actually enjoyable. My head cleared and most of the sickly symptoms were gone. At mile twenty, I actually sprinted ahead of John. But then the last six miles were hell. I felt skeletal, my shins were exploding, there was no energy left. It actually felt worse than having the flu!

I concentrated on just how badly I felt, but in a twisted way that made me even more determined to finish. If I could run three-quarters of a marathon with all the symptoms of the flu, I certainly could finish one now that the symptoms were gone. And of course, I reached way back to my youth, when I had to gut things out to feel accepted, so I knew that somewhere inside me was the drive to finish, to make it happen. It had nothing to do with saving face, not being able to face the congregation and say I couldn't do it. At thirty-two years of age, I was over those issues. It was just a matter of determination, sheer willpower to complete it.

When I crossed the finish line, I was extraordinarily tired. I can't remember ever feeling that tired in my life. However, I do recall telling John that it was the greatest rush I ever had. My body fought the flu, I fought the 26.2-mile monster, and we both won.

There were victories celebrated on a couple of different levels that day, but unfortunately, my celebration meal consisted of ibuprofen and chicken soup.

I've often gone back to that day for inspiration. I've woven the metaphor of the marathon into quite a few Sunday homilies, drawing on the fact that the nature of the goal determines how the race is run. In sports, a marathon is run differently from a hundred-yard dash because the goal is different; the race goes not to the swift, but to the steady. In life, if your goal is to follow Christ, your daily existence draws inspiration from His Spirit so the goal eventually is attainable.

Even the Bible has its doses of running metaphors. St. Paul uses running as a metaphor in his letters to the Corinthians, 9:24: "Do you not know that in a race all the runners run, but only one gets the prize. Run in such a way as to get the prize. Everyone who competes goes into strict training. They do it to get a crown that will not last; but we do it to get a crown that will last forever. Therefore, I do not run like a man running aimlessly."

Running changed me in many ways, but then everything we do changes us in some way, every experience helping to strengthen the resolve. The other metaphor I like to use is that life itself is a marathon journey, with a beginning, a middle, and an end. For me, the beginning and end were the most difficult parts of the race. But what keeps us all going is the ultimate knowledge that the goal is worth the supreme effort it takes to achieve it. If it were easy, it wouldn't be as valuable. We all need goals. Life is hard to live without one.

I truly believe I am living my life's goal, to be the person God dreamed me to be. All of us have been made for a purpose. And at the core of that purpose is to be at home with God. The gifts and talents He so freely gives us will help us find our way back home.

A BRASH BEGINNER

BILL BEGG
RESIDENCE: NEWTOWN, CONN.
OCCUPATION: EMERGENCY ROOM DOCTOR, DANBURY HOSPITAL
FIRST MARATHON: 1991 MARINE CORPS MARATHON, WASHINGTON, D.C.
D.O.B.: 8-16-63
AGE AT FIRST MARATHON: 28

Bill's work at the hospital is constantly challenging: He handles everything from stitches and broken bones to sudden surgery and the reality of signing death certificates. And on top of all this, there are the thirty-six-hour shifts. Getting in a daily run is not always in the picture. But he can be seen on the weekends running around the neighborhood, pushing the baby jogger with both kids tucked inside. A doctor with a bedside manner that includes off-the-wall humor, Bill took on his first marathon as a challenge. With a strong conviction and determination to back up his brash statement that "any wimp can run a marathon," he started off on a journey that would change his life.

I GOLFED IN HIGH SCHOOL. That was the extent of my organized sports career. I am a big fan of all sports but a player of few. My parents were bigger proponents of academics so except for my brothers' football games, I paid more attention to the schoolbooks. However, I played lots of backyard football and baseball with my three brothers. Also, I knew early in my schooling that I wanted to be a doctor so I was always studying hard to get into college, medical school, then residency. In 1985 I entered New York Medical College and hung out with a bunch of guys who played rugby, so I joined them. But in my senior year I tore my knee cartilage and needed surgery. I was on crutches for three weeks and that was the end of my rugby. After that I went to Johns Hopkins for my residency. One weekend I ended up going to the University of Pennsylvania for a party and met Leah. We started dating and were inseparable. Leah was a track jock and one day my pride got the better of me and I foolishly decided to join her. To my surprise I was able to keep up with her. Secretly, I think she slowed down a bit for me. After all, we were still in the dating stages of our romance.

That was the extent of my running until 1991, my second year of residency. A group of my friends had just registered to run the Marine Corps Marathon on November 3, four weeks away. They were bragging about it like they were Olympians, so I said, "Any wimp can run a marathon. All you have to do is run for a couple of hours and you get free water and food. Big deal." They countered with, "Oh yeah? You couldn't." That was it. The challenge had been thrown and I told them I would prove my point and run it.

Leah, now a second lieutenant in the army, having gone to college on the ROTC program, was stationed at Aberdeen Proving Grounds in Maryland, not far from Johns Hopkins. I called her to tell her what I'd done, looking for support and some enthusiasm. Instead, she told me I was crazy, that no one should run a marathon without proper training.

Despite her good advice, I wasn't about to back down. I had to prove it to my friends that I could do it. Back then, I was a bit of a hot shot with a heavy dose of ego thrown in. I also love a challenge and couldn't pass this one up. On October 3, I registered for the marathon and went out to buy Jeff Galloway's book on marathon training and the cheapest pair of running shoes I could buy, preferably on sale. That weekend, I set out for my first official training run, two and a half miles. It killed me. I ended up walking more than running. It took me twenty-five minutes to finish and all the time my lower legs were on fire, I was short of breath, and my lungs hurt. It felt like I was sucking wind and I couldn't move for an hour. This was not a good sign. Then I received a code blue to report immediately to the emergency room and I couldn't even walk up the stairs at the hospital. All I could do was wobble as fast as I could.

The next day I ran the same course again and felt better, but on the third day of training I decided I needed a rest. I didn't want to overdo it. The next week I got up to seven miles but ran very slowly. My legs and thighs were still sore but my time was better. I also started stretching. One week prior to the marathon I did an eight-mile run, my longest ever, and thought I was really getting the hang of it. I was in the running groove now. And just as the book suggested, I tapered off the last two days prior to the marathon.

Leah couldn't believe I was actually going to run. She told me I was a lunatic. The training book didn't even have a chapter on preparing for a marathon in three weeks with a zero base, but I was determined to not only run it, but finish. We were engaged at the time and I thought, well, now she knows how stubborn I can be. But on a more positive note, she also knows I will follow through on my commitments. I have an abundance of tenacity.

My friends were laughing at me for going through with the challenge, but I took it very seriously. I knew I could do it. I had lots of confidence. All through medical school I had to rely on myself to get through some tough times. And after having to stay alert during 36 hour shifts in the emergency room, I thought the marathon would be a piece of cake. I knew my medical training would come into play and help me out when I was running. When I make a decision to do something, I go after it with all my heart and soul. I was voted Emergency Resident of the Year at Johns Hopkins, an honor that I am most proud of. I work hard, plan hard, and play hard. The marathon had a piece of all those aspects in one event. I may have appeared crazy to tackle it, but I did have a game plan. I was prepared. On the back of the race number there is a medical form for emergency purposes. I filled it in with four different contact numbers and under the listing for allergies, I wrote "interns and medical students." That way, if I did end up unconscious at a hospital, hopefully I'd get a seasoned doctor.

The day of the marathon, I was very nervous. Mostly, I worried about hurting myself. My three brothers and Leah were at the starting line and it was exciting to see them there. I was getting pumped up. I started at the back of the pack with the rest of the riffraff runners. My game plan went as follows: After every three miles I'd take a five-minute break and rest or lie down, stretch and eat something. Actually, on one of those breaks I called my friends back at hospital and said, "Hey guys, I've done ten miles already."

I studied the route and knew where every mile marker and every historic monument would be and the expected time I would approach them. I gave my family a copy of my schedule so they could meet me at different intervals of the race.

At thirteen miles my legs started to tighten, but I was right on schedule, 2:31. My thighs really started to burn, but my endurance was fine. At sixteen miles I had to make a slight adjustment to the schedule and started to take breaks after every mile. I just couldn't keep running with the pain in my thighs. I stopped for a while and ate a hot dog from one of the food vendors. As part of my prerace preparation I had pocketed about twenty dollars for such emergencies!

I drank at every water station. In fact, at the end of the race I gained ten pounds of fluid weight. I had a total of thirty-nine drinks. On the downside, I also had to make five bathroom stops.

Haines Point was the worst part of the race. There aren't any fans allowed out there to cheer and I had to force myself to keep running. It was a real struggle. At twenty miles, I can't even put into words how miserable I felt. The pain was constant, but I stayed focused. I guess I've developed a rather thick skin working the emergency room. As a doctor, you quickly learn not to acknowledge pain. If my patient is screaming in agony, I can't give in to the emotional aspect. I have to block it out so I can concentrate on treating the source of the pain. Also, the pain I experienced in the marathon wasn't the type where I felt a sense of helplessness, like being in a car accident. I had control over the pain, could have stopped it if I chose to. My other focus was that I only had six more miles to go and an entire year to recuperate. At that point, I never wanted to run anywhere at any time again.

Then came the Fourteenth Street Bridge. The slight incline became a mountain and I couldn't make it. I had to lie down three times while crossing. I can still feel the gravel cutting into my back as I lay across the road. When I finally made it to the other side, my brother Michael was there and that was a real shot of adrenaline for me. He screamed out, "You've got two more miles. Suck it up, buddy!" His energy helped carry me the rest of the way, even though I was dead tired. I must have looked like a drunken sailor trying to run, slowly weaving in and out of everyone around me. I just kept focused on the finish, knowing that my family and Leah were waiting for me. The final loop of the race goes around the Iwo Jima monument and that is so emotionally stirring, I started to cry. It was such a powerful moment for me. I could see the finish line and knew I had done it.

I decided to go for a big ending, despite how tired I was. I didn't want to drag myself across the finish so I hit the gas pedal and sprinted across on the last few fumes of energy left. It was definitely one of the top ten moments of my life. I never doubted that I could finish, but when it was finally over the tremendous strain of the last five hours suddenly lifted and an incredible weight left my body and disappeared along with all the mental pain and exhaustion. It was exhilarating.

But then the hunger kicked in and I just stuffed myself with candy bars, oranges, bagels, anything I could find. Later on, Leah told me just how miserable I looked when I finished running 26 miles, 385 yards. She has a vivid memory of me leaning on the fence, wrapped in my space blanket, looking pale and ghostly, sweaty and gross, shoving candy bars in my mouth. My family had a huge party for me, but unfortunately the next day I had to work a twelve-hour shift at the hospital. I refused to call in sick. I was proud as a peacock of my accomplishment and I wanted to share it with my doubting friends. Actually, some people didn't know how to react to the news. They'd say, "You ran what? A marathon? How many miles is that?" It really takes the wind out of your sails when you have to explain it. Heck, I know women compare it to having a baby. Well, when Leah had our babies I gave out cigars. I felt like someone should have given me a cigar for running the damn marathon!

On a more serious note, running the marathon reconfirmed that I can accomplish anything in life if it is within my grasp. I have the courage and the power and the drive to make it happen. I ran this race under the worst possible conditions; I set a goal and achieved it. As a result of the experience, I became hooked on running—but I wanted to learn how to run the right way! I took a year to train properly and then ran my next marathon. I have become a running fanatic. I look forward to my long runs on the weekends. It's my time to slow down the hectic pace of the week and start to notice things that otherwise I don't have time for. I'll appreciate the beauty of a simple stone wall set in a field and I find myself wondering, "Who built it and why?" I probably drive by that wall every day on my way to the hospital but my mind is so clogged I never see it. On my runs, I can empty my mind of the day-to-day events that get in the way of seeing my surroundings and appreciating them.

Running gives me the balance in life that I need, especially when I am dealing with pain and death every day. I need to get out and see life being renewed.

BE ALL THAT YOU CAN BE

LEAH BEGG
RESIDENCE: NEWTOWN, CONNECTICUT
OCCUPATION: FIRST LIEUTENANT, ARMY RESERVES;
MOTHER OF TWO PRESCHOOLERS
FIRST MARATHON: 1994 MARINE CORPS MARATHON, WASHINGTON, D.C.
D.O.B.: 6-9-69
AGE AT FIRST MARATHON: 25

Leah manages the day-to-day household affairs while chasing after her two toddlers. As a first lieutenant in the army, she's well equipped to handle the job, and just about anything else that comes her way. Meeting her husband, Bill, at a party while attending the University of Pennsylvania, she had no idea what she was getting into. Not just romance, but eventually marathons, too. Leah, a seasoned and serious runner, watched her husband stumble his way through his first marathon and instantly made the decision to run her own. However, like a Hollywood grade-B movie, everything from a hurricane in Florida to a famine in Africa kept her from her goal. Leah finally did cross the finish line—not without a few laughs along the way, and inspiration from Oprah Winfrey.

MY MOM IS FROM THE LOST GENERATION of female athletes who never had an outlet for their sport. So when I entered high school, she was determined that I take advantage of the new era of female sports and join a team. I chose running because I used to run with my dad when I was a kid. He wanted to lose weight so picked up running and I would go along as company. Those memories were dear to me and I thought, "Well, why not run on a team?" I ran cross country and I took my running very seriously. We were a serious team. Even though I was living out my mom's desire to be on a team, I didn't like the competition, never enjoyed the pressure of racing. I love running for the sake of running. It is an art form to me and that's how I like to run. At a race, I have to perform. It's different. I'm no longer doing it for myself but for my coach, or to beat the clock, or the girl next to me.

I quit competitive racing after high school, just wanted to kick back and enjoy running once again for my own pleasure. I was fortunate enough to get into an Ivy League school, but money was an issue. Mom and Dad came to the rescue with some practical advice and suggested I join ROTC, which would pick up some financial payments if I was willing to give back eight years of my life. I was very naive about what I was actually getting into, but it was better than taking out all those loans, so I signed up. I thought it was a romantic notion: young woman officer in the army. My four years of college flew by. Not only did I have my basic schoolwork, I had the army and basic training to deal with. It was rare that I took a night off, but when I did, I met Bill.

The first thing that struck me about him was his competitive nature. Maybe it's all those backyard ball games he played with his brothers, but he sure does love a challenge. I knew he wasn't a runner, only did it once to impress me. So when he called to tell me he was running a marathon, I told him he was a lunatic. He wasn't taking it seriously, and that bothered me. I was the serious runner and there was no way I would tackle a marathon.

By this time in our relationship, I had graduated from college and was attending officer training school at Aberdeen Proving Ground in Baltimore, Maryland. I went to Washington, D.C., to lend my support for his marathon, but still couldn't believe he was doing it. Watching Bill cross the finish line, I was actually getting angry with myself for not running it. I always thought the marathon was a serious event for serious runners. Now I was seeing all walks of life cross the finish line: fat ones, skinny ones, out-of-shape and in-shape ones. They had all completed this amazing feat. Heck, I knew then I could do it.

The seeds were planted and I planned on going through with my own marathon, but the army had other plans for me. After Aberdeen, I was transferred to Fort Drum in upstate New York and put in charge of the motor pool, responsible for the maintenance and upkeep of about three hundred pieces of army equipment. I had forty men reporting to me. Every morning we would have to do some form of physical activity, whether it was a three-mile full-pack run or working out in the gym. I was really in good shape. Every three months we had to pass a physical test: a two mile run in twenty minutes. Well, for me that was a joke, as I did the two-mile in 12:30 in high school. But still, it was good training.

Bill and I finally got married in 1992. He joined me in New York, taking a job at a local hospital. We started to train together for the '92 Marine Corps Marathon, but the army had other plans for me. Hurricane Andrew hit Florida and I was sent down to help out with the army reserves and I ended up missing the marathon. I was so angry and disappointed. Bill ran it anyway and I was glad he did. Then I started training for 1993, but was sent to Somalia as part of the food relief airlift program. That was quite an experience.

I finally returned home three months later and had a heart-to-heart talk with Bill. We wanted to start a family and my career was putting a damper on that. I was just as unhappy as he was, so I put in for reserve work so we could settle down without the unexpected call of Uncle Sam getting in the way.

It was now spring of '93. For almost three years I had kept my marathon dream on hold, never giving up but never able to make it a reality. Now that I knew my life would be manageable, I went back to school for my masters degree. I also got pregnant. Although that was a blessed and anticipated event, it was another year prolonging my dream. I was beginning to think it would never happen for me. But, if anything, I am determined. I gave birth in May and started training in June for the October 1994 Marine Corps Marathon.

I followed the advice in Jeff Galloway's training book and did long runs on the weekends. My longest run was fifteen miles. Bill was really into racing and signed me up with him at local events, but I was very reluctant. I got so nervous when I'd have to race. I felt like I had to beat my inner clock to do well. It was like being back in high school and I had to perform for the coach all over again.

With one week to go, I didn't think I could do it. I constantly doubted myself. The night before the race I couldn't sleep. I kept thinking the alarm wouldn't go off and I'd miss it, something really silly like that. It was just nerves but I was a wreck. The morning of the race the alarm did go off in time, but what I didn't expect was the torrential rain. It was pouring with no relief in sight, but we decided to run anyway. We had come the distance and there was no turning back. We started out slowly, with a nine-minute pace. I really enjoyed the local scenery and somehow the rain didn't dampen the spirit of the crowd. But I guess I owe that to Oprah Winfrey. It was big news that she was running this race as her first marathon and the media was everywhere. She got to start at the front! The crowds were out in full force, even with the ever-present rain, to see her.

The first seven miles seemed like seven seconds. I was pumped, ready to fly, although in reality we were running a very slow pace. At fifteen miles we stopped to stretch and I suddenly realized I was starving. Then I remembered Bill had put a Snickers bar in his pocket at the start of the race. I kidded him about it, but now I was desperate for that Snickers. When I asked him about it, he hesitated. I think he was saving it for himself and we started to fight over who was going to eat it. As he took it from his pocket I grabbed it and ate the whole thing. I couldn't believe how nasty I was, but I was so hungry! Bill just laughed at me and said, "Hey, I wanted that Snickers, too."

I felt absolutely no pain the first twenty miles. Despite the rain I was really having fun. Bill and I talked the entire time. Having run it twice, he was an old hand at this by now. He had told me to expect some low periods of emotional upheaval when we reached Haines Point, and he did not exaggerate. It was desolate. That's when I saw injured runners getting pulled off the course on stretchers. It's mentally depressing but I just kept thinking, "Not me, not me. I am going to make it." Bill had made a schedule again, but this time we didn't need any breaks. I hit the wall at twenty-three miles, crossing the Fourteenth Street Bridge. I didn't think I had the strength to go on. I was cramping and aching all over. I have a very high threshold of pain but this was miserable. It was worse than my baby's delivery, just barely five months before. My knees were sore and I was so hungry. I ate everything in sight but I was still starved.

I knew then that through sheer willpower I was going to finish. At twenty-five miles, we started to hear the crowd getting louder and louder just up ahead and I realized we were closing in on Oprah, that she was just a few yards ahead. I couldn't resist the urge to pass her. So I told Bill I was going to leave him and run faster so that I could see her.

He couldn't believe that after all my whining about him not leaving me, I was kissing him off with one mile to go just so I could pass a celebrity. But I am a big Oprah fan. I wasn't passing her to be a smart-ass, I wanted to see her! Just knowing she was ahead of me gave me that extra boost to run faster. As I passed her, I turned around to say, "Hey, Oprah!" and waved, but she was so focused and had so many people around her she never noticed me. So I just kept going until I saw the Iwo Jima monument and knew I was just a few yards from the finish line. I started to cry. I know that sounds overrated and corny, but seeing that statute gave me a real sense of power; I felt as if I could do anything I wanted at that point. I had reached the pinnacle of my running career. The surge of emotion was powerful and I almost started to falter. It took everything I had to make it to the finish. I was so depleted of energy, food, and fluids there was nothing left inside but a wonderful, awesome, total feeling of accomplishment.

The marathon changed my outlook on running. I no longer cringe at the thought of doing a race. I feel more confident about my running, in fact about everything I do. After my first marathon I said I would never do another, but after a while I started to get psyched thinking of doing one. I wanted to capture that winning moment all over again. It is such a thrill. When I need a lift during the day I take myself back to the marathon, back to the wonderful moments Bill and I shared together. Sometimes we'll be at a party and start talking about running the marathon. We get so involved with it, so giddy with big smiles on our faces as we recount the miles, that the listeners start excusing themselves long before we're finished!

Now that I'm a stay-at-home mom, I need a little something to get me through the day. That something is the realization that I ran a marathon.

EXORCISING THROUGH EXERCISE

ELLEN BELLICCHI
RESIDENCE: NEW LONDON, CONNECTICUT
OCCUPATION: NUTRITIONIST, PERSONAL TRAINER,
OWNER F.I.T. (FEMALES IN TRAINING) GYM, SPRINGFIELD, MA
FIRST MARATHON: 1992 EAST LYME (CT) MARATHON
D.O.B.: 7-3-50
AGE AT FIRST MARATHON: 42

Ellen's philosophy is simple. No matter what you do in life, you won't achieve your goal unless it comes from within. No one will lose weight or get in shape unless they want to. Ellen works from the inside out and that's why the membership of her gym is constantly growing and her members love her. It's also her philosophy regarding the marathon. You have to really want it to run it. And the clock is always ticking as she counts down her miles, trying to beat the clock and get on to the next event.

THE ALARM GOES OFF AT SIX EVERY MORNING. Even though its piercing pitch has broken my sleep for the past twenty years, I still don't want to believe it's time to get up. On automatic pilot, I grab my faded black sweats, fumble into my Sauconys, and, while the rest of the house sleeps, head out the door. Just barely getting a stride going, I run down Pequot Avenue and wonder what the hell I am doing out here. My breathing is irregular, I'm not warmed up yet, and I've only had five hours of sleep. How can I possibly consider myself a serious runner, or even a good runner, when I can't even find the energy to do five miles? But slowly, the salt air seasons my senses, and I watch the beacon from the lighthouse at the mouth of the Thames River take a few more sweeps before fading into daylight. My first mile marker is the huge house under construction for a year now. The crew and I exchange morning hellos. I'm almost awake now, but still feel sluggish. I really hate the first two miles. At times like this, I question how I ever made it to a marathon. It's got to be all mind-set, the challenge of achieving an impossible goal. As for now, I'm making the best of a forty-minute wake-up call. By mile three I've rounded the bend onto Montauk Avenue and slowly get a rhythm going. My mind starts to drift away from my body and I finally relax into a pace that moves me effortlessly. I've got twenty minutes left to just float and be me, no pressures, no guilt, no cares. Sometimes I feel I could run like this forever. On those nerve-racking days when I am really at the breaking point, I daydream about going for a long run and never coming back. Just run and run and run. The dream is never completed because I never know if I am running to something or from something.

Before I know it, my house is in view jutting out from the rocky point on the seawall and the reality of a long workday ahead sets in and I get really sad. My treasured time is over.

I wasn't always a runner. In fact, I spent my high school days hiding from gym class because I was one of those fat teenagers that everyone made fun of. I begged my mother to write notes excusing me from gym. I was very self-conscious of my body, always feeling awkward and uncoordinated. I would be the last person picked for a team. No one in my family was athletic. I had no role models, no incentive to exercise.

As a recollection of those days, I keep a picture of my fat self as a reminder of what I had to overcome. My kids always laugh when they see it. They can't believe that I changed from a balloon, as they call it, to a lean and healthy person. My overweight body image surfaces every now and then to haunt me, and it wasn't until I ran my first marathon that I truly convinced myself that I can overcome anything in life that stands in the way of my accomplishments and dreams.

After those horrid high school days, I attended the University of Connecticut and fell in with a group of friends who exercised and were health conscious. I did what they did. Not as well as first, but I started to lose the baby fat and liked what I saw. I got married in my senior year and my mother-in-law owned an Elaine Powers Figure Salon. After I graduated, I went to work for her as an aerobics instructor. That was something. Me, the girl who wouldn't go to gym class, teaching aerobics. I threw myself into it and wanted to do the best job possible. My background as a nutrition major helped me work with people who not only wanted to tone, but wanted to lose weight. I was really good at reaching them because I had been there.

Later that year my husband, Richard, and I bought our first health club together. I was twenty-two years old, had no employees, and was totally in charge of everything. I cleaned the bathrooms, paid the bills, taught all the classes. I quickly developed a very demanding work ethic. I tend to bite off more than I can chew, but it works for me. I need to be driven. Richard was running a few mornings a week, so I joined him to keep him company. I hated it at first. I only did it to be a good wife. It was difficult, but I stuck with it and soon was loving it. I would start my day with a run and then felt totally invigorated to work at the gym all day long. It made me feel better.

I continued to run every morning, even when Richard didn't. He tended to view running as a leisure activity but I had moved on to become a running addict, never missing a day and increasing my mileage. I ran through both pregnancies despite negative comments and concerns from family and friends. I needed that feeling every day. It was my special time to be just me—not a mom, a wife, a boss, just Ellen. Sometimes I would finish five miles and run two or three more with Richard. After running a consistent pattern for about fifteen years, I entered a race on a dare and was immediately hooked. The adrenaline from the crowd was such a great high. As an added bonus, my pace improved. Racing became routine. In 1992, I did my first twelve-miler and decided right then and there to run a marathon. I had to do it, to take that challenge. I had no doubt that I could run the distance, but could I stay mentally focused for all those hours? Would I break down and quit under stress? It was a control issue, mind over body. I had to know if I was mentally strong enough to take the challenge.

Once the commitment was made to run a marathon, I became a different person, totally focused on my new goal. I am very disciplined, so the intense training was a natural attraction for me. The physical release I experience from a long run is like being in an altered state. I start my run, pounding the same path I've followed for years, and slowly I find myself transformed into another dimension, a calmer state of mind where I let myself go and allow all sorts of thoughts to process through my senses. The air is easier to breathe, the summer grass smells especially potent, and I experience the natural beauty of my surroundings in a new light. I think about my kids, my career, what I want to be when I grow up. I don't even realize I've been gone for over an hour. Reality comes back when I start to get thirsty or tired. Then, with the transformation gone, running seems like drudgery and I try to recapture the moment.

The damn alarm was permanently set at 6 A.M. so I trained while the family slept. I was conscious not to take time away from them, so I was constantly squeezing in my training around their schedules. My two kids were old enough to leave at home alone if necessary, which was a real benefit. Training is such a huge time commitment. Richard was very supportive and would run with me, but it was an effort for him to do distance, even six miles. My kids, on the other hand, were not supportive. They thought I was crazy. I think it was difficult for them to see me in such a determined, competitive role. No other mother was out there running like a lunatic. They were at the age when they wanted me to be normal and I wasn't. I was doing fifty to sixty miles a week and as many races as I could find. As the race date grew near, I knew I was physically ready but I was still unsure of the mental part.

The night before the race I was extremely nervous. I just wanted to get it over with. Like the racehorse at the starting gate who kicks and goes into a last-minute frenzy, I couldn't focus. I kept eating all sorts of different foods, hoping for a magical meal, an elixir that would provide instant energy when needed. Richard had decided to run the marathon with me, but instead of being a positive influence, we were direct opposites. I was nervous and tense, he was relaxed. After a restless night waking up every hour, I couldn't wait to get to the course. In contrast, Richard casually made himself breakfast.

When we arrived at East Lyme High School, I got totally caught up in the marathon fever. It was so exciting to be part of a group taking on the biggest event of their lives. The crowd of about two hundred runners, most of whom are locals, were doing last-minute stretches, getting last-minute hugs, or saying a silent prayer for an extra ounce of courage. The collective energy was fuel for me. Richard and I started at the back of the pack with a very slow pace. At mile nine I developed a blister. Being a novice at marathons, I wore new socks that morning and quickly learned a lesson about the importance of the correct, and worn-in, footgear. Richard was already struggling at twelve miles. He didn't want to hold me back so I took off and started running my own race with my own rhythm. It finally felt great.

I was warned the real marathon starts at mile twenty, but for now I was flying. Occasionally I would talk with other runners who were at my pace. We'd talk about how scenic and pretty the course was, what our goal was, chitchat stuff, anything to take our minds off the distance, the exhaustion, and the mental fatigue. Some were here to try and qualify for Boston, others were doing it as a training run for the New York City Marathon or Marine Corps. Most, though, were people like me who just love to run. Then it happened. At mile twenty, as predicted, I ran out of gas. I was so tired. The mental burden to keep going was incredible. Physically, I wasn't hurting except for the stupid blister, but I was wiped. I looked around at other runners who were suffering and in severe pain. Some were literally screaming from the cramping. Others were throwing up on the side. It's a real downer to experience the pain of your comrades. I really felt for them and it didn't do anything to lift my own mental strain.

But I had prepared for this moment. I knew I would need something special, a strong commitment from inside my heart to keep me going. I dedicated each of the last six miles to people that I love, that I would never give up on in life. I had to finish their mile or it would be as if I let them down. It got me through the most difficult part. I don't think I could have made it without them mentally by my side.

When the finish line came into view, I sprinted for all I was worth, even though I have no idea where I found that last bit of energy. I think I was just overjoyed that it was over. And for me, crossing the finish line of a marathon meant exorcising that overweight teenager harbored in the recesses of my mind forever. Here I was, a nonathlete, feeling so athletic, so exuberant. I was overwhelmed with emotion at my accomplishment. I earned every step of that race. No one can ever take that feeling away from me. It was the next best thing to childbirth. You spend all that time and energy preparing for the big moment, whether it's nine months or 26.2 miles, and the outcome is pure heaven.

When I started the race, I set my watch alarm for twelve-thirty, hoping I would finish in four hours. I totally forgot about it until I was in the parking lot walking off my stiffness and fatigue and suddenly the alarm went off. I was thrilled to hear the sound, which came to signify my win, especially since I had beat my time by fifteen minutes. It was such a great musical reminder of my accomplishment that I keep the alarm permanently set at that time. It makes my day to hear that little beep on my wrist, taking me back to the one of the best moments of my life.

However, my day was not yet over, as I anxiously waited for Richard. I walked off my tension and fatigue, drank juice, and just enjoyed the moment watching the other runners finish, cheering them on. After half an hour, I began get worried, but sat in the bleachers with the other spectators. A truck was pulling in the stragglers or the injured, and I started to get concerned. When I finally saw him coming down the last few yards, I was overjoyed for him. I had been waiting for over an hour but he had been running for that extra hour. I stood up and cheered as loudly as I could for him.

I continue to run every day and have completed seven marathons so far. Every year I still get that urge to see if I can do it. It's my personal challenge, my permanent New Year's resolution. Some people make a goal to lose weight, stop drinking, be a better parent, make more money. I resolve to run a marathon every year. It's really no different from other people's goals. But the decision has to come from the heart. No one can talk you into losing weight, or running a marathon. It has to come from within or the drive won't be there when you need it.

HOW NOT TO RUN A MARATHON

RICHARD BELLICCHI
RESIDENCE: NEW LONDON, CT
OCCUPATION: OWNER, WORLD GYM HEALTH CLUB, CHICOPEE, MA
FIRST MARATHON: 1992 EAST LYME MARATHON
D.O.B.: 10-6-47
AGE AT FIRST MARATHON: 45

Richard does not describe himself as a runner. A few mornings a week he goes out for two or three miles to get some fresh air. However, he does describe himself as a tough competitor. All through life, he has taken on challenges that others would walk away from, and in most cases has succeeded due to an overabundance of tenacity and a firm belief that he is right in his decisions. However, running his first marathon may not have been the right decision on this particular day. But being Richard, he turned what was destined to be a failed run into a challenge and achieved his goal.

I WAS ALWAYS TOO THIN AND TOO SMALL for most high school sports, so no one ever thought of me as an athlete. I was the skinny kid, the scrapper, never having the endurance to pull my own weight on the playing field. Football, the be-all-and-end-all of high school sports, was allegedly out of my reach. Part of that was due to my allergies, which can really affect sports, but I had real difficulties at building muscle mass, getting physically strong. Because of that weakness in me, and perceived by only me, I needed to prove to myself that I was as good as the football kings. I desperately wanted to be an athlete, to be recognized as they were. I was always testing myself against their strength and abilities on the field. I chose football because it offered the greatest challenge for me to succeed.

Despite all the odds against me, I started preparing for football try-outs by building up as much speed and endurance as I could and ran the hundred-yard dash. Believe me, I didn't break any records, but to everyone's surprise I made the team and actually won some trophies.

After high school, I was recruited to play football for the University of Connecticut, a dream come true. However, when I reported to training camp at Storrs and saw the size of the other players on the team, wisdom prevailed and I gave it up. I knew I could never compete against those players and come out alive. They were huge, and I tipped the scale at 150 pounds after dinner.

I continued my running a few miles a week and played some basket-ball, my real passion in sports. But endurance continued to be a constant problem. During my senior year of college, I got married, and after graduation Ellen and I took the plunge into the fitness industry and bought a health club. We did very well from the start and kept expanding. I had 127 employees across five states and it soon consumed us, putting in long days and not getting home till very late. We were burning the candle at both ends and with that type of schedule, getting any form of daily exercise is tough. Running was the most logical routine. It's not that I loved it, but it was the best alternative; I didn't have to wait for anyone, buy expensive equipment, or fit into someone else's schedule. I just got up a half hour earlier and ran. There was a sense of satisfaction knowing that my exercise had been completed for the day by nine in the morning.

I realize that running can get boring, so I try to make it interesting. First of all, my run is very scenic. I run along the water where there is always a different view, whether it's the ferries crossing to Orient Point, a few morning submarines on patrol, or a sailboat on its way into Long Island Sound. Running also keeps me in shape for other activities I enjoy such as tennis and basketball. And although I didn't start out thinking this way, running is a hedge against aging. I'm forty-eight now so that benefit becomes a positive factor in my outlook on running. And for someone whose business is the exercise industry, staying in shape and being on top of the latest trends in physical fitness is a job requirement.

When Ellen decided to run her marathon, I encouraged her but had no desire to run it myself. I couldn't see spending four months doing all that intensive training. And besides, I knew I didn't have the endurance. With six weeks to go before the race date, Ellen asked me to keep her company on a ten-mile run. I agreed, but only if she paced herself at a ten-minute pace. Even with that, I was dying the entire way. A few weeks later, Ellen decided to run a 15K on Block Island and asked me to keep her company on the ferry ride. Since I had already done the ten miles, I decided to enter the race with her just to see if I could handle more. That was a big mistake. I was miserable. I hated it. The island is beautiful when you're on a bike or driving around, but it sure is hilly and windy when running around it. When I had to slow down to a walk, Ellen kept running. Now I was on my own, doing something I didn't even enjoy. It was a horrible experience. I didn't think I would ever get off the island that day.

With two weeks to go, I still didn't even think of running the big one, but I then read somewhere that if you can run sixteen, you can run a marathon. The seeds were beginning to take hold and I actually contemplated the run, only because it would be a terrific challenge to do a marathon without really training. The next weekend I decided to do a split sixteen—I ran ten, went home to shower, ate a big breakfast, then went out again and did six. My legs were so sore afterward, and to make it worse, my allergies kicked in and I was wheezing and felt miserable. I started coughing and couldn't stop. Later on, I called a friend whose opinion I trust. This guy worked for me as a personal trainer and told me a marathon is the worst thing physically you can do to your body. He'd never ran one and would not recommend it. I rationalized that if Doug, who is in great shape and a very strong athlete, won't run a marathon and I do, I would be on par with him physically, perhaps even a better athlete. I know that sounds strange, but I guess I never got over comparing myself to others.

I still wasn't sure I wanted to do it. By now, Ellen was ready in every aspect. She had trained hard for four months and could hardly wait. The morning of the race, I decided to do it.

East Lyme is a great first marathon course, although very hilly for the first twelve miles. It's like running with friends in your backyard. We started out at a snail's pace, but by five miles my allergies were too much for me and I had a coughing fit. I knew I was holding Ellen back, so at twelve miles I told her to run her own race.

I kept plodding along, not having a very good time. I remember going up this big hill and could barely breathe. I kept thinking, "Dear God, just let me make it up this hill." Well, I made it up, but at the crest there was another hill. That was it for me, I was done. I was ready to pack it in and get a lift home. Then, as if fate stepped in my way, I saw one of the local running gods, who was considered a shoe-in for winning, walk off the course. He walked over, slapped me five, and said one of those runner things like, "Go for it." I couldn't believe he was quitting. What a coward. I knew he had done all the proper training. What reasons could he possibly have for giving up? Here I was, barely breathing, hadn't trained, wasn't one of the so-called local elites. I figured, if I could finish, then I would be a better man than him.

That gave me the incentive to continue. My quads were killing me, I was at my physical limit, but I decided to keep going.

For the remainder of the race, I walked a hundred yards, then slowly ran for about a quarter mile, then walked again. With no endurance left, it was the only way I could make it. I was totally alone out there. It was pretty much me and officials. The hardest part of the race was sixteen to twenty miles. I kept thinking Ellen had probably finished, and I thought about her courage in committing to this Herculean event and how much she had endured to get this far. Just thinking of her gave me the inspiration to go on. I admired her strength and fortitude. Then I started focusing on my own character, how I had never backed down from anything before. I needed to find the part of me that would get me through this; I wasn't going to be a quitter. I knew this race was bigger than me, but if I could beat it I would be my own hero.

At twenty miles I wanted to cry. At this point, I knew I would finish, but I was in such pain and I was suddenly so hungry. I kept saying, over and over, "It can't get worse than this." I needed nourishment in the worst way and then I spotted a Dairy Queen across the street. Soft ice cream, the perfect food! Like a crazed nomad who was too long in the desert, I crossed over the line and went to the D.Q. It was crowded, but I had lost all inhibitions and went to the front of the line, where a woman was ordering for her son. I begged her to buy me an ice cream. I must have looked pretty scary, you know, when runners get that glazed look in their eyes, mouths covered in dried sweat, T-shirt soaked and ill-fitting. But I did have my East Lyme number on so she took pity on me and bought me the sweetest and most needed ice cream I ever ate.

For the last six miles I savored my ice cream for as long as it lasted, counted telephone poles, and shuffled along with dogged determination. At twenty-five miles, my parents drove by and waved. That meant a lot to me, and inspired me to shuffle my feet a little faster. When I finally crossed the finish line, five hours and fifteen minutes after starting, I felt proud that I hadn't let myself down. And the sight of Ellen waiting for me, well, let's just say she never looked more beautiful.

After we cleaned up and took some photos, we headed home to a hot shower and bowl of pasta and our neighborhood-famous Bellicchi sauce, prepared with my father's homegrown tomatoes. And believe me, I really needed that pasta. I lost eight pounds during the marathon and was sick for weeks afterward. My immune system was shot, I was a physical wreck. I don't even feel entitled to say I ran a marathon. Basically, I completed the distance and almost killed myself doing it. I have no desire to do another one.

The marathon event requires more will than skill to survive. If you anticipate that it won't be so terrible, you can make it, but I wouldn't recommend my method.

My next challenge was skydiving, which was a hell of a lot faster to the finish line than the marathon.

THE PATH LESS TAKEN

HEIDI L. WINSLOW BUTTS
RESIDENCE: TELLURIDE, COLORADO
OCCUPATION: MOTHER OF TWO TODDLERS, FREELANCE PAINTER
FIRST MARATHON: 1986 FIESTA BOWL, SCOTTSDALE, ARIZONA
D.O.B.: 9-8-57
AGE AT FIRST MARATHON: 29

Even though her first and only marathon was twelve years ago, it was a high point in her life and Heidi had no problem recapturing every moment. Escaping the path of the corporate world after college, she took the less traveled road to Colorado to become a ski instructor "just for a while," but the landscape was too breathtaking and she never returned East. She found a job and a passion for running, inspired by a friend and the splendor of the Rockies. Nowadays Heidi is most happy when she is in the mountains with her husband and children, teaching them to love, honor, and respect the beauty that surrounds their lives.

I GREW UP ON A SMALL FARM IN ESSEX, Massachusetts, and in Vermont with two younger brothers. We were always skiing, making rope courses in the woods and rambling around the fields making up games. I played sports all though grade school and high school. It was important for me to excel in sports because in first grade, I was shy and didn't have much confidence. Sports was the only thing that made me feel good about myself.

When I was in high school I was asked to run the relay for the track team because I was fast, and they needed girls. Running came naturally to me. I never planned on running track; my only experience with it was as a foundation or preparation for other sports, especially my chosen ones, lacrosse and hockey, which I played all through prep school and college.

During college, in 1977, I sat down and wrote my life's goals: 1) Run a marathon, 2) climb Mount Kenya, 3) skydive from an airplane, 4) start my own business, and 5) write a children's book, among other things. I wanted to incorporate these goals into a job. I was lucky enough to go with the National Outdoor Leadership School to Kenya for two months, where I tested my skills at climbing and mountaineering.

When that ended, I wanted to get a job with UNESCO. I also applied to the Peace Corps, but something else always seemed to get in the way. When I was younger, I worked in a hospital and helped build a school in the West Indies. I was definitely more the save-the-world type than the corporate type and fortunately, my parents have always been incredibly supportive and encouraging in all my pursuits.

I moved to Colorado and became a ski instructor at Aspen. It was a great life. I was in my early twenties and doing what I loved. Sometimes I felt guilty as most of my college friends were in advertising or working on Wall Street and here I was, a ski bum. However, I would wager that I had more fun and felt better about what I was doing.

A tennis club had just changed hands in Aspen, owned by Dick Butera and his wife, Julie Anthony, Billie Jean King's doubles partner. Julie and her husband renovated the club, transforming it into the Aspen Club Fitness and Sports Medicine Institute along with Dr. Bruno Balke, who is credited with starting treadmill stress testing. At the time, I was thinking of going to the American College of Sports Medicine, but Julie offered me on-the-job training and a salaried position with her institute so I took it and worked there for the next six years.

Most of my time was spent skiing and working. It was a perfect life for me. I was dating a guy who was a coach for the U.S. ski team and he loved to run, so I started to run with him. He was one of the most inspiring people I've ever met in my life. He made running so much fun for me. We would run through the woods, into the mountains, across streams, meadows, jump fences, it was absolutely beautiful. I became addicted to these runs. I'd go out on my lunch break and run six of the most gorgeous miles I could find. We decided to take a drive to

California together and every four hours or so we'd stop at a scenic spot, slip into our running shoes, and take off. I never would have viewed running with the same intensity or emotions, almost as a separate entity from other sports, until I saw it and experienced it in this way. I owe him that.

My six-mile run during lunch became my routine. While my co-workers went into town to grab takeout, I'd be running through meadows and up and down the mountain. It was also my time to sort through thoughts, to meditate and find that inner peace most of us struggle to discover. Running kept me grounded.

I started to race some 10Ks, thinking it would be fun, a challenge to test myself. I only did about two a year, but I did well, usually finishing in the top three. Doing well was great, but then I would be afraid that the next time I wouldn't do so well, that maybe my winning streak was just luck. I never had the confidence to believe I was good, that I deserved to win. I remember being on starting lines and having people point to me and say, "Oh, there's Heidi, she's one to watch." Then I would feel so much pressure. What if I didn't win? It got too distracting. I was definitely addicted to the high of running. If I couldn't get a run in every day, I'd go nuts. But at the same time I also loved running for the pleasure and sense of calmness it brought me.

By the mideighties the institute was booming. I worked with Martina Navratilova, Buddy Hackett, other celebrities who came to recondition their bodies. Julie assigned me to a woman in her sixties who came in every day to work on the treadmill because she was training for a marathon. I was very impressed and thought, "Hey, if she can do it I can do it." That planted a little seed in my mind to run a marathon. However, I didn't tell anyone, I just kept running my regular routine, but would push the distance. While my friend was coaching a ski team camp in Oregon, I used to hitch a ride with them to Mount Bachelor and then run down, traversing the meadows, running through the woods and down steep embankments. It was an exhilarating experience.

My longest run prior to the marathon was sixteen miles. Deep down inside I believed in myself, believed that I could finish. Of course there were times a few doubts crept in, but I also knew about conditioning and training because of my work at the sports institute. The thing that made the marathon different from other sports events I had done was that my whole life I played team sports and now it was just me. It was a big challenge to do something all on my own.

I chose to run the Fiesta Bowl Marathon in Arizona because people in the institute talked about what a neat race it was. I went alone as my boyfriend had to work. I flew to Arizona the day before the race and stayed in a hotel room. Lying in bed the night before the race, I suddenly felt so alone. What was I doing here? My family was back home on the East Coast and my boyfriend, who had inspired me and wanted to be there with me, couldn't come and I felt, this is it. I'm on my own. But the next morning when I got to the start and saw all the other participants, I felt a great sense of belonging.

It was still dark out and we had to take a bus through the desert to the start. I was kind of groggy on the bus ride, just catching glimpses of the desert through the moon's glow. When we finally got to the start, the sun was just about ready to come out, casting shadows on the cactus. It was dewy and chilly. A subdued energy was rustling through the crowd. It felt as if I was on another planet. It was so surreal. The land formations were different from anything I had been used to. This was a strange land.

I couldn't believe I was finally at the start of my first marathon. I wondered what it must feel like for people in the Olympics or others experiencing a really big event. I started out fast, right up there with some of the elite runners, doing just under seven-minute miles for the first three miles until I realized I had to slow down. I was moving so swiftly, I couldn't even feel my legs, like I was floating detached from the crowd, moving in a mass of bodies. The air was cool, the sun was breaking through, the gentle breezes were blowing my hair. It was amazing. By seven miles I started to calm down and get into a pace. I kept my mind busy viewing the incredible scenery around me. Having grown up in New England on a farm, I was mesmerized by the landscape of the desert. I couldn't believe there were no trees. I was consumed with how different it was from anything I had known or seen before. These thoughts occupied me until about twelve miles. I didn't talk to many people because I was keeping a pretty fast pace. I started out telling myself my goal was just to finish. But then I thought, heck, I'm out here, I might as well see just how good I am. Maybe I can do it under 3:30. So I pushed myself, but I also felt that whatever time I finished in was going to be fine. I knew I was playing head games, but I did want a strong finish and at the same time I needed a comfort cushion just in case I didn't.

I concentrated on my breathing, as Dr. Balke had taught me. Prior to the race, I had a few sessions with him and he concurred that I had mostly fast-twitch muscle, which isn't necessarily conducive to running marathons. He taught me breathing techniques to maximize my energy. He believed that by changing training techniques and following a different breathing pattern for a long period of time the body would adapt, for better endurance. Whatever it was, it was working.

At about thirteen miles, the course enters the city of Scottsdale, and I suddenly tensed up. The landscape changed from a relaxed surrounding to the noise and cacophony of a city. I wanted to withdraw inside myself and find the more peaceful oasis of the desert. The city surroundings made me claustrophobic. The next seven miles were tough and I needed some mental stimulation to get me through. I started to sing "Every Breath You Take," by the Police. I kept repeating that one line, "Every breath you take, every step you make," over and over in my head, and it seemed to help.

By mile twenty my legs seized up like steel. I'm used to physical pain but I had never run this far before. My glycogen was depleted and I needed something to bolster my energy level. I remember reading somewhere to carry aspirin and hard candy in case of an emergency. I forgot the candy, but at the next aid station I took the aspirin, ate an orange, and drank Gatorade. It helped somewhat.

I was determined to keep going, but I had to talk my way through it. I kept telling myself, "Don't blow it. You've worked so hard, don't give up." I slowed down to a jog for about a quarter mile. I felt like I was running on empty but mentally I was still strong. At mile twenty-two, I came back full force. I knew I could do it. By now a crowd had gathered, cheering all the runners and that definitely felt good. I felt like Rocky running up the steps of the museum, with the music blaring—I could hear the theme in my head—and people were reaching out to me, cheering me, supporting me. It was wonderful and I choked up, almost crying. How I wished my friends or family were waiting for me at the finish, at this most incredible moment in my life, but no one was there, and I found it didn't matter. It was very overwhelming. I don't know which was more compelling: the fact that I had accomplished my goal, or that I was part of this amazing demonstration of the human willpower. I just couldn't believe it.

After the race, I jumped right into a taxi to catch my flight back to Colorado. I didn't have time to mingle around soaking up the euphoria from the other runners. When I settled into my seat, I sat back and thought, "Wow. What did I just do?" It was crazy. An hour later, the plane landed and my boyfriend ran out onto the tarmac and greeted me as I came off the plane. For me, at that moment, it was like crossing the finish line all over again. I ran into his arms and he hugged me and told me how proud he was of me. He knew how much it meant to me.

A few years later he was killed in a car accident. He's not with me anymore, but in a way he is. Often when I go for a run in the mountains I think of him. I got married in 1988 to the greatest guy, who loved the outdoors as much I did. We did some traveling together before we had children and we would run in some amazing places, past rice paddies in Bali and up volcanoes. He was always more of a skier than runner, although he enjoyed our runs together. But due to a back injury suffered from a ski racing crash when he was young, he had to finally give up running altogether. Now, he just enjoys hearing about my runs while he stays home playing with our two girls. Skiing is our family sport, although I'm sure the girls will want to pick up snowboarding any day now.

At night, right before bedtime, I get all cozy with the kids and we read one of their favorite books, *The Little Engine That Could*. I loved that book as a child and I definitely remember repeating some of those lines during my marathon. The book has an important message for everyone from five to ninety-five. It teaches us to strive for whatever in life is important and not to give up without giving it our all. I want my girls to grow up knowing that whatever their goal, it is within their reach if they just "think they can, think they can."

BLOOD IS THICKER THAN WATER

ILETA COLEY
RESIDENCE: BILLINGS, MONTANA
OCCUPATION: CO-OWNER, G AND C AUTHORIZED AUTO SERVICE
FIRST MARATHON: 1995 GOVERNOR'S CUP "GHOST TOWN"
MARATHON, HELENA, MONTANA
D.O.B.: 8-27-45
AGE AT FIRST MARATHON: 50

Having the courage to question whether your life is working for you isn't easy. Especially when you think the path you've been on since childhood may need an alternative route. Ileta and her husband, Gary, had the strength and fortitude to make the changes in their lives that would best benefit their children. In doing so, they built a strong family bond that continues to this day and includes, among other things, family marathons. Ileta credits her children with instilling in her the strength to keep getting out the door to run. After she spent years watching them perform at the high school meets, they wanted to give back the same support and encouragement to their mom. Inspired by her two daughters, who ran their first marathon together, Ileta wanted to share the experience.

I GREW UP IN JOLIET, MONTANA, a very small town with a very small high school. My graduating class had twenty-one kids. In a school that small, there was little opportunity for organized sports, especially for girls. My family wasn't very athletic either. My older brothers and younger sister were more the book type than the sports type, and tended to lean more toward the overweight side of the scale. Although we lacked a drive toward exercise, we were a close-knit family.

I dated a guy all through high school who shared my strong beliefs in family and church values. We attended a theology college in Kansas, but Gary dropped out after being somewhat disillusioned with the strict rules and rigid teachings. We met again at a Billy Graham conference a few years later, started dating again, and got married. Our lives were quickly consumed with three kids, work, and church. Every night there was something to attend, whether a church committee, choir, services, it was all very demanding. Finally, one night attending yet another church function, our youngest son rebelled. He just refused to come along. And our older daughters weren't too happy with the extensive role the church was playing in our lives either. Gary and I sat down and analyzed just what direction our lives were taking, and we didn't like what we saw. We had stopped questioning what we were practicing, content to just follow in the steps of the elders.

We made a decision to stop all involvement with the church and instead spend Sundays and weeknights with the children, doing activities that interested all of us. Weekends and vacations were now reserved for family camping trips, snowmobiling, motorcycling, lots of outdoor family-related activities. We were always close, but now that we were devoting more time to our children, the bond became stronger. We were finally taking into account what was important to them.

As the kids got involved with high school track, we attended all their events. I loved the meets, cheering on the kids with the other parents. At this stage of our lives, Gary and I were going through our forties and definitely doing the weight-gain thing. We never took time away from our family life to do any exercise on our own, such as joining a gym. It just didn't fit into the scheme of things. The kids were the ones who first encouraged us to get out and walk or jog with them. That's actually how we got interested in running. It felt so good being outside enjoying nature that soon we started running more than walking. Then we started doing races. I guess all those years watching the kids perform at the meets rubbed off on us.

Gary and I found a nice two-mile loop and we were very satisfied running our course at our own pace. We thought we were doing great, making more progress than we imagined possible. Then our neighbors suggested we try a local 5K race, and since we didn't know what distance a 5K was, we asked them. When they told us it was 3.1 miles, we were concerned. Gosh, can we really run another mile? It seemed so much longer. And since we were so happy with our little loop, we weren't sure we wanted to find a longer one. Could we, should we venture out into the world of racing? We decided to give it a try, and to our amazement, we really enjoyed it. At first, I was thinking, "What am I doing out here? I am forty-five years old and taking up a new sport." But it was fun. I am not a competitive person so even in the races, I never ran for time. I didn't want the element of competition to override the enjoyment, the fun of running for me.

My first 5K was an all-women race and I never saw more women of every size and shape gathered in one place. Some of them didn't even look like they could run a mile, no less three, but who am I to judge the performance of others? I was just really captured by the energy and spirit of the women. After that first race, I was hooked, I loved it. I especially liked the social aspect of the race. Everyone stands around chatting, sharing tips and running stories. I just soaked up the enthusiasm of the crowd, hanging out, saying, "Hey, I did it!" You rarely hear a negative word spoken.

After that, I started reading about running techniques to improve myself. Gary is very scientific minded, so he was the one who really studied the articles and passed on the information to me. He was doing most of the road races with me so he was also interested in improving his training techniques. By now most of our kids were in college so we had more time to dedicate to our interests. Our two older daughters were attending college close by so we were able to visit on weekends, and still attend their track meets.

Although the idea of a marathon started to roam around our thoughts, we didn't think there was time to train for one with our son still at home. We just kept racing and learning, increasing our endurance and concentrating on the cardiovascular benefits. Health was a big factor in our dedication to running. We saw the pounds disappear and felt better. It was definitely becoming a lifestyle change for us. Our eating habits also changed, reflecting our newfound healthy lifestyle. Foods that once were appealing, like hamburgers and french fries, just didn't taste good anymore. I learned to listen to my body and it definitely was telling me to eat more fruits and vegetables.

I started to increase my race distance from 5Ks to 10Ks. I also made a habit of running more distance than the actual race during training, just to make sure I could do it. Now that our son had moved on to college, leaving us with that empty-nest syndrome, Gary and I had more time on weekends and in the evenings so we started to increase the distance. Running was now part of our lives. We entered races as often as possible.

One drawback to being out here in the boons, away from big cities, is the lack of scheduled race events. We had to travel long distances every weekend if we wanted to race, and that became too much for us. So we stayed content running with friends, doing our loops and waiting for that occasional local race.

I guess it was my daughters who first inspired me to run a marathon. When they left home, I missed them dearly and thought about them every day. When they called with the news that they were going to run a marathon together, there was no hesitation, no doubt that Gary and I would be there for them. The morning of their marathon we drove them to the bus area and watched them take off in the pitch black for the starting line, twenty-six miles away. We then went and had some breakfast. I kept looking at my watch all morning, thinking, "Well, they've just started." One hour later I'd look at my watch and say, "Gary, it's time to leave for the finish line. Gary, do you have the camera? Gary, we can't be late. Gary, do you think they're halfway yet?" I was so caught up in the excitement of what they were doing. When we got to the finish line and saw the crowd that had gathered, it added to our already-high level of enthusiasm. I really got caught up in the fever of the event. This particular course ends at the bottom of a downhill, so you can see the runners coming into the last quarter-mile straight line to the finish. I remember straining through the crowd, focusing on the road and waiting to get my first glimpse of the girls. When I saw them, I just started jumping up and down, grabbing onto Gary and screaming. It was such an exciting moment. I was so proud of them and when they crossed the finish line holding hands, I wept. I was also thinking, "Wow, I want to do that. Yeah, I think I can do that!" I was driven by the excitement. It looked like so much fun and I felt that if I did run a marathon it would connect us in some strange way. I don't know, I just wanted to be a part of that, to share an experience that seemed so special.

My decision to run a marathon was also made out of sheer ignorance. Heck, everyone was smiling when they crossed the finish line, how difficult could it be? When we got home and shared the events of the race with our neighbors, and I mentioned my desire to run one, they immediately jumped on the bandwagon and said they were registered for the Governor's Cup Marathon in Helena, and why didn't we all run it together? So my thoughts for running a marathon escalated from a "someday" time frame to seven months away.

Now that I was committed, I started to take it seriously. My longest run to date was eight miles and I had seven months to train. I was relying on my neighbors' advice since they had run a few marathons. They were going to be my unofficial coaches. Gary trained with me, although he wasn't sure he was going to run the marathon. Our training was very simple. Every other weekend we bumped the mileage up by two more miles. We went from eight to ten to twelve and so on. We did a half marathon in March, in the town of Moab, Utah. As I mentioned before, races are far and few between out here. To get to the half marathon, we drove eight and half hours to Salt Lake City, spent the night with our daughter, and the next morning drove another four and a half hours to Moab. It was a beautiful run and well worth the drive. The course has the Colorado River on one side and sheer red cliffs on the other. It's a desert run with incredibly beautiful scenery. I saw different species of flowers and birds that we don't get in Montana. It helped take my mind off the aches and pains I was feeling, especially on the bottoms of my feet. I think my shoes were worn down and I hadn't gotten around to replacing them and now I was paying for it. Overall, it was a positive experience and I started to look forward to the marathon.

I now felt it was doable. I did a few more 10Ks during the spring and felt totally ready. I didn't want to overtrain.

My marathon debut was going to be a family reunion. All the children were planning on being there to cheer for me, giving me their support and love. The night before the race we packed up the camper. Since there was so much extra room, I overpacked, taking one of everything. I even threw in a case of Gatorade. When we got to Helena, my daughters were already there waiting for us and we had a little reunion. Then we went to register and pick up the race packet. While there, one of my daughters had to use the ladies' room. When we got back to the hotel room, she realized she had left her wedding ring on the sink counter. We all raced back to the registration center hoping and praying it would be there, but the ring was gone. This was not a good way to start the marathon. We were all crying and carrying on, feeling her loss. But she finally looked up at me with a tear-stained face and told me she wasn't going to let this ruin my day. She said, "I'm over it. It's gone. Let's move on." We never mentioned the mishap again and she truly did seem to forget the whole thing. I knew she was being incredibly brave for me, which made me want to hug her.

Helena is an old mining town, but so is every place in Montana. It's also very hilly, which should have been a clue for me about how difficult this race was going to be, but as I said, I was clueless on all aspects. The race only draws about 250 participants, and again, I was clueless as to why, until it was too late to turn back.

I slept well, got up early, and headed to the bus, which took us to the starting point. The ride seemed to take forever. Gary had decided to run the marathon with me and we sat there together wondering when would we ever get to the start. We finally stopped in the town of Marysville, which resembles an abandoned movie set from an old western. We were way up in the mountains and it was very cold and still dark. I wasn't nervous; in fact I was in a great mood. Again, I chalk this up to my total ignorance of the event. While others were doing warm-up runs, I walked around humming to myself, wondering why anyone would want to start running now when we had twenty-six miles to cover? It seemed like a silly idea to me.

Gary started out fast, so I was left to myself. The first six miles of the course is all downhill and by then, the sun was out, there was a light breeze, and it was quite pretty. There were pine trees and all sorts of pretty wildflowers. I was feeling very happy, very satisfied with myself. Occasionally I would strike up conversations with other runners, but mostly I kept to myself.

After the downhill, the course levels for a few miles, and then starts going uphill. The course is described as "lots of rolling hills," but this was turning into nothing but hills. I hadn't done any hill work in my training so I was not enjoying this. My inexperience really hit hard as I thought I had to run fast up those blasted hills. I passed a couple, younger than me, who said, "Hey, slow down. You're working way too hard with a long way to go yet." I immediately slowed down. I was dying out there and it was only twelve miles. I was also really hot and couldn't cool off. Again out of ignorance, I wore the wrong clothes. I had on spandex running shorts with a long cotton T-shirt that came down to my hips, which created a double layer around my stomach. The heat was making me weak and tired. On top of that, my feet were in absolute agony. I kept thinking, some lucky runners are already finished, showered, and having lunch with their families while I'm stuck out here in hell.

By eighteen miles I was doing the walk-run pace. I wanted to end it all, quit the race, lie down and die, but unfortunately there was no one in sight. I couldn't see another person on the course in either direction. I wanted to just give up the ghost, cuddle up to the curb and fall asleep, but I was afraid the vultures would get me.

Why didn't anyone tell me about this part? This was not the way I imagined it would be. I hated it. I swore I would never do it again. I was so depressed and disillusioned. I'd been out there four hours and had eight more miles to go. I started to cry.

The course continued to be covered with gruesome, grueling hills. I had long lost any desire, or ability, to run. However, I'd never been a quitter and I wasn't going to let this race get the better of me. I had to finish, even if it meant walking the remaining way. Finally, at about twenty-two miles the course leveled out for a while and looped through a National Guard armory. Some of the military men were on duty, thinking they had seen the last of the runners and then I showed up. I could see the pathetic look in their eyes as they watched me run through the base. I kept thinking, "God, I hope I don't look as bad as I feel."

Then, just when I only had three miles to go and I was actually getting my strength back, the course went uphill again. Now I was really pissed. This sucked. It was awful, I didn't think I could take another step, and I figured since I'd already been out five hours and no one had sent a rescue squad for me, the race must be officially over, the banners taken down, and everyone dispersed for home. But then, in my darkest hour, I saw my son running toward me, encouraging me to finish. "Come on, Mom, you can do it, you've come so far. You're doing great! You're looking good." The only response I could muster was, "Like hell I look good." Then my daughters showed up to run the last two miles with us, and then my husband, who had long since finished, also came out to help me, so there I was the last two miles being escorted and coaxed along by my family. I was so touched by their support that I was actually able to run the last yards and fake a strong finish through the chute.

I was so burnt that the only enjoyment I felt crossing the finish line was that it was over. I was done. My cotton shirt was soaked, I was dehydrated and needed to change out of those clothes immediately. In fact, I wanted to burn them. My kids formed a circle around me and I peeled off my clothes right there at the finish, enjoying the refreshing feel of cool, dry clothes. Even though the clean clothes helped to lift my spirits, I was in agony. My quads hurt, my feet were on fire, and I was walking like a penguin. One of the volunteers offered to give me a massage. That turned out to be a big mistake. She killed me. I know she was trying to help, but she applied a lot of pressure and I ended up feeling worse. I wanted to scream, but she was being sweet and I didn't want to scare her. I really don't think she knew what she was doing.

We were all starving by now, and went out to eat. The conversation centered on what an absolutely horrible experience this had been for me. The kids encouraged me not to give up marathons, and next time choose a nicer, gentler marathon course. "Next time?" I gasped in horror. A running coach who had attended the marathon came by our table and confirmed that the Governor's Cup is known as one of the toughest marathon courses to run. So I gave it some thought and decided to try another one and picked the St. George Marathon in Utah, which was the same course my daughters used for their first.

I trained the same way, but did more hill work, drank more fluids, and wore the proper clothes. I also practiced a technique where I slowed down on my long runs and ran faster on my short ones, which is supposed to build more muscle mass. Everything paid off because in St. George I beat my time by almost an hour. The following year I ran the Twin Cities Marathon in Minneapolis, which was a lot of fun. I'd have to say that is my favorite course to date.

Now that I have run a few, I pay more attention to my time. If I feel I didn't do well, my kids are the first ones to sit me down and say, "Mom, do you realize how few women in their fifties are out there running marathons? You are extraordinary." They give me a wake-up call and I realize just how fortunate I am. There is a positive side to starting so late in life: I have no past record. Everything I do is a personal best.

I have always had a very positive outlook on life, but running marathons has given me a new perspective, something else to be thankful for. When I'm doing a long training run, I tend to reflect on the role religion has played in my life. I used to feel guilty about leaving the church, wondering if I made the best decision for my children. Basically, they grew up with no designated religion, although they do remember the fundamentals from their early indoctrination. And I know they pray, but they incorporate their own logic and conscience into their prayers. While I run, I'll say a prayer to keep my kids safe, another prayer of thanks for the natural beauty that surrounds me, and other prayers reflecting my thanks for things in life I have been blessed with. It's a very spiritual experience. Sometimes I'll choose a prayer, like the "Our Father," and try to figure out what it really means, what the message is. I strongly believe that events in our daily life are meant to teach us about our experiences and why we go through them. I am always searching for meanings in my life that will make my journey more comprehensible. I'll tell you one thing, I felt like I really experienced death during that first marathon!

My younger sister recently called to tell me she started running and wants to do a marathon with me. I guess we'll have to follow the family tradition of sisters running together and crossing the finish line holding hands and have my two daughters meet us at the finish.

A WILLINGNESS TO SUFFER

TED CORBITT
RESIDENCE: NEW YORK, NEW YORK
OCCUPATION: RETIRED PHYSICAL THERAPIST; DISTANCE RUNNER
FIRST MARATHON: 1951 BOSTON MARATHON
D.O.B.: 1-31-19
AGE AT FIRST MARATHON: 32

Often called "the pioneer of ultramarathoning," Ted Corbitt not only helped to break the color barrier in his sport, but has also set national records at twenty-five, forty, fifty, and one-hundred-miles, and in the twenty-four-hour run. Running was a scientific endeavor for Ted. Fascinated to find out just how far the body could run and endure, he kept pushing himself beyond the limits of the times, using his own body as a human laboratory. Born in Dunbarton, South Carolina, Ted spent his early childhood picking cotton and doing other chores after school on his father's farm. However, during harvesttime, children didn't even go to school, as they were needed to get the job done and school was canceled. He first learned about running as he ran and walked to and from school. His grandfather, a former slave, used to run everywhere. He was also a good jumper, but there are few remaining details of his life. The Corbitt family lived by the motto: Be the best in whatever you attempt. Soft spoken and reserved, at seventy-eight years of age Ted still goes out for a bit of a run. He still lives in upper Manhattan, on the island that he used to loop around for training. It is rumored he has never smoked and only tasted beer once in his life. Every athlete should know the story of Ted Corbitt; he helped pave the way for the sport that has captured the hearts and souls of millions.

BACK WHEN I WAS RUNNING RACES, no one ever made any money. Heck, it cost us money. And time, and pain. Most of the road races in those days were in New England, and I was always asking for a ride as I didn't own a car. It wasn't until 1958, when the New York Road Runners Club was formed, that the level of local competition improved. Then the running boom took off in the late seventies and early eighties, but ironically, my personal boom was just about over by then.

There was very little knowledge in the area of professional training available to runners, so most of my early training was experimental. I tested theories and techniques on myself. If they worked, I'd pass them on to my friends. If they didn't, well, then it was back to the drawing board. And I didn't just want to run, I wanted to run as far and as fast as I could, as was humanly possible. Many times I was accused of running too much. However, I always believed that if I had the proper amount of rest and didn't get injured I could survive just about any distance. Yes, some people have better bodies for running, but the key is to rest. In order to cash in on all the training, get the rest. If you can't run as fast as you want to, you haven't rested enough. You'll become dull.

I started competitive running during my high school years in Cincinnati. I guess I was good, because as a senior in 1938, I received an invitation to join the prestigious Cincinnati Gym Club. The letter was obviously based on my records alone, not by any club member who had attended my meets, because the club was restricted to whites only. That was only one of many color hurdles I had to cross to be accepted in my sport.

The first time I heard the word *marathon* I was a sophomore in high school and saw a picture of Ellison "Tarzan" Brown, who had won the 1936 and 1939 Boston Marathons. He was a dark-skinned Indian and at first, I thought he was another black runner. The idea of a long-distance race intrigued me, as at that time a four-mile race was considered long distance.

During college, segregation kept me out of many interstate meets and even some American Athletic Union (A.A.U.) competitions. Arthur Newton, a Rhodesian who pioneered ultramarathoning in the twenties, said blacks would never run distance; they just don't have what it takes to do the distance. At the time, I was running a revolutionary two hundred miles a week. I am a fan of Newton's running and learned a lot from what he did. I would use his books to get myself psyched. His comments about black runners are unfortunate, but he was a man of his times.

Graduating college with honors, my plans to become a physical therapist were put on hold when the Japanese dropped their bombs on Pearl Harbor. Eventually, I was on a troop ship in the Pacific, with rumors flying that we were headed for Okinawa. We did land there, but that night America dropped the bomb on Hiroshima, virtually ending the war. I spent six months on Okinawa and then was transferred to Guam for another six months. During this time, I was desperate to stay in shape and even considered running through the jungles. But with occasional rifle fire as U.S. Marines hunted down unsurrendering Japanese soldiers who didn't believe the war was over, I decided against it. Instead, I built a gym inside my compound.

Upon arriving home, the first thing I did was get myself to New York to find my Cincinnati sweetheart and get married. Between a new wife, working, and getting my master's degree at night from New York University, my running wasn't as consistent as I liked, so I joined a running club founded by a black mortician called the New York Pioneer Club. The name was based on the fact that members were accepted without regard to race or qualifications of any kind. It was totally unique and for that reason it attracted many elite runners who wanted to be part of a club that stood for sound principles.

I was working full time as a physical therapist and never took time off to train. Instead, I incorporated my training into my day, running twelve miles one way to work from my home in upper Manhattan to the Institute for the Crippled and Disabled. Sometimes I'd lengthen the route to twenty miles one way, depending on my schedule. I don't remember ever being late for work.

The only downside to this was constantly being stopped by the police. There wasn't much I could do about it, and anyway, I didn't look like a runner as there were no specific running clothes back then. Sometimes I'd run in chinos, a work shirt, and brown shoes. Actually, I preferred to run in my street shoes, as I have a chronically sprained ankle and the support from the street shoes was better than a pair of running shoes. No one was out there running like I was. One of the most memorable times I was stopped was back in Cleveland in 1949, where I was working at a hospital. I went outside to take a break, wearing my sweats, and a woman called the cops thinking I was an escapee from the mental ward. I was approached by two policeman with guns drawn, pointed right at me.

Another time I was doing a training run over a new Yonkers Marathon course for the final Olympic Marathon trial race in 1952, and as I ran through the town of Hastings, New York, I was confused at an intersection as which way to go. I had passed a parked police car with two officers in it, which suddenly pulled up next to me. They asked what was I doing so I explained, but again I was dressed in chinos and street shoes. They told me they were looking for someone who had stolen a car. I responded, "Well, as you can see, I'm not driving, I'm running." I did feel as if they were just doing their job. It was a part of the culture I grew up in and we don't get a choice as to the times we live in. I don't have any lingering anger and I didn't choose to be an advocate. I just wanted to run.

When I joined the New York Pioneer Club, the thought of a marathon was still in the recesses of my mind. In 1947 I competed in the 25K Junior National Championships and finished. I had a tough time, but I did it. In 1950 I finished my master's degree and made the decision to train for the 1951 Boston Marathon. My philosophy was to train to run thirty miles, so I knew I would be able to run twenty-six. But for some reason I couldn't get past twenty miles. It was very frustrating.

Then I had my breakthrough, which I remember as clearly as if it happened yesterday. It was a snowy February day and I set out to try for thirty again. I started to get thirsty and stuck out my tongue to catch some snowflakes. I did this all through the run and that day broke through to thirty miles. It was those snowflakes, the water that did it. I never drank water before on my runs and now realized that I was terribly dehydrated. From that day on I always made sure I was properly hydrated. The other factor that was inhibiting me was the heavy, stiff pants I was wearing. After a few miles they would rub the skin off my legs.

April finally arrived and I felt ready, having run several thirty-mile runs. I shared a room with another runner I met on the train. Back then you could get a cheap room. I had no time in mind, no expectations for my first marathon. I just wanted to get through it. That year the race was dominated by the Japanese marathon team. It was exciting for me to be there, to meet some of the runners I'd read about. But mostly I just concentrated on finishing.

I stayed with the pack for the first ten miles. After that we strung out single file. I didn't know the course, so I just kept following the runner in front of me. I'd heard about the Newton hills, but I had done hill training, so I wasn't particularly worried about them. At about twenty miles, there was a gap between me and the runner in front and behind me. We were really spread out and the only way I could gauge where they were in relationship to me was to listen to the clapping of the crowds. I knew the person behind me was about thirty seconds back because that's how long it took the crowds to start clapping again after I'd pass. I knew when he started to gain because the clapping started to come faster and faster.

By twenty-three miles I wanted to quit. I was so tired. Although I had trained hard and ran thirty miles several times, I was running faster than I ever did in training. Distance wasn't my nemesis; it was the speed. I didn't run recklessly, but I ran fast. There were no mile markers then, so I had no idea where the finish line was. It wasn't till I rounded the bend onto Exeter Street that I saw the finish line. I finished in fifteenth place, in 2:48:42, and was very relieved.

I was glad it was over, but I immediately started to think how I could beat my time. I was also thinking of the 1952 Olympic Trials, which started the very next month at the Yonkers Marathon. I was thankful that I finished my first marathon. It's not a simple thing to do. You have to incur a certain amount of risk if you want to go fast, if you want to win.

British runners call distance running "having a go at it." They have a wonderful spirit about them. I always considered ultramarathoning a disease and the British had it with fever to spare.

I was once asked to represent the United States at the 52.5-mile London-to-Brighton road race. This was a great honor for me, especially after Arthur Newton's statement, and also being denied entry to the 1958 Boston Marathon due to a heart problem the doctors thought I had. I ran anyway as a bandit and finished in an ineligible sixth place with a time of 2:43:47. I went back to Boston over twenty times in my career. I guess my heart was strong after all.

Preparing for the London run was critical. On weekends, I would go out for thirty to fifty miles, or loop around Manhattan Island twice. I'd leave my lunch and some juices in my mailbox and take a bite as I passed by. I knew I'd never come back out if I went up to the apartment for lunch. One Sunday, when I passed by for a bite, my lunch was gone! I never found out who took it.

By July of 1962, half the airfare to London had been raised by sponsors and I knew there was no going back on my commitment to run from the Parliament Building in London to the beaches at Brighton. One month prior to the race I attempted a massive workout schedule that opened with Hell Week, 198 miles in the summer heat and finished with back-to-back 50s. The next day, I did a seventeen-mile run commute to work. I hated these extreme workouts. I kept sane by counting miles, beating myself up and thinking of Arthur Newton's racist comments.

There were no other Americans in the race, and I received a warm welcome in London. As I stood at the starting line with seventy other men, listening to the chimes of Big Ben, I thought to myself, "What am I doing here? I should have stayed home." The course was dogged with hills, and soon I was dog tired. At twenty miles, my so-called "effort mask" appeared. This is the part of the race when my features would contort, my brow become wrinkled, my eyes twist, and I groan. It sounds and looks like I am one step from death, but I'm not. It's just the way I run. Actually, it scares some of my opponents which I guess is a good thing. At forty-five miles, the biggest hill of all awaited my wrecked thighs and dead legs, but somehow I kept going. Descending into Brighton, I thought I would buckle under if I ran any harder. Just then, my handler caught up with me and said, "Show me what an American can do. My five-year-old sister can run faster than you." For the first time all day, I laughed. I was grateful to have finished the race and in a decent time, and to set an American record. The first newcomer to the race who doesn't finish in the first three places gets a newcomer trophy. So for my fourth place victory, I received the trophy and newcomer record.

Afterward, we all soaked in a hot tub, trying to erase the pain from our run-ravaged bodies. Fourth place didn't seem worth all the effort I put into the event. The next day, my legs felt crippled. I didn't think I'd ever run again. Two days later, I had to crawl a quarter mile. However, an amazing transformation was taking place as I recuperated. I was suddenly filled with enthusiasm. I vowed to return to London and beat Brighton in 1964. That's another story.

I flew to Zurich the night of the race and then took a train to Germany for a physical therapy course. That late-night flight was more difficult than anticipated. When I got off the plane the next morning, I felt like a very old man. The course work was in advanced massage. I had always been interested in massage work and felt it was a necessity for recovery. To this day, I give myself a pre-warm-up massage before any running is done. However, with all my training in massage therapy, I never did get a massage after a race. One day, after a particularly long walk I decided to get a massage, but couldn't find a place that looked legitimate!

I went on to run London-to-Brighton a total of five times, and at the end of each one, I would say, "Never again."

In 1968, I received an invitation to the hundred-mile run at Walton-on-Thames, England, scheduled for October 1969. I pulled out all the stops for this one, running every marathon possible and enduring unheard-of training mileage when not racing. In July alone I ran a thousand miles, two hundred short of my goal. At the 1969 Boston Marathon, now fifty years old, I was becoming the guru of marathoning, right up there with the other legends, Clarence DeMar and Johnny Kelley. I was surprised the spectators, who called out my name, even knew who I was.

My final training plan was to run my fifth Brighton-To-London race, and then three weeks later tackle the hundred-miler. Along the way, I went for a complete checkup by Dr. David Costill, a physiologist and former track coach. After tests taken on pulse rates, leg spring, oxygen absorption, heat tolerance, and heart findings, the data indirectly confirmed that more than physical well-being, it was motivation and competitive drive that made the difference in a winning performance.

Approaching the midnight start of the hundred-miler, another runner summed up my feelings exactly: "I've looked forward to this race for two years, and now I don't want to do it." My only goal was to break the existing American record of 16:07:43. The most crushing period of the race was between seventy and eighty miles. Fatigue was overpowering and strength was definitely on the decline. There is a fear that either the legs or the mind will snap, permanently. How I wanted to quit at sixty-eight miles. I couldn't believe there were still thirty-two miles left. At ninety-seven miles, I was wobbling uncontrollably. The crowds cried out, "Don't stop now. Keep going." I could barely hear them.

Finally, I heard the bell announcing my last lap to complete one hundred miles. Later on, I wrote in my journal: "Reaching ninety-nine miles gives one a good feeling but hearing the bell . . . try it sometime." Among the many refreshments offered, such as beer and sandwiches, what I really needed was a new pair of legs.

Most runners would have retired at this point, but I knew there was more in me. As president of the New York Road Runners Club, I pushed for a masters category for runners over the age of forty, knowing that it would bring out the retired racers who couldn't compete successfully any longer in the younger arena. There was resistance from the A.A.U., which feared that a four-mile race would harm the over-forty crowd. We all proved them wrong and I won my first masters-division marathon in 1970 with a new record of 2:52:32.

When I was fifty-four, I received another surprise invitation in the mail, this one to run a 24-hour run in November of 1973 at Walton-on-Thames, the same track site as the 1969 hundred-miler. Without bothering to think, I sent back my reply: "Yes, count me in." Sixteen competitors started the race. My trainer for the event was John Chodes, an adviser from the Pioneer Club days. Replacing nourishment was a critical factor in the run. John developed a concoction consisting of two hard-boiled eggs mashed in a cup of orange juice, which could be swallowed easily. Intermittent treats of chocolate bars, orange and pineapple slices, blackberry juice, and a can of sardines rounded out the gourmet menu. I kept my sanity by counting laps, using visual imagery to improve my posture, and working on arm movements. Willpower alone kept me going. John had a special technique for alleviating stiffness, by stroking my legs with a hard hairbrush to release neural energy. It worked. At twelve hours, halfway, I had covered eighty-one miles and was in second place. Events at the race changed dramatically after the halfway mark. Once competitors, we now all shared our food, reserve, and encouragement with each other. The realization that we were all in this hell together turned us from foe to friend. By mile 100, I was physically exhausted and didn't think I could continue. It was humiliating to feel so impotent after all the training I put into this. I came off the course and instructed John to perform a type of massage called "Pae-Roe," a judo revival technique using thumbs to bore down into the middle of the skull.

With seven hours to go, I said to Chodes, "I can't go through this another seven hours." I was referring not to dropping out, but slowing down due to severe quadriceps pain. I knew I could no longer perform at the level I needed to reach my personal distance goal. Then, as if we hadn't suffered enough, at the twentieth hour a sudden downpour flooded the track. We continued on, chilled to the bone, in two inches of water. It seemed as if I was only half alive. By the end of twenty-four hours, I had covered 134.6 miles, a third place victory. It almost killed me.

I've never really retired. In 1994, I was invited to the twenty-fifth anniversary of the Walton-on-Thames hundred-miler, but decided to walk it. A reporter asked to follow me with a cameraman for an interview. I agreed, but when the interview was finished she wasn't happy with it so I had to walk a few extra miles so she could get her story. I completed seventy-odd miles then had to quit due to an inflamed anterior tibia muscle. I had never dropped out of a race before.

What is the mind-set, the secret, to running a hundred miles? When Roger Bannister broke the four-minute barrier, setting a world record, he wasn't the most talented runner of his time. However, as soon as he broke it, others followed, breaking his record. There have been some experiments done on rats that prove once one rat has been taught something, other rats soon learn the procedure at an easier rate. There is a related force in the universe that is at the center of this theory, but I am not the person to explain it in depth.

The marathon demands patience and a willingness to stay with it. You must be willing to suffer and keep on suffering. On a good day, the running seems to flow effortlessly. On a bad day, it's the pain that flows. I truly believe that if you can run a marathon, you can continue for another twenty-five miles. Of course, you must be in shape and have put in the training, and endure the suffering. I would do it all over again, but I would do it smarter, having learned from my mistakes. Of course, I'd make new mistakes along the way. I have led a full life and was blessed with a wife who was a great help and support to me. I am a widower now, but she really helped make my career. She was very tolerant.

I guess I've run over two-hundred-thousand miles. I've lived through many changes, but the biggest observation I'd make is women's running. I thought that would be a fluke, that they would quit. I give them credit.

I used to have a fantasy about winning the Boston Marathon that

I've never shared with anyone but my son. Here goes: I was going to train hard enough to stay out front the entire race, refusing to let anyone pass me. I'd speed up and rather die than let someone pass by. In this fantasy, to make sure that no one was gaining on me, I wore a pair of specialty glasses with side-view mirrors to see who was behind me. I ran Boston twenty-one times but never won, so I guess my fantasy can still be put to use!

I regretted not acting on the Boston fantasy. However, I came up with another one for the double marathon London-to-Brighton race, which I attempted to do in 1968. I was on a crash training program in June, July, and August, attempting to do three hundred miles a week. I didn't reach that target but I was only two and a half weeks away from concluding the heavy training, leaving the month of September to do active resting in preparation for the race. An encounter with a dog left me unable to run at all and I canceled the trip to England. The heavy training had left my body fragile, like a boxer with a glass jaw. But here's where the fantasy comes in. In this "burnout run" in London, I would have taken the lead in the first five miles and stayed there, passing the first marathon marker in 2:31 to 2:33. No special eyeglass mirrors this time, I imagined a handler on a bicycle, and he would kept me informed of what was happening behind me.

I was able to resume training after the dog encounter in time to compete in the National Championship fifty-miler that year, 1968. I am prouder of that than any other race. At the age of forty-nine, I became the oldest man ever to win a national long-distance title.

Intellectually, I'd like to run another marathon, but I'd have to get fit first. My Boston record of twenty-one entries all with a finish under three hours was recently broken. Actually, I was more shocked that people knew of my accomplishment than that it had been broken.

I look back at when I was running in the thirties and forties, when most people weren't interested in it. Now I read that we are going through another fitness craze. I am flabbergasted by such things. Running is something you just do. You don't need a goal, you don't need a race, you don't need the hype of a so-called fitness craze. All you need is a cheap pair of shoes and some time. The rest will follow.

AGAINST ALL ODDS

TOSHIKO D'ELIA
RESIDENCE: RIDGEWOOD, NJ
OCCUPATION: ELITE RUNNER
FIRST MARATHON: 1976 JERSEY SHORE MARATHON, ASBURY PARK, NJ
D.O.B.: 1-2-30
AGE AT FIRST MARATHON: 46

Toshi d'Elia has already lead many lives, some of them more interesting, complex, and tragic than most people will ever experience. Growing up in war-torn Japan during the thirties and forties, she lived on the edge of starvation. She was raised in a traditional Japanese family: Her father forbade education for women and she was destined for an arranged marriage. However, fate stepped in and offered her an option. But like a pact with the devil, the option turned out to be even worse. Toshi metamorphosed into an elite runner late in life, taking her first jog at age forty-two. She was the first woman in the world over fifty to break the three-hour barrier for the marathon. With fifty-one marathons behind her and more to come, she has covered ground all over the world. One of her greatest achievements was surviving cervical cancer at fifty years of age and three months later running the 1980 Boston Marathon.

ONE OF MY STRONGEST MEMORIES from childhood is constant hunger pangs; there was never enough food for us to eat. Japan was struggling though the devastation of its seemingly continuous war years, a country ravaged and depleted of its resources and spirit. It was especially tough during the post-World War II period. Everything was rationed. We never saw certain items such as bananas or sugar for five years. My mother would stand on food lines for hours and come home with one cucumber for a family of six. The only other foods I remember having were sweet potatoes and porridge. I guess I should be thankful that my family at least had that. We were lucky.

Being extremely traditional, my family upheld every aspect of our culture. I attended high school, which most women did, but when I announced that I wanted to continue my education and attend college, my father said, "A woman's voice is just a waste. You will follow your destiny and marry into an arranged marriage. No more talk of college." Mother interjected on my behalf, a strong stand for her to make, and offered to pay my tuition out of her own money. Although she followed the customary rituals of a Japanese wife, she wanted something better for her daughters. She taught us to go after our independence, to follow our dreams. As a child, I dreamed of being a bird, to be able to go wherever I wanted, to have that taste of freedom. Then as a young woman, I dreamed of being a man because only they had the ability to be free.

I shared my mother's spirit for independence and after graduating college, I won a Fulbright scholarship to study special education for the hearing impaired at Syracuse University. My father forbade me to go and once again my mother interceded. My father did not want me exposed to the disrespectful, rebellious ways of Americans. I incurred his wrath for disobeying, and it would not be the last time I would do so.

Coming to the United States at twenty-one years of age was like a dream come true. I finally tasted freedom. There was so much to see and learn. First, I could eat whatever I wanted, whenever I wanted. That alone would have been enough of a satisfaction, but then I discovered men and dating. I had never been on a date, never allowed to be alone with a man. It was very overwhelming and I was totally unprepared, but at the same time it was also thrilling and exciting. Probably a little too overwhelming because I ended up marrying the first man I dated. I was so unrealistic, so young and naive. In retrospect, we were not suited to each other at all. I completely misjudged his character.

Things did not go smoothly from the start, and then I got pregnant and gave birth to a baby girl, Erica. Two years later, I was divorced. He disappeared completely and I never saw him again. The financial and emotional consequences were devastating as I struggled through my long commute to work while taking care of Erica. Finally, my family suggested I come home so I made the decision to return to Japan.

Once under my family's influence again, I knew I never should have gone back. My father was furious. Not only had I disobeyed him by going to America in the first place, I had brought shame on our house by marrying a Caucasian and giving birth to a half-breed. I had disgraced him and a family meeting was held to decide my fate. Things were not going well. While the elders met in secret, I was left alone to reflect on my mistakes and ask for forgiveness. When the meeting was over, my father and my oldest brother called me into the room and told me, "You reached for stars that didn't belong to you and now you must be punished. You have brought shame into this house. In order to clear our name, you must give up your daughter to adoption and enter into a contractual marriage. This is the only way. If you do not do as you are told this time, you must leave here forever."

I was shocked. How could they possibly think I would give up my daughter, my own flesh and blood? And for what? To uphold the honor of the family? Again, my mother came to my defense, saying she would raise Erica as her own. She understood the bond of motherhood and knew I could never give up my child. She begged for my mercy but was silenced. With a swift glare, my father announced she was being too emotional and not to ever interfere again. The sad irony of it all was that in the end, I kept my child, but she lost hers.

I sailed back to America with Erica. At night, I would walk the ship's decks, wondering what my bleak future would bring. All those wandering nights must have helped, because as we sailed into the harbor, I felt no loneliness, only a sense of starting over.

Back in the Bronx, things began to look up. I was fortunate to get my teaching job back, and also our apartment. But every day, as I left the apartment at five in the morning and returned at six at night, I had to leave my three-year-old daughter all day in nursery school. I lived with a deep sense of guilt and doubt. She was an outsider, teased by her classmates for having slanty eyes and no father.

I had long given up the idea of ever having another relationship. I was too jaded, too serious, and too tired. Then I met Manfred d'Elia, twenty-two years my senior, and after a three-year courtship we were married. More important than loving me, he loved Erica and became her legal father.

Fred took my life on a completely different course, taking Erica out of New York City to the tree-lined suburban town of Ridgewood, New Jersey, where he taught piano lessons to gifted students. I felt a great sense of relief with Fred, as if the heavy chains I had been carrying around the last seven years were suddenly taken off my body. Now I had to learn how to become a housewife. This was my first step into living the American Dream.

Fred was an avid mountain climber and on weekends we would all go hiking. After a while, we made the decision to tackle the hiker's dream: Mount Rainier. I was forty years old and thought I was in good shape, but two-thirds up I suffered extreme altitude sickness and had to quit. I was devastated, especially since Fred continued on. After that, I worried that I wouldn't be able to keep up with him. This was a bad thing since hiking was such an integral part of our marriage, a mental and emotional rope that held us together. I feared that our marriage would start to unravel and I would end up divorced once again. This must sound silly, that Fred would leave me for not keeping up on hikes, but I was still fragile inside.

After returning from Mount Rainier, I sought advice from a highly respected female climber who told me she ran a mile every day for stamina. I embraced her advice with the utmost enthusiasm and that day I bolted out the kitchen door for my first run wearing one-dollar Japanese sneakers, sprinting as fast as I could for one mile. For the next three days, I couldn't move. I hurt all over. Erica was amused at my effort, but also sympathetic and said she would teach me to run. I had never heard of such a thing. Doesn't everyone know how to run? Erica explained about pacing and starting out with a slow jog until I could build up to a fast run. I jogged religiously and gradually gained the stamina needed for high-altitude climbs.

By now Erica was in high school and had become captain of the track team. Under her supervision, I was running five miles every day without effort. One day she suggested I enter a race, but her motive was underhanded. Her team was running an open, cross-country event and they thought if I entered, then no one on her team would suffer the humiliation of coming in last, because I would! I went along with it, but to everyone's surprise, I finished in third place. I was doing seven-minute miles, not ever realizing I was fast. That was the beginning of my next life.

Erica sensed strong running possibilities within me and became my official coach. She taught me interval training, pacing, stretching, speed work, everything I didn't know about the sport. It was fun, but very difficult. She was a demanding coach.

In August of 1975, Erica registered me for the World Masters Track and Field Championships in Toronto. This was going to be my debut. There were hundreds of athletes and it was a very stimulating event. I felt out of place and didn't expect to do well, but ended up wining a silver medal in the five thousand meters. And Fred, who was sixty-three at the time, won a silver and bronze medal in his events. This was a very special moment for our family. I was awestruck.

After Erica left for college, I continued running on my own and Fred picked up the coaching. Back then, women weren't running as much and I had only one female friend, almost fifteen years younger than I, who ran. In January of 1976, Carol suggested we enter the Jersey Shore Marathon. I could never conceive of such a thing. I told her twenty-six miles is only meant for horses to run, not people.

Carol was determined to run, so out of sheer friendship I agreed to run fifteen miles of the course; that was it, no more. January of 1976 was a particularly cold month and this day was the coldest ever, ten degrees below zero without the wind-chill factor. Carol's husband, Enver, offered to ride his bike alongside to keep his eye on us. He also agreed to meet me at the fifteen-mile marker with warm clothes so I wouldn't catch cold. It was very thrilling to be at the starting line, but I felt sorry for all the runners who were going to run the entire course.

Since I only planned to run a little more than half, I started out strong and ran fast. Also, it was freezing, and it helped to keep me warm. The cold was a major factor that day, so cold in fact that at the water stations, the water was frozen in the cups. At fifteen miles I pulled off to the side in expectation of meeting Enver and getting some warm clothes. But there was no Enver. I waited and waited until I was literally freezing to death, so in order to keep warm, I started running again. I stopped at every mile marker, hoping to see Enver, but he was nowhere to be found. The temperature was getting dangerously colder. All the runners had on gloves, hats, and pants, unusual multiple layers for almost any marathon. Any exposed hair on heads or faces was covered in sheets of ice. Finally I reached the twenty-mile marker. Still, no

Enver. I kept running. Then someone yelled out, "Only two miles to go!" I couldn't believe it. I was almost at the finish. With a burst of excitement, I picked up my speed and ran as fast as I could, crossing the finish line of my first marathon in 3:25.

I still wonder what bit me that day. I never even entertained the notion of doing a marathon. It was thrilling. After that experience, I gave up track and became obsessed with distance. Another phase of my life had dawned, one that would ultimately take me back to Japan.

Someone told me my marathon time qualified me to run Boston. I wasn't exactly sure what that meant, but when I understood I was eligible to run the Boston Marathon, I got excited all over again. When I became a runner, I followed the career of Michiko "Mikki" Gorman, a Japanese woman who won Boston in 1974. Her life seemed to chronicle mine, being raised in war-torn Japan, settling in the United States, and picking up running late in life.

In a time frame of three months, I went from running one of the coldest marathons on record to one the hottest ever on record, 110 degrees in Boston, in April. At the starting line, I was standing near George Sheehan, who kept repeating, "Heat can kill you! Everyone be careful out there." It was so hot we were hosed down while waiting to begin the race.

Out of a field of thirty women, I came in eighth place at 3:15. The heat never bothered me, although my feet kept squishing from the sweat. I ran hard, but it was fun for me. It almost felt easier than a 5K or 10K on the track. I was hooked on the marathon.

Just as my life was settling down to a nice, easy routine, and I thought the demons had moved on, I was diagnosed with cervical cancer. Why me? I lived such a healthy life. I didn't understand and was in deep despair. As always, Fred and Erica were by my side and the operation was a success. I remember waking up Christmas morning, groggy from all the drugs, and seeing Erica handing me a present. It was a new pair of my favorite running shoes.

Little did anyone expect that I would wear the new shoes so soon. I was determined to put this disease behind me and concentrated on my running as a form of therapy. Just as I never thought of running easy, I attacked my recovery with the same zest.

Four months after my surgery, I ran the 1980 Boston Marathon. I was running with caution, not my usual abandon, and still managed to finish in 3:09. A Japanese reporter from the Associated Press was there and was surprised to see a Japanese woman running. He asked for an interview and as I told him my story, including the cancer surgery, he was most impressed and kept writing and writing and writing.

The following morning, my brother called from Japan to announce I was on the front page of all the newspapers there. He was shocked, as he didn't know anything about my life here, such as my marathon history or the cancer.

I returned to Japan to speak at the Women's World Sports Symposium in Tokyo. I had been away from my country for sixteen years and the trip back was emotional for many reasons. My beloved mother had passed away and finally Erica and I had the opportunity to visit her grave and pay respects to the woman who gave me so much courage, wisdom, and strength throughout her life. She remains with me always.

I don't define myself as a runner because running was always a supportive tool to get me somewhere else. For instance, it made me a better teacher. It brought me closer to my daughter. It took me places I would never have seen otherwise. It was also fun for me, something that I consider my true companion. It also made me physically strong; I have lots of stamina to get me through my busy days.

Sometimes I think back to that moment when I was asked to give up my child. My father tried to convince me that the decision would make my life easier. Little did he know that I have never done anything the easy way. All my decisions, from keeping Erica, to marrying Fred, to running, have brought me more joy and happiness than I ever could have imagined at a time when I thought my world was about to end.

As I go through life, making the inevitable mistakes that take me on unexpected journeys, I remind myself of two Japanese proverbs: "Tap on the stone bridge twice before you cross." And my other favorite, "When you are in a hurry, go around and take a longer route."

SOMETHING ALL MY OWN

LAUREN FESSENDEN
RESIDENCE: MANHATTAN, NEW YORK
OCCUPATION: MOTHER OF TWO; SCHOOL VOLUNTEER
FIRST MARATHON: 1994 NEW YORK CITY MARATHON
D.O.B.: 10-23-55
AGE AT FIRST MARATHON: 39

Lauren drags out the big black garbage bag that is stuffed with race collectibles such as race entry numbers, space blankets, race brochures, autographs of Tegla Loroupe and Anne Marie Letko, and I think I see a half-eaten orange somewhere in there. The bag of running goodies is used for her postmarathon talk at her children's elementary school. She feels it's great for the kids to see and talk to a mom who ran the marathon. It makes the race seem more real to them; something they could do someday. The first question they always ask is, "Did you win?" She tells them everyone who runs is a winner. Busy with two children, a willing volunteer at school, and the author of a budding wine newsletter, Lauren needed something in her life that would help balance the chaos. Running was the answer.

I WONDERED HOW I WOULD BE ABLE TO REMEMBER the specifics regarding my first marathon experience. It was three years ago and I have trouble remembering what I did last week. I started to go over it with my husband and suddenly it all came gushing back. As I went through each mile, details such as entering Manhattan at the sixteen-mile marker and seeing a friend in the crowd all came back to me. I can't believe this, but I started to cry, right there in my living room three years later. I realized I had total recall of the entire twenty-six miles. It's as if my first marathon had become permanently imprinted in my brain.

I didn't start really running until the summer of 1993. I competed in figure skating as a teenager and I am an avid skier, but I always thought distance running would be boring and never had the desire to do it. A friend of mine was a runner and thought I'd like it. I took the challenge and to my amazement I did like it. A lot. In fact, I ran every day that summer in Cape Cod and started to notice how the daily routine of running was beginning to change my life. I became more focused; getting that run in helped to structure my entire day. I would return from my run feeling less stressed, more mentally alert. Running was a way to defuse stress or frustrations and clarify thoughts. On the few occasions my husband and I get into a heated discussion about minor household stuff, the conversation can quickly take a wrong turn into the territory of defense tactics. I don't think we're unlike any married couple with two kids and daily life situations. But now, instead of falling into that trap, I'll go for a run and think things through. I work my problems out by pounding pavement instead of yelling. I let all the issues percolate to the top and then simmer for a while till I digest them and then go back and calmly discuss things again with a clearer head. It works for me.

After my summer initiation, I continued my morning runs in Central Park. My basic routine was the six-mile loop around the park. I decided to really push myself one day and do two loops, or twelve miles. It was a big hurdle for me, but I wanted to try it. At the end of the second loop I was really dragging. Being mostly a solo runner by choice, I didn't have anyone to turn to for an easy distraction or a bit of the psychobabble that runners seem to engage in while running down the miles. Suddenly, out of the blue, I found myself shoulder to shoulder with another runner, this guy who was sort of strange looking. My first impulse was to avoid him, but I was so tired I couldn't even get out of his way. "Are you okay?" he asked.

"Yeah, I'm just trying to make it around the park twice and I've never done this before. I'm kind of wiped."

"Well, I'm going around three times to train for the marathon, so run with me if you'd like. You know, the first New York City Marathon was four loops around the park."

"Oh, I could never do that."

"Yes you can. Just think, you're halfway through it now."

The realization that I was running a half marathon was a break-though. Something clicked for me. At that moment, I knew I could finish a marathon and decided to do it. I never saw that runner again and always wanted to thank him for giving me the mind-set to go for it. He did it for me, got me believing that I could do it.

I was already a member of the New York Road Runners Club, so I went to them for advice. They gave me a training schedule that was very intense and included five twenty-mile runs and some speed work. I had never done this sort of thing before so I signed up for a course. It turned out to be so gruesome that by the end of the first day I was praying for someone to deliver me from the hell I found myself in. We concentrated on interval work, which was new to me, and I pushed myself beyond any boundary I had known in athletics. It was pure anguish. I started dreaming that I was dead just to avoid the pain, but it didn't work. Hot, searing, flames were shooting up my legs and my lungs were bursting. I was thinking, "Shoot me now," near tears. My confidence had been shattered and I started doubting my ability to finish the marathon. I'm a forty-year-old woman with two young kids. What the heck am I doing out here running fartleks like some high school track star? I wanted to quit, but realized if I stopped on such a negative vibe I might never recover from the humiliation I felt. So I went back the next day and we did hill work. A guy behind me kept saying, "You can do it, just run through it." But how could I run through something that had no limitation, no end? I wanted to shed my body, it hurt so much. I thought my lungs would explode if I took another breath. I had never experienced such physical pain while running, ever. But I did keep going. I didn't want to be last and I didn't want to not be able to do it. Somehow my body never failed me, although it was the most terrible thing I ever put myself through voluntarily. Childbirth is also painful, but that's a ride you can't get off once you get on. As I reflected on why I did that, voluntarily suffer the pain, I realized I had tested my body and my strength beyond any level ever experienced in training and I won. I did it. It has changed my way of approaching new things in life. I won't back away, worried that I can't do it or that it will be too hard. In fact, I recently started playing the piano again, something I've been wanting to do but kept putting off because I thought it would be too difficult to get back into it at a satisfying level. Back in 1972, I was at a near-professional level and didn't think I could settle for anything less. I now know nothing can be too difficult if you just give it a try.

Anyway, after that brief experience, I gave up on the group training and continued to do my loops through the park and also trekked throughout New York City on my long runs.

This is going to sound really weird, but once in a while when I'm in the park where I know every curve, every pothole, every inch of pavement, and I'm running particularly strong, I start to feel very light and airy and I can literally feel myself float above my body. I'm not the runner anymore. I'm floating above this person named Lauren and watching her run. And then it really gets crazy because I don't run near the reservoir, but yet I have a perfectly good view of it. How can that be? Some runners call it a buzz, or a high. It is an incredible experience.

With the hard training behind me, having completed five twenties and various other long and short runs, I was now ready. I couldn't sleep the night before M-Day. I knew I had the endurance to finish, but I was worried about the mental part. Would I mentally last for four or five hours? When I arrived at the starting area, I went to the women's waiting section. There is a unisex area, but a friend of mine who'd run the marathon a few years before told me they had better coffee and more bathrooms in the women's area. It was so inspiring to be surrounded by, literally rubbing shoulders with, thousands of women all attempting this inhuman feat, this incredible challenge of wills. Some didn't have the look of a runner, but they were out there being as heroic as the leanest, fastest runner on the line, and I was soon to learn that physical body proportions don't mean anything when it comes to endurance running.

On that morning, we were all one if not in body then most certainly in spirit and determination. When the race was about to begin, the men and women section off for their own starting points. The woman next to me said to no one in particular, "Oh-oh, I have to go to the bathroom again."

I told her, "Well, it's too late. You can't move out of this mass."

"You're right, but I really have to go."

The next thing I know, she made one swooping move and was squatting next to me, urinating. I couldn't believe it. But then, like a domino effect, I noticed all the women around us were doing the same thing.

Everyone was pulling their shorts down and peeing. I know the men were doing the same thing. Where else but a marathon could I be surrounded by total strangers who feel so comfortable with each other that they do something that is so socially incorrect but somehow becomes acceptable behavior?

The Verrazano Narrows Bridge covers the first two miles of the race. I was shocked at my first mile time, seven and a half minutes. I was going out way too fast and slowed down. I don't think I was consciously running that fast, but I was swept away with the crowd. The collective tempo seems to carry everyone in a single mass. At eight miles, we were in Brooklyn and I started to lose my bearing. I knew it was way too early to let my mind start wandering, so I focused on the varied ethnic enclaves along the route. I've lived in Manhattan for a long time, but never saw New York up front and personal like this. All the families, the cheering, the music, even the costumes of the onlookers kept my interest for quite a few more miles. At the halfway mark, running along McGuinness Boulevard in Queens, I felt exhilarated to be a part of this event. I belonged here. This is my town and my race and I was becoming a part of running history. It rated right up there with marriage and childbirth. This was truly a shining moment, everything I had trained for and anticipated. I was sky high.

Then, in the midst of my euphoric moment, an unexpected hill in the middle of the Fifty-Ninth Street Bridge caught me by surprise and I started to lose energy. Somehow that minor hill, never noticed before, became a mountain. After too many miles, my mental and visual perspectives blurred and something as small as a curb became a barrier. At sixteen miles, the route enters Manhattan for the first time and I started crying, overcome with emotion. I felt like I was on home turf. The crowd seemed bigger, bolder, louder. And it was! I caught sight of a friend and ran over to give her a hug. I remember hoping that I wore my waterproof mascara because it truly is an emotional event.

At twenty-three miles, the route enters Central Park and for some reason I started to get fuzzy. I wasn't in pain, but I guess I had used up all my glycogen and was totally depleted. All my mental wattage was burned out like a lightbulb. I felt like I wasn't connected to myself. I kept asking, "Where is Central Park?" A part of me knew I was coming to the park because I trained here every day, but a bigger part of me was in trouble. I started to get tunnel vision; things were closing in on me. I passed a food stand, reached for the sweetest supplement I could find and grabbed a cookie. It did the trick and I could think clearly again.

Soon after, I encountered another hill. I was familiar with this hill, and had run it many times during training, yet it never seemed so big or so insurmountable as now. My legs had already given up and I was running on an adrenaline rush. I didn't know how I was ever going to be able to finish. And before I knew it, there was the finish line. It's an amazing thing, but sometimes under the most adverse conditions, we blossom to our fullest potential. As I crossed the finish line, my first thought was that I had fulfilled my quest. It was a very enriching moment in my life.

As I walked home, proudly displaying my medal and space blanket, I anticipated the celebration party my husband had prepared for my victory against all odds. He had gathered old friends, new friends and family, a festive collection of well-wishers and party revelers that toasted me well into the night.

The next day, I could barely walk. I remember crawling out of bed and lying on the couch all morning surveying the wreckage from the party. There was no way I could move to clean up the mess. I lay there, entombed on the couch for hours until it was time to pick up the kids. Now I really had to move. Slowly, ever-so-painfully, I crawled toward the stairs, which had suddenly turned into a deep, long, winding mine shaft. I had to walk backward to get down. I was stiff and sore for two days. But it was all worth it.

I've run the New York City Marathon for three years in a row and look forward to the next one. I want to make this a yearly event. The feeling of personal satisfaction and accomplishment lasts about six months and just when it starts to fade, I start training again. My intensity and love for this race is a yearlong affair. This is not about instant gratification. You have to work hard for it, sweat for it, give up sleeping in on Sunday mornings, bear pain, and accept the mental challenge. And in spite of all that, there isn't anyone I can think of who wouldn't benefit from experiencing the thrill of a marathon. It is something you will talk about the rest of your life. I learned something about my own level of strength and courage that was extremely rewarding. It changed my life forever.

ULTRA MAN

WAYNE GIBBONS
RESIDENCE: HACKENSACK, NEW JERSEY
OCCUPATION: CHIROPRACTIC SPORTS PHYSICIAN
FIRST MARATHON: 1978 JERSEY SHORE MARATHON
D.O.B.: 6-10-59
AGE AT FIRST MARATHON: 19

Wayne and his wife, Christine, have participated in over 110 marathons with sub-three-hour times and have completed eighty ultramarathons. They don't appear to be crazy, don't have that glazed look about them. They are just normal, healthy, hardworking people who happen to love running. About 70 percent of his patients are runners. He is also a purist when it comes to running; it is not something he does, it is part of him.

WHAT DO YOU DO WHEN YOU'RE SIXTEEN years old, 5'10" and two hundred pounds, hanging out with the hoods and bad dudes, smoking cigarettes, drinking beer on street corners, and flunking out of high school? That was my life. I desperately needed a wake-up call to break out of the negative influences surrounding me. My freshman-year gym class still registers as one of my more mentally painful experiences. I hated gym because I was so fat and uncoordinated. The teacher asked me what size gym shirt I needed and I ordered a medium. He said, "Kid, you're way too fat for a medium. I suggest an extra large. And you'll probably get fatter if you don't do something about it."

I stole my parents' rent money and ran away from home thinking that would be a distraction. I got as far as Missouri before the police caught up with me. Back in school, some of my friends were already in jail by their seventeenth birthdays or going the way of drug dealers, alcoholics, and junkies. I decided to turn my life around before it was too late. First I tackled my weight and started losing through dieting first, then jogging. I always liked the track guys. They were in great shape and I thought running was kind of cool. By my senior year I lost forty pounds, quit smoking, and brought up my grades. I realized that running was the ticket for staying in shape. Dieting can only do so much. By the time I graduated high school I had my act together and went to college.

I kept running and steadily increased my distance. I read books to learn about proper form and training techniques. At eighteen I ran my first race, a half marathon, and I ran much better than I thought I could. And as an added bonus, I was fast. After that I got the bug. Finally, here was something I was good at doing. The marathon was the ultimate challenge and being competitive by nature, I wanted to see if I could do it. Never having accomplished anything of significance in my life, the marathon offered me the opportunity to excel at something. If I could run a marathon, my self-esteem and self-image would be raised to a level I'd never felt before. It is such a physical and mental feat. Most people don't enjoy running at first and give up. It's really difficult to dedicate yourself to finding that time every day to run. For most people it doesn't come naturally. That included me, until I got hooked. Running has a lot to offer if you just stick with it long enough to like it, or at least see the benefits. More than any other sport, running offers the opportunity to come alive again, to experience a rebirth. Some of my patients are former high school or college running stars who gave it up and have now hit their late thirties or forties and don't like what they have become: out-of-shape corporate types who have a couch-potato attitude toward life. I convince them to get back to running, to take charge of their lives, and it's as if they become alive again. Running can be a person's wake-up call to recharge the batteries that have been left dormant. It certainly was mine.

The other interesting aspect of the marathon is that it's about the only sporting event where the average runner has access to a race where they are on the same course as the greatest runners of our time, Olympic contenders. You may not be going head to head with Alberto Salazar or Anne Marie Letko, but you know they're out in front somewhere. It is a thrill just to be part of the program.

I wanted to be in top shape for my first marathon. The books suggested I strive for a training routine of sixty miles a week and I was doing forty. The marathon was in December and by then I brought my distance up to eighty a week, with one long run of twenty miles. Here I was, one year out of high school and just starting to fall in love with running and I was entering a marathon. I really felt good about myself for the first time in my life. I had a direction, I was focused, and I was challenged. Training started to dominate my life. That's a difficult balance when you have a career, a marriage, or dependents. I think that's why most people don't run distance. But being in college, training was easy. I could run just about anytime I didn't have a class. Training is a painful, self-absorbed journey. It slowly takes you toward your goal, but away from everything else in your life.

Anyway, back to December 8, 1978. I really wasn't sure if I could finish. Running back then wasn't the same as it is now, where there are twenty-five thousand weekend warriors coming out to run a big city marathon. Back in the late seventies, early eighties, only the serious runners were doing marathons, and the finishing times were significant. No one went out just hoping to finish. Everyone had a P.R. in mind, and it was usually a sub-three-hour time. I didn't know if I had that in me; it was an unknown for me, never having put my mind and my body through the test before. I heard all the horror stories about The Wall, but I hadn't talked to a lot of runners about it. I didn't really know any other runners. I was out there alone. I was young and naive but I think that actually helped! And not having anyone to talk to and break up the monotony of the race, I had to focus. From the moment the race started, I was just doggedly determined to finish no matter what.

At first, my mind just wandered around all sorts of feelings regarding the race: why I was doing it, the satisfaction I would feel when I finished, the glory I would reap. And then came the pain. I ran the first half at a seven-minute pace and when it was too late I realized I had gone out way too fast. I was spent, gone, nothing left. I thought it was over for me. I had to take walk breaks and then run backward to relieve the pain in my legs. They were on fire. I felt incredible pain. It was cold that day and since running gloves were not in vogue yet, I had a pair of socks on my hands to keep them warm. I still remember so vividly the last two miles of the marathon. I was in such intense pain that I had to pull off the socks and stuff them in my mouth to keep from screaming. Quitting was not an option. I had to finish. I went into my survival mode, dulling all the senses and focusing on only one thing: to finish. But the pain I felt during the marathon differed from other types of pain. The intensity of the pain was real enough, but it's self-imposed. I can't stop a tooth from aching or a cut from bleeding but I could have stopped the pain by quitting or resting for a period of time. I consciously chose not to. I guess that's what makes the pain endurable. But on the positive side, there's nothing like running a great race and feeling euphoric afterward. If I am running strong and at the halfway point I am ahead of my goal, the second half of the race is like having a thirteen-mile orgasm.

I used to have little rituals. If I ran a great race with a terrific time, I would wear the same clothes in my next race, trying to re-create the winning situation down to the same socks, shoes, shorts, whatever, until the luck wore out and I'd switch to something else. I remember working out with an elite runner one day and afterward I drove him home. While we were driving, he changed out of his sweaty top and put on a clean one. He left the running shirt in my car and even though it didn't fit me, I wore it from time to time, subconsciously hoping his talent would rub off on me. Now I consider myself lucky if I can find a pair of matching socks.

Crossing the finish line at my first marathon was like ending one life and starting another. Now I was a runner. A whole new world opened up to me. I no longer identified with that fat, rebellious kid in high school. I had a new identity and I loved it. It also enhanced my other life as a student. I had new confidence. I felt invincible. I had a more positive outlook on life in general. I kept running and maintained a goal of two marathons a year. Racing became a part of my life.

My personality is very goal oriented and I need a challenge to keep me motivated. Running became the carrot. It totally filled my life. I needed that high and I kept pushing the envelope, running farther and harder. I was studying to become a chiropractor and the more I learned about the body and how it works, the more I was convinced that we are capable of much more physical output than we think. Previous standards of excellence are continually being surpassed. The advance of athletic records provides evidence that the human body has potential for greater development in the area of athletic prowess. There are many recorded cases of men and women who would be considered past their athletic prime setting incredible records. In 1987, Priscilla Welch from Great Britain won the New York Marathon at age forty-two with a time of 2:30:17. At age ninety-five, Herb Kirk ran 800 meters in 6:03. The passion of sportspeople to exceed themselves reflects a drive that all of us share to some extent. And I am certain that we haven't come close to knowing the full story of what we are capable of doing.

At this point in my life, thirty-seven years old, I've completed about two hundred marathons and I do an ultra every summer. The positive energy I felt from that first marathon continues to stay with me. When I run distance somewhere out there I cross over into a spiritual world where there are no distractions, no pressures, no stress. I feel like I've walked into heaven. Some people call that an alternate state, but I view it as the way our lives should be. Every day I live an abnormal life filled with chaos, pressures, commitments, and a continuous game of beat-the-clock. I need to escape to another zone.

Lately, I've been doing all my running on mountain trails. I get up at five in the morning and head out with my wife and our two dogs to the Ramapo Mountains and run about ten miles of paths through beautiful woods. I feel like primitive man again. Shouldn't our everyday lives be peaceful and calm? Maybe I have too many caveman genes and I long for a place and time that doesn't exist anymore. But my nine-to-five day, which almost always goes to six or nine at night, isn't what I'd care to consider my "normal" life.

The feeling I get from running is a good thing. I wish more people could experience it. I've been called a "running addict" and "obsessive" by some people, usually nonrunners, and they say it with a negative slant. Our society tends to give negative labels to people who live out their passions. But every day we continue to do what we love. I'm just your average runaholic and workaholic. I wouldn't have it any other way.

TEACHING THE GOLDEN RULE, STEP BY STEP

TINA GORDON
RESIDENCE: NEWTON, NEW JERSEY
OCCUPATION: SPECIAL EDUCATION TEACHER
FIRST MARATHON: 1994 CHAMBERSBURG (PA) MARATHON
D.O.B.: 1-24-60
AGE AT FIRST MARATHON: 34

Tina Gordon's golden rule is that life is a series of "purposeful coincidences." An exemplary teacher and role model, Tina stood firm in her pursuit of running the Boston Marathon although it meant quitting her twelve-year tenured teaching position after the district refused her a personal day to run the race. Even with her near-perfect attendance record and Teacher of the Year honors, the district was unrelenting, so Tina heeded the advice she always taught her students: Follow your dream no matter where it may lead. Her gutsy decision led her on a series of purposeful coincidences, including landing another job within weeks of her resignation at a school system that readily accepts her personal day to run Boston. Tina now has the best of both worlds: She has found a way to combine her passion for running with her passion for teaching.

AS A FRESHMAN IN HIGH SCHOOL, I desperately wanted to be a cheer-leader. But as fate decided to play its hand in a long series of purposeful coincidences, I broke my collarbone in the tryouts. So during the fall when all my friends were on the squad, I sat out feeling sorry for myself.

Finally I realized I had to do something, but I had no sports experience. Track seemed like the most logical to attempt for a few reasons. First, at least I knew I could run. And it didn't matter if I was fast or slow because track is one of the few sports where you don't get "benched"; everyone participates. It's also the type of sport where you can only get better; the self-improvement can be measured both in the way you feel physically and in faster finishing times. As much as you put into it, that's what you'll get out of it. It's really a sport for anyone. It doesn't discriminate.

One of the unexpected outcomes of joining the track team was the camaraderie I developed with the other girls and the coach. Mr. Valentine, or Mr. V, as we called him, took us on road trips to races in the area and throughout the East Coast. We got to know girls from surrounding towns and developed a bond that continues today. It created lifetime memories for me and my two best friends, Mary and Lisa. After high school, I attended a college that did not have a competitive track team for women so I ran sporadically, mainly just to stay in shape. Noticing a few extra pounds creeping on, I joined field hockey because at least I would be running again. But never having played a team sport, I felt very incompetent and didn't continue. So for five years, while plugging away at my bachelors and masters degrees, running was more of a staple than a major focus in my life. At the same time, my best friends from high school track kept a rigorous running program and started training for a marathon. I admired what they were doing, but I was still stuck in a three-mile rut and dismissed the idea of a marathon. I have to admit that part of the allure of running back then was to get in great shape, run hard, and run fast. I missed that as I watched my best friends outperforming me, being fit, and having a goal, a focus.

I believe that the idea to run a marathon enters the mind long before the commitment is made. For me, seeing my friends train was the first subconscious entry that triggered my thoughts of a future marathon. The second and final event that fueled the marathon engine was watching my husband, Guy, run the Long Beach Island (L.B.I.) Commemorative Run, an eighteen-miler established in honor of the Israeli athletes killed during the 1972 Olympics. Guy was already a good athlete and runner when I met him after college and our dating routine always included a run. We set a great foundation for a future together as we established early in our relationship that running was going to play a big part in our lives. We would spend hours running together, talking and getting to know each other. Even now, after fifteen years of marriage, we always make time to run together. It takes on a new form of intimacy when it's about the only time we have to catch up on the daily events in our lives. Guy got me going beyond my three-mile routine and steadily brought my mileage up to twelve. So in 1992, with our five-year-old daughter in tow, we drove to L.B.I. for the Commemorative Run.

I remember watching the runners cross the finish line and being overwhelmed with emotion for them and what they had accomplished. When Guy finished, I had tears in my eyes and continued crying all through the applause and awards ceremony. I stood there watching all these people who had run so hard, thinking I would never be able to do that. The pain I saw on those agonized faces was too much, but then again I didn't realize that behind the pain was the glory and exuberance of their personal achievement. I only saw the pain. I didn't want to go through that struggle. Even Guy said he would never run it again. However, on the way home he started talking about how he planned to do better next year! And a year later not only did Guy run it again, but I ran with him and I loved it. I knew then I was ready for a marathon.

A lot of thought was put into choosing my first marathon course. I wanted a small, local, and obscure one just in case I dropped out. That way if I failed, only my immediate friends would know. We decided on Chambersburg, Pennsylvania, which satisfied all factors, and was scheduled only three months after my eighteen-mile L.B.I. race. A January marathon meant training in cold weather, but I actually prefer that to any other temperature. The last three months of training were intense. I would get a few miles in before work while Guy stayed home with Amanda, then after work she was in an after-school program so I had another hour there, and on weekends I would either swap time with Guy, get a baby-sitter, or run with my friends. I've heard many people say they could never find the time to train for a marathon, but all it takes is some creativity. My two friends also had children so we worked out a rotating system where one of us would be the designated baby-sitter while the other two ran. It was a great way to accomplish our goals. A support system is extremely important throughout training, for both the physical requirements and mental stability.

The day prior to the race Guy, my daughter, and our baby-sitter, Kathleen, piled into the car with our running gear and drove the four hours to Chambersburg. It snowed that night and we woke up to freezing precipitation and temperatures thirty degrees below zero. The race officials wanted to cancel but sixty-five of us were willing to run, so off we went! I hate the start of races and was all butterflies the first mile. I get so nervous, which is really silly because my performance only matters to me. I'm not out there to impress anyone, but I still get the jitters. The race director kept cracking jokes because he couldn't believe we were running in such conditions. He was great and had a way of putting us at ease. Mentally, I had prepared for the race by breaking it down into small pieces, measured by the people I would meet and talk with to get me through. This way I could visualize that I was really at home on a long training run with my friends; it just so happens that "my friends" were total strangers. The first six miles I ran with a woman named Leanna, who was delightful. We talked about our initial nervousness, had a few more interesting conversations, and then after six miles I moved on. Ironically, she was the first person I bumped into at my next marathon! Next I met Pam and ran with her from seven to twelve miles. It was Pam's first marathon also, so we had lots of fun wondering if we were doing it right. And talk about coincidence, her husband was also running the marathon, and at a point in the race where there is a loop we saw our husbands running together and talking it up. Sitting here now, I can't believe I remember everyone's name.

As Pam's pace slowed slightly, I moved on and ran with an older gentleman for the next four miles. He was so interesting and had run a marathon in every state! After I told him I wanted to qualify for Boston, he said at the pace we were running I would have no problem. I was now at fourteen miles and feeling great. I had no pain, I wasn't tired. Also, the loops in this course allowed me to see my family at frequent intervals, up to the twenty-mile marker. That really kept me going. At this point I was running with Britta, but she didn't want to converse so we didn't hit it off as well. She was concentrating on her pace and was not receptive to my incessant chatter. She pulled away at eighteen miles and now for the first time in the race I was alone. There was no one around to run with and without the distraction of a conversation, I began to feel the pain and the fatigue. My shoulders and neck were stiff and sore. When I hit twenty miles, two things happened.

First, I was exhilarated with chills because I had never run that far before. But then I got simultaneously depressed because I wouldn't see my family until the finish line. I panicked and lost faith in my abilities. I thought, "Now I am going to crash, now my legs will buckle under from exhaustion and I'll have to walk the rest of the way. Next my breathing will start to go. What if I get in trouble and they forget I'm out here?" These awful thoughts kept jumping into my mind and I knew I had to fight hard to focus on more positive thoughts, mentally pull it together. At twenty-one miles, despite the subzero arctic chill and the fact that I saw icicles hanging from some of the runners' faces, I started to shed my layers of clothes. Off went the gloves, the headband, one of the T-shirts and the neck band. The shedding of the layers psychologically rejuvenated me and I began to run stronger. I concentrated on just putting one leg in front of another. Feeling somewhat refreshed, I caught a glimpse of someone out in front of me and set a mental challenge to catch him and did so at twenty-three miles. We were struggling just to keep moving. I was so glad to find a new friend again that I could have easily stayed by his side and talked the remaining three miles, but he encouraged me to keep moving and not loose my strong pace. He inspired me not only to keep moving at my pace but to pick it up. With two miles to go, I reflected on the fact that my source of energy throughout the race came from my fellow runners and the friends and families of the runners who were also braving the cold to cheer us on. They were my focus. My piece-by-piece psychology worked and now this seemingly insurmountable goal was going to be realized.

The last few miles I played a game with myself to see how many people I could pass. I knew a big hill was coming up at twenty-four miles and I started to get nervous again. I thought it would be my undoing. How much more could I endure? I was so overly fatigued at this point I knew I had to do something creative so I turned it into a challenge. If I could just crest this hill, it would be all downhill from there and my family would be waiting for me at the finish. The thought of seeing them was the hook and I flew down the hill. When I finally crossed the finish line, I felt as if my head was detached from my body. I was so weak I could barely walk through the chute. And when I realized I had qualified for Boston, I was really thrilled. Everything was settling in at once and I totally lost it. A volunteer was handing me a plaque and I couldn't even hold onto it, I was so out of it. At that point, walking seemed harder than running twenty-six miles. Guy helped me inside the center, where we found warmth, sandwiches, a keg of beer, and a hot tub. Everyone gathered around and celebrated. It was so wonderful! I loved that race.

After celebrating, we were going to drive home but a snowstorm moved in and we had to stay over. I remember lying on the bed surrounded by Guy, Amanda, and Kathleen, our sitter, and just staring at the ceiling thinking, "Isn't this great!" The next day it took us eight hours to drive home. By the time we arrived, I was so stiff and achy from being immobile it was worse than running the marathon. But the following weeks were euphoric. We called everyone we knew and related our marathon story many times over. We never tired of telling our tales. Of course we had a huge phone bill, but it was worth it. Months later I was still talking it about with my girlfriends on our runs. I never tired of reliving it. The beauty of postmarathon accounts is that we forget the pain and only remember the greatness. It's something I got through on my own. I lived through the months of training, the moments of doubt and despair, the mental challenge to keep going, and the realization that I did. It took over my entire being. For those few months it became my life's purpose.

Guy and I ran Chambersburg again, and in 1996 we both won our divisions. I ran a P.R. of 3:13, which I am very proud of. I've also run Boston, which is a thrill, but none of the runners want to talk there! They take it so seriously. But nothing has ever come together for me the way it did at my first marathon. Call it beginner's luck, but it was the most perfect day. I've been running for twenty-two years now, a longer period of time than any relationship I've had. It's a part of who I am. It's a part of my life I've shared with my two girlfriends since we were in high school. When we spend time running together, we discuss events in our lives, share our troubles and our achievements. I guess you can say we measure our lives not with coffee spoons but with strides.

There are some days when I do run alone, and those are most special for a very private reason. Nine days after my daughter, Amanda, was born my father died suddenly of a heart attack. He never even got to see her. I hadn't run since my delivery but I knew I needed to run then. I needed to be alone. I had to get out and run through my grief, through the tears and the anguish I was feeling. Now when I want to spend some time with him, I'll go for a run by myself and we'll talk. I see him in the sun as it filters through the leaves on the trees or he'll just pop into my mind and I'll see his face. It's our time to be together.

Running has also helped me with my special education class. I've developed a motivational program especially for them that covers geography, reading, physical education, a bit of math, plus a bit of discipline and focus by using the T-shirts I've received from local races. First we find the location of the race on the state map. Then the kids get to choose what shirt they want to "earn" by reading the requisite number of books and running the number of miles that is on the race shirt. If someone wants the 10K race shirt, they have to read ten books and run ten miles. They plot their progress on a graph and at the end of the year we hold an awards ceremony and present the T-shirts. The kids love it. I'm not looking to turn them into marathoners but I want them to learn about setting goals and going after their dreams. I teach them the "piece-by-piece" psychology and they soon learn that even a seemingly insurmountable goal is within their grasp. Isn't that what life is all about?

MY WORST NIGHTMARE

SCOTT GREELEY
RESIDENCE: RENTON, WASHINGTON
OCCUPATION: ENGINEER, BOEING
FIRST MARATHON: 1995 SEATTLE (WA) MARATHON
D.O.B.: 4-28-59
AGE AT FIRST MARATHON: 36

Growing up with three brothers in the Puget Sound area of Washington State, Scott was good at many sports but a master of none. He played the usual top three: baseball, basketball, and football, but running as a sport was not an option, as he had asthma and didn't have the endurance to go the distance. Then he started biking and the cross-training made him stronger, allowing him to try a marathon. However, Scott's first marathon was not as easy as anticipated, and he learned the hard and humorous way that no one has the upper hand when it comes to running a marathon.

LIVING IN THE SUBURBS OF SEATTLE and growing up with my brothers, we were always doing whatever sport was in season. We were very close in age, and since I was number two, I tried harder. And I definitely believed in quantity, not quality, when it came to my abilities: I was consistently mediocre at many sports. In junior high I ran track but suffered from a congenital knee problem, chrondromalatia, which required surgery. Since running was not my best option, I took up swimming, competing in high school and at the University of Washington.

After graduation and a few consulting jobs, I joined Boeing in 1984, settling into my job, marriage, and becoming somewhat sedentary. I didn't succumb to being a total couch potato, but I certainly wasn't in collegiate shape either. I missed the athletics, but found a new challenge, common among suburban dwellers. I was now captain of the lawn team, competing against the weeds and bugs that invaded my garden and lawn every weekend. It's a very competitive game and most of the time, I lost.

During the week, I played on the softball and volleyball intramural teams at Boeing, where the employees are encouraged to participate and the goal is to have fun. We play against other Boeing teams in the region. I took my intramurals seriously and after the first few games realized I was not in the best of shape. I wasn't able to do what I wanted to do and others were outperforming me. I didn't like that. It was my wake-up call to get in shape. I started to run a little bit, as that was the easiest way to get back in shape. And because I wasn't good at it as a kid, I thought this would be a challenge. I wanted to break through my hundred-yard barrier! I worked up to two miles and it felt good. I think it gave me a slight competitive edge. Whether it did or not, it certainly was a nice feeling that I was finally able to run a respectable distance. And it was certainly better to get out and run rather than just sit around.

I kept a running routine of two miles twice a week for about five years. Boeing started to relax their dress policy and since I didn't need a jacket and tie every day, I started to bike to work. So now I had an even better physical routine, biking to work three days a week and running my two miles twice a week. I started to notice an increase in my endurance and my running was getting easier. The combination of biking and running was definitely working for me. My nine-minute pace was picking up. This may not sound like a big deal, but because of my asthma, I could never run past a certain distance or pace. It was like this physical barrier I could never break through until now. I was beginning to feel like a real athlete. I was going beyond the imposed limits. Keeping in shape is the best way to control my asthma. It works better than any doctor's prescription I've taken.

I don't want to give the impression that I can be seduced by the mere presence of a couch and a good TV show; I really do think of myself as an athlete. I play in an over-thirty soccer league, but even that is getting a little too competitive for me. I want to stay in shape but I don't want to die or sustain a bad injury like the time my thigh got kicked and blew up like a watermelon, or when I broke a few bones in my foot, or, worse, when I blew out a major ligament in my knee. I think most guys are in denial about their sports prowess and keep participating out of vanity. It's taken me a while to figure this out, but it's time to give it up. I'll stick to biking and running.

I was feeling very confident about my new running abilities and decided to enter a half marathon. I guess I did it to prove to myself that I could. I started reading training guides, and although I didn't follow everything, it helped. I started to race because I needed to push myself. A race is a lot different from a training run; it gives me a goal. I run much faster, I push myself, I don't want to come in last. It appeals to my competitive side. I'm racing against myself, to prove that I can do it. It is a great sense of accomplishment.

I started running during lunch, at work. We have an incredible facility with a recreation room, gym, showers, and an outdoor cinder track. The employees use the facilities as much as they can. In fact, at one point we complained that there weren't enough showers, so Boeing brought in a couple of trailers with showers and parked them next to the office.

A friend of mine from work also ran, so we started running together at lunch. We did a 10K together and after that we started talking about a marathon. He ran track in high school and didn't think he would have the stamina to run a marathon. I wasn't interested in running one either. I didn't need to. I liked where I was. Besides, from what I read and heard about marathons, it would be way too painful. But we kept bringing it up, kind of kidding about it and in a subliminal way challenging each other. Finally, we gave in to the lure and agreed to do it, to go for the ultimate runner's quest. I guess it was just the logical thing to do when you like to run, or perhaps it was the beginning of a midlife crisis, or most likely I thought if I was ever going to do one, do it while I was still able. Seattle is fortunate in having what would be considered marathon weather all year long. I do triathlons in the summer and didn't want to overtrain during that period so we picked a marathon in November, over Thanksgiving weekend, which gave us three months to train. After I went public with my marathon quest, people started relating stories from their past marathons, and I was somewhat spooked by the fact they all had unhappy endings. I heard horror stories of bleeding nipples and required hospital recuperation. Some people just looked at me like I was crazy. A limited few thought it was admirable. I tried to follow the marathon training guide but my life is too complex to stay on any schedule. Sometimes I would substitute biking for a long run or if I had a soccer game I wouldn't run later on. I guess my training came down to a basic pattern: some of this, a little of that, and none of the hard stuff. In the middle of training, I suffered the unfortunate experience of pulling a hamstring and for four weeks had to convert the training schedule into my own schedule of stretching, biking, and light running. Then the pain started traveling up my thigh, somewhere around the Buttocks Maximus. When I told my family where it hurt, my kids started rolling on the floor, pointing at me, and saying, "Dad pulled a butt muscle." It wasn't the kind of sympathy I needed, but they are at the age where butt jokes are funny. I don't know how many of their friends they told, but I could feel the neighbors look at me after I ran by, thinking to themselves, "Is that the guy who pulled his butt muscle? I wonder which side was affected."

My longest run was twenty miles and I hated it. It was raining, I was miserable, I wasn't into it, but I had put it off for so long it was a matter of now or never. I had already cheated so much on the schedule, I just had to do it. And I have to admit I wasn't in shape to take on twenty miles. I tried to cheat the schedule and paid for it.

A week before the marathon, I was confident that I could finish without feeling miserable and hold a steady pace for about four hours. However, I did make one big mistake the last week. I was carbo-loading and began to feel really heavy so I decided I had put on too much weight, which would slow me down, so I started to diet the last few days. The Thursday before the race was Thanksgiving and now that I had the perfect excuse to pig out, be a complete sloth, I dieted. I stayed away from the pies, the gravy, the butter and rolls, and even forsook all the leftover turkey sandwiches crammed with cranberry sauce and stuffing the next day. In retrospect, I should have eaten everything in sight.

The night before I slept well. I wasn't feeling nervous but I was anxious to get started. It was freezing out on marathon morning when I finally arrived at the race with the other five thousand entrants but I didn't feel the cold; I was too pepped up, like all the other high-metabolism, scantily clothed runners packed around me. Someone way up front, a race director I imagine, was speaking through a loudspeaker that was so inaudible the transplanted New Yorkers thought they were back on the subways. The race was being delayed but we couldn't figure out why. Everyone kept asking questions, getting no answers. My biggest question was, "Why am I here?" I was suddenly feeling less bravado and more mortal as the minutes crept by. But then the gun went off and I thought we'd all start running but only the people up front started moving. I tried to tell my body, "Don't start the adrenaline yet, I won't be needing you for a few more minutes."

As I cross the starting line, I get into a nice moseying pace, working up to a full shuffle that I think I can hold for twenty-six miles. This is going to be a piece of cake. At mile two I am feeling good and start reviewing my goals for the race. Finishing is most important, but I also want to hold an even pace for the entire race. I don't want to die at the end, flopping across the finish line with all the grace of a fish in a puddle. The goal is to finish with style. At mile four I calculate that I am one-sixth of the way done. This is too easy. At this rate, I'll probably have so much energy left over I won't even need a ride home. I'll tell my wife, "No thanks, honey, I'll just jog home to cool down and stretch out those tendons." I feel like laughing out loud at this personal joke, but the runners around me won't understand and will possibly think I'm already losing it. I pass mile eight and wonder if I started out too fast. I haven't slowed down yet, but I'm considering it, and the macho idea of the leftover energy is gone. I'll definitely need a ride home.

At mile nine I'm one-third of the way and I think I'm going to be fine. I feel strong; my stride is fluid and graceful. But as I look around me, my fellow marathoners look tired and their strides are disconnected and rough. How can they possibly be keeping up with me? I wonder again about the finish, not because I'm anxious or anything but I still have that goal in mind of a strong, sharp finish. So far the weather has been cooperating, with mild temperatures and a light breeze.

As I pass mile eleven, it starts to rain. I'm cold and wet, but I visualize that I am wearing a two-hundred-dollar waterproof, breathable running suit that keeps me dry and warm. And since this is my visualization, I'll also imagine that I bought it on sale for $129.99. That makes me feel even better and before I know it I've passed the halfway mark. Part of me is ecstatic that I'm halfway, the other part is crying because I have thirteen more miles to go. I'm beginning to wish this was a half marathon and I was finished by now. This full-marathon thing was a stupid idea. Suddenly, my body starts talking to me. "Scott, this is your right foot and I'm not happy. I have an inflamed nerve in my second metatarsal and you better do something about it right now or I'll really start to complain." So to make my right foot happy, I compensate the body weight and put more pressure on the left foot. Then I start hearing it from him. "Scott, this is totally unfair. I've never given you any problems, never complained of nerve endings or bunions, not even when you slam me into soccer balls. So don't start abusing me now just because Mr. Right over there is a wimp." I decide my left foot has an inferiority complex and to hell with both of them.

By mile fifteen I'm definitely slowing down, so I decide to rethink my first goal of running at an even pace throughout the race and change it to being able to run at all toward the end and not get passed by too many people. I don't want to find myself in the pathetic situation of crawling toward the finish line while droves of people pass me thinking to themselves, "That guy started out too fast and is paying for it now."

By mile seventeen I am so tired I can't even wipe the sweat off my face. I tell myself there's only nine miles to go. I am definitely going slower, but if I can hold this pace the rest of the way, I'll be happy. Suddenly, my body starts talking again. "Scott, these are your groin muscles. I know you haven't heard from me in a while but you've gone too far this time and I am resurfacing all those old injuries you thought were healed. Remember when it hurt just to roll over in bed? Well, consider that a roll in the hay." (My groin has a great sense of humor.) My old injuries seem to be staging a reunion and all body parts are welcome to attend.

Mile eighteen brings despair. I may as well admit to myself that I indeed started out too fast. I've still a long way to go and I keep slowing down. But wait a minute, I think I'm getting a second wind. Yes, my breathing seems stronger, steadier. Now all I need is a second pair of legs to go with it and I'll be all right. As I pass mile nineteen, I'm feeling trepidation about reaching mile twenty. Everyone says that's where I will hit the wall. Actually, I feel as if I've already hit a dozen walls and figuratively fallen flat on my face a number of times, so what could be the big deal? It can't get any worse, right? Wrong. I'm reaching new depths in self-punishment. I can't believe I have six more miles to go. My stride has long since stopped being so fluid and graceful. In fact, there is nothing graceful about me. I think it's time to alter my finishing goal for the third and last time: Try not to get passed by anyone with a cane.

At mile twenty-two I contemplate suicide. Why am I doing this? Why didn't I train more? Why did I sign up in the first place? I try to remember my new finishing goal but can't. I think I'm brain dead. I wish I were a race director instead of a runner. They've probably all gone home by now, showered, had dinner, and are preparing the race results for tomorrow's papers. My running pace is now a walk. I wonder if this is what childbirth feels like and I want to ask one of the female runners who are passing me, but I don't have the energy. It doesn't even bother me that I'm being passed.

At mile twenty-four I wonder if I will ever get the desire to run another marathon in my lifetime. I worry that I'll forget all this pain and suffering and in a few weeks start thinking about the next one. If only I could bottle this feeling and administer doses of reality whenever I get delusions of marathoning. Maybe if I go home right away and write down what this is really like I will have a record to serve as a reminder. I'll use words like *masochism* and *self-mutilation*. I'll want to remember the looks on the crowd as they take pity on me. Although they're supportive, I am in a bad mood and don't want to hear, "Come on, you're looking good." No way do I look good.

Finally I saw the finish line and yes, I still wanted to have the look of a superstar crossing with the grace and stride of a Bill Rodgers, but I was more like Quasimodo. I saw my wife and kids and that was a real boost. In fact, my older daughter ran the remaining few hundred yards with me and I got an incredible burst of energy from her presence. I actually finished with some semblance of style. At least that's the faint memory I have, but I actually don't remember the last part of the race very well. I think my body was shunting blood away from my brain to the needier parts of my body, realizing that it was my brain that got me in this predicament in the first place. I certainly don't remember how my hands and knees got bruised and dirty.

When I finally stopped running, I realized how cold I was. All I wanted to do was go home. I was disappointed with myself and didn't want to hang around doing the finale thing. I was miserable. I didn't feel good about my performance. It certainly isn't the marathon I wanted to remember. There was nothing worth remembering about it except the pain and humiliation.

Overall, I'm glad I did it because now I never have to again. But as James Bond says, "Never say never." I shouldn't entirely rule out running another but it won't be for a long time, long enough for this memory to fade into the distance.

ALWAYS THE COACH

ROB HEMMEL
RESIDENCE: RIDGEWOOD, NJ
OCCUPATION: HIGH SCHOOL ART TEACHER, GIRLS TRACK COACH
FIRST MARATHON: 1981 JERSEY SHORE MARATHON
D.O.B.: 9-5-48
AGE AT FIRST MARATHON: 32

A veteran of eighteen marathons, countless bi- and triathlons, and usually seen around town in running shorts and T-shirts from obscure races, Rob shows up for the interview with a bulging backpack filled with race memorabilia: every entry number, official finish results, photographs, brochures, newspaper coverage of the more special events, awards, George Sheehan books, you name it. If it is race-related, it's in there. In 1971, a year out of college, Rob received an invitation to join the Marines, no RSVP required. Scheduled for Officer Candidate School at Quantico, Rob started running to get in shape for the grueling months ahead. At the last moment destiny swerved, as a double compound knee fracture from high school football caused a medical deferment. This past summer, Rob celebrated his twenty-year anniversary of daily runs. He hasn't missed a morning.

AFTER I WAS TURNED DOWN BY THE MARINES, I decided to keep up the running a few days a week. Just being able to run was a bonus, as the doctor who performed the knee surgery back in 1965 predicted I would never do sports again. I was always active in sports like football, basketball, and tennis, but never running. Now that most of the other sports were off limits, I became a runner by default. Actually, running made me feel really good. I noticed health benefits from the start. At that time, running was unique, it was different. I liked that about it. Now I didn't have to wait for anyone or rely on anyone to get my exercise in. It was just me out there. This was new to me and I liked everything about it. I remember buying my first real running shoes, a pair of blue New Balance, with the N printed on the side. I also bought a pair of Tigers. I wish I had kept those, they'd probably be worth something today.

One of the characteristics runners have in common is that little nudge to compete, to see how good we really are and I'm no different. After my first 10K, I was completely hooked on the racing experience. I loved it. I started running longer distances to challenge myself, always pushing a little bit farther. It was the summer of 1972, and Frank Shorter had just won the Olympic gold in the marathon, the first and last for the U.S. since 1908. He was a big influence on my decision to run a marathon. There was a certain mystique about it that intrigued me. I wanted to measure myself against the best runners out there and this was the race to do it. However, having recently married, busy with teaching and coaching soccer and track, I wasn't ready yet.

By 1981 the Marathon Sirens were still calling me. By now I considered myself a serious runner and competitor, but I didn't confide my dream to run a marathon to anyone, including my wife, not knowing how she would react to the change in our daily routine such a challenge would mean. Judy was supportive of my athletic lifestyle, but training for a marathon? That's asking for major sacrifices. Ultimately, I had to confront the challenge, had to prove to myself that I could do it. Not just anyone can finish a marathon.

My cousin had just run the Jersey Shore Marathon, and after speaking with him I decided to enter. For me, it was a perfect first marathon; close to home and a nice flat course. And as a teacher, I could spend most of the summer training. The race date was December 8.

I started researching training techniques. Marathon guidelines in the late seventies were totally different than we know today. The standard training routine for top runners was 120 miles a week, which included two 10s on most days. The diet consisted of protein and starches with a recommended depletion technique four days prior to the race, then bulk up the day before. There were no bagels, no breads, no prerace spaghetti pig-outs. This was really the dark ages of training.

Being a track coach, I knew how important the training would be and tried to follow the methods, but I added my own instincts to the mix. I was up every morning at 5:00 A.M. for a run. I never really measured my distance; I've always been a believer in time. The longest training run I did was two hours and I didn't do any of the new stuff they recommend today such as separate days for speed work, fartleks, hill work, et cetera. I kept doing races and ran lots of 10Ks and a few half marathons. As a vegetarian, the protein-based diet was a real problem. No matter how many bean dishes Judy and I devised, it just wasn't enough. I was hungry, irritable, and weak. And it got worse. During the four-day depletion diet I ate nothing but eggs and bean curd. I was a nasty s.o.b., just ask Judy.

Training took over everything, it consumed me. Judy was semisupportive but was worried about my health. She said I looked like hell throughout the training period. In fact, right after the race she said, "You look liked you've just aged twenty years."

Today most people set out just to finish the marathon, without a time to compete against. But back in the seventies, only serious runners tackled the 26.2 miles. Looking through my old race brochures and listings of finishing times, almost 50 percent of the runners did it in under three hours. That was the mark to beat, and I felt confident I wouldn't be too far off. However, I was really nervous.

Race day dawned cold and windy. As we were queuing up, I met an older guy who had done it before and he gave me some great advice: "Just pace yourself throughout the race. Let everyone pass you the first ten miles. If you keep the steady pace, you'll be passing them at twenty miles." I was worried, though. I'm not used to letting people pass me. But I followed his advice. I kept focused and never stopped running my own pace.

For most runners, the first ten miles don't present any major difficulties if you've trained. The hardest part is reining in all the adrenaline. At fifteen miles, though, I began to break down. Things hurt that I never knew I had. My quads hurt, my shoulders and arms hurt. At mile twenty, the fun was over and the bottom of my feet were burning. It was extremely painful but I just kept shuffling along. I was waiting to hit the wall, since I had read about it in all the books, but nothing happened. I guess I never hit it. Maybe the anticipation of worrying about it was worse that the realization that I had just run twenty miles.

Over the last six miles, it all boiled down to a game of wits, of total focus. I knew I couldn't disassociate myself from the task at hand. One slip, one ounce of self-pity or whining and I'd be done. So I kept looking down at my feet and repeated over and over, "Just keep moving." I knew that if I just kept my feet slip-sliding in front of each other, no matter how slowly, I would finish. Finally, the end was in sight. However, the finish of this marathon was a real mind teaser. The last two miles is a double loop, so I could look to my left and see the lucky ones crossing the finish line. God, that was such a draining feeling. I wanted to be done in the worst way and there, right alongside of me I could see people already being rewarded. But I persevered.

Nothing but nothing will ever look so good as the words FINISH LINE. Crossing was the best feeling of satisfaction in the world. I checked my official time, got hurtled into a mass of well-wishers and headed over to a table of free food and drink. It was truly a euphoric moment.

Where does the satisfaction come from? Knowing I did this all on my own. Nobody helped me. I worked hard for this. Everything I got out of it I put in myself. No one can ever take this feeling away from me. At the eighteenth mile, I couldn't imagine ever doing this again in my whole life, but after crossing the finish line and getting that incredible high, I started grabbing the applications for the next one. My finishing time was 3:27 and I was already figuring out how to beat it.

The days after were exuberant and the high lasted for three days. I wore my pain and marathon scars proudly. But eventually the letdown occurred, when I could walk down the stairs without holding onto the railing for support and stopped wobbling side to side. I knew I had lost the glow when I could walk straight again. Then depression set in. It seemed that overnight, gone were all the months of training, then the experience itself, then the unadulterated after-bliss. The loss of that high is difficult, and the body is too busy rebuilding itself to give any positive support.

For me, the marathon experience has had long-term benefits. I feel I can meet any challenge life throws me. It has given me such self-esteem. If I can run a marathon, I can do anything. And I do believe it is something within everyone's grasp. It is the most pure, beneficial, rewarding experience you can do for yourself.

Being a coach, I can't help giving out some advice for first-timers. First, talk to people within your capability level who have run it. Don't listen to the trials and tribulations of the sub-three-hour group. They aren't your peers. Don't force yourself into regimented training routines. Listen to your body. Then don't think of the race as twenty-six miles, break it up into three pieces: Miles one to five just enjoy the thrill and look around at the surroundings. Miles six through nineteen run a mental half marathon and just stay focused. Then for the last twenty to twenty-six run a slow 10K. The input is considerable but the rewards are unbelievable. It was one of the best moments in my life.

The last marathon I ran was the Marine Corps in 1992. My neighbor's son, who was very close to our family, was a marine and had planned on running that marathon with his dad. However, he never made it to the marathon. He was killed in a car crash a few weeks before. To honor his memory, I gathered a group of neighbors and we ran the marathon with his dad. It was a very rewarding experience. I hadn't even been training, but I didn't care. I just wanted to be there for him.

With eighteen marathons behind me and a personal record of 2:53, my marathon days are over. I have nothing else to prove to myself. I'm really not a textbook marathoner, feeling I have to run one every year. The training is just too intense to fit into a normal lifestyle. I've run marathons where I hadn't trained properly and got injured. You can't cheat a marathon. I'm content doing my bi- and triathlons and a few fun races on weekends. I judge a race by the quality and quantity of the free food. Fajitas and beer? I'm there. Besides, despite the new so-called running boom of today, there are no American running idols. Gone are the days when Shorter, Rodgers, and Kelley were household names. I'll wager a bet that if you did a "person-in-the-street" survey, you'd be hard pressed to come up with just one American name attached to the marathon, or track in general for that matter.

I must admit, the feeling I got from those marathons was a better high than any other sports endeavor I've participated in. I think it boils down to the fact that a marathon is run from a completely inward focus. There's no bike or body of water or any other element to contend with; just my mind and my body. And I have to make them work together as a unity in order to finish. The marathon is one rare opportunity to make such a connection, and make it work successfully. That is pure satisfaction. The input is considerable but the rewards are unbelievable. And don't forget, you get to burn almost a pound of fat in one morning!

YES, THAT'S ME, AND I'M WALKIN'

DONNA ISAACSON
RESIDENCE: ROGUE RIVER, OREGON
OCCUPATION: NEUROTRAUMA NURSE
FIRST MARATHON: 1997 PORTLAND (OR) MARATHON
D.O.B.: 6-1-53
AGE AT FIRST MARATHON: 44

For Donna, the patients in her intensive care unit are living proof that life is full of possibilities. She sees the worst cases and the most fragile patients turn around and make a better life for themselves. Donna has also gone through the best and worst of life, enjoying the perks of being the last sibling at home with very devoted parents and then watching her father die. Fond memories of long hikes with her dad were used as a balm to soothe the pain of his death. Life became bleak and meaningless after his passing. Coping with a nasty divorce and raising two sons, Donna put on weight. Filled with a deep despair, Donna was not only mourning her father, she was also mourning the loss of her own existence. Salvation appeared in the form of an old Native American shaman who got Donna back on the right path, and she continued to walk that path straight through to her first marathon. For those of you who think running a marathon is tough, try walking one for seven hours.

I WAS THE BABY OF THE FAMILY, the afterthought. My closest sibling was eight years older so by the time I was ten, my sister and brother were out of the house. Because of that, I think I got the best of my parents. My dad was fifty-seven when I was born, but he was a very active man. He loved the outdoors and would take me hiking up in the Pryor Mountains in Montana. I have very vivid memories of sitting on his knee watching mesmerized as he dusted off some ancient relic he had uncovered while on an archaeology dig. He was a wonderful collector of Indian artifacts and taught me to identify the different arrowheads he'd found. An expert in the state on Indian artifacts, he received blessings from the various Indian tribes for his efforts. Dad was the one who dragged me off the couch and into the outdoors and I owe him a great deal for that. On the other hand, my mom taught me mental strength. I can still hear her saying, "There isn't anything you can't do." She taught me to set goals and not give up.

In high school, I was the typical geeky girl who just wanted to have fun, stringing along three or four boyfriends at a time. Needless to say, I wasn't very studious. My mom had big plans for me to be a concert pianist, and although I did have talent, I wasn't about to waste my high school days taking lessons. But in a case of a modern day O. Henry-esque story, I sold my piano during my first marriage to help put my husband through school. He was going to buy me a bigger and better piano when he got a job. Instead, we ended up divorced and I never got my piano.

By 1988, I found myself starting over and needed an outlet, a way to channel the seething debris of rage left over from the divorce and my slowly deteriorating self-esteem and confidence. Running seemed to fit the bill. That and a martial arts program. Between the two, I was beginning to feel better about myself. My two boys were on the track team and gave me encouragement. They were always there for me. When they were at practice, I'd be on the road logging in my own miles. I wasn't as gifted as them, but I looked forward to my time alone, running a few miles just to unwind or think about what was ahead for me. My job is very stressful and sometimes when a patient dies, it's hard to let go. Once they enter my care, they cease to be strangers. I look after them like family and quite frankly, wouldn't know how to do my job any other way. It's the same with my boys. They are my best friends, the two finest reasons for getting up in the morning. I am 100 percent committed to them and don't think there has been a day in their lives when they didn't go to sleep at night without knowing they were loved.

God gives us things in life we don't always ask for, such as a divorce. And sometimes He tests our strength even further. For me, that ultimate test was my father's death. He passed away four years ago at the age of ninety-eight and there was no consolation in the fact that he had lead a long, fulfilling life. If I heard that one more time during his funeral, I thought I would lose it. It didn't matter to me how and when he died, he was gone. The one person on earth who gave me uncondi- tional love was no longer there for me. With his passing, a huge hole was ripped out of my heart and I plunged into that deep, dark hole with uncontrollable grief. As my mourning period continued, I went deeper and deeper into that black abyss. For four years, I engaged in a death wish, slowly dying inside. I had no social life. My life consisted of two things: work and sleep. At night, I'd crawl into a cave under the sheets and get into a fetal position, hoping sleep would come and for a few moments I could forget that he was gone, dream that he was still with me. It hurt so badly. And I put on fifty pounds.

Out of desperation, I met with an old Indian shaman who thought she could help. As part of the healing ritual, I spent a night in a sweat lodge on the top of a mountain while she prayed over me. As sweat mixed with a steady stream of tears slogged off my body, she prayed that my grief be lifted and for an inner peace and healing to take its place. She told me to stop punishing myself, that I would never bring him back and I needed to let go of my grief. The final thing she told me, which hit home more than anything, was that he wouldn't want me to suffer this way, wouldn't want me to live this way. To honor him properly, I needed to take back my life and make him proud of me. I realize her counseling was not something that any professional grief counselor wouldn't have expressed, but somehow she got through to me when others couldn't.

The next morning I felt renewed, better than I had felt in four years. I decided to celebrate my new self by taking a walk. At first, it was hard to walk around the block without getting winded, but I stuck with it and eventually found a friend to join me. Our first walk together was six and a half miles, and finished uphill. When we reached the top, six hours later, there wasn't even a bench where I could collapse. I lay down on the grass and thought I'd die. A month later, after walking every day, we repeated that first walk and it took us half the time with breath to spare. The realization of just how far I'd come was exhilarating. Another plus was losing fifteen pounds.

In April of 1997, some of the nurses at my hospital suggested I walk the Portland Marathon. By now, everyone knew me as "The Walker," and the idea of walking a marathon appealed to me. The first person I called to discuss the possibility with was my sister, who had run a few marathons. If I decided to go ahead with this crazy plan, she was the person I wanted by my side. Living so far apart, our relationship had boiled down to seeing each other at funerals and weddings. What kind of connection is that to have of my only sister? I wanted more and thought this was the perfect vehicle to renew our bonds. She immediately said yes. In comparison, others greeted the news with the comment, "You should have your Prozac levels checked. Are you nuts?"

I started a walking routine in anticipation of the marathon. All through the spring and summer, I walked. My base was ten miles a day, longer on the weekends. In the beginning I had tons of blisters and shin splints but after a while they went away. My wardrobe took on a new look as the contents of my closet boiled down to three pairs of walking shoes and various sweatpants and tops. Out here in Oregon, towns are at least fifteen miles apart, so generally I'd just walk to another town to get in my miles. Most of my walks were in very remote areas, so remote that I worried about cougars. I always took a cellular phone and left a note for the kids as to what direction I was headed.

My walks became adventures out of the old television series, *Wild Kingdom.* On many days I was privileged to see eagles, bobcats, ospreys, lots of deer, at least one rattlesnake, and salmon jumping in the rivers. One of the most special wildlife scenes I saw was a mother opossum with her babies lined up on her back crossing the road. Every day was an escapade, something to look forward to. On a clear, cloudless day, I felt as if I was walking through paradise. In the distance there were snowcapped mountains peeking through the conifers. Even on rainy days, and we do get rain, I walked through wet mist or heavy downpour, taking in the changes of the scenery.

By September, marathon month, I had lost a total of fifty pounds. Some of that was due to a change in diet. I was eating better, not like the little piglet I had let myself become. As for the race itself, I was somewhat worried that my sister wouldn't be able to keep such a slow pace. For her, it would be a different mind-set to be walking in almost double the time she could run it. However, she didn't seem fazed, so I stopped worrying.

Two days before the marathon, I picked her up at the airport and we spent some time catching up. The night before the big event, we went line dancing, drank beer, and stayed up late. We didn't turn out the lights till 2 A.M.,setting the alarm for 5 A.M. By 5:30 of marathon day, I was up, dressed, and ready to go. Before we left the hotel, I presented my sister with a gift of a gold chain with half a heart on it with the engraving, BIG SIS. I was already wearing my necklace, the other half of the heart engraved with, LITTLE SIS.

There were forty-five hundred walkers and fifty-five hundred runners at the marathon. We, meaning the walkers, started at a different spot than the runners, but eventually both groups merged although they quickly passed us by. It was slow-going at first as we couldn't break through the swarm of walkers for the first three miles. I was getting antsy, wanted to get a pace going, so I foolishly left the road and tried to get around the walkers by cutting across someone's front lawn. Bad idea. I tripped over a ground-level sprinkler head and started to go into a head-first fall. I quickly used my martial arts training and went into a tuck and roll position to avoid cracking my head. That took some of the wind out of the fall, but I still separated two ribs. It hurt, but I kept going. I think the pulsating adrenaline and endorphins disguised the pain.

The first ten miles was a little boring so my sister and I spent the time doing more catch-up, discussing our lives, Dad's death, kids leaving the nest, my summer romance that had just broken up, things that were special to our lives. Then we played Remember When, taking turns reminiscing about funny happenings from our childhood. "Remember when Mom made you wear that ugly red dress? Remember when we snuck into the kitchen and ate the entire pan of just-baked brownies and Mom gave us hell?" We got the giggles so bad we could hardly walk. At mile twelve, I had to use the Port-a-Potty, and bumped into another woman who took a quick glance at me and said, "I know you, you saved my life!" Turns out she was a former intensive care patient of mine and the last time I saw her she had tubes coming out every part of her body, lying there near death. Before I could reply, she continued, "You probably don't remember me, but I knew I was dying and you were the only nurse who could get my I.V. in properly. I really do think you saved my life." With that, she gave me a big hug and off she went.

I had a camera with me to capture moments along the course and when we spied two motorcycle policemen directing traffic, I knew I had a Kodak Moment. I climbed onto the back of the motorcycle and as the

surprised cop turned around, I explained that I wanted a picture taken
with one of Portland's Finest. "Well, that would be me," he responded
with a smile.

During miles fifteen to twenty we sang every show tune we knew.
Actually, I take that back; we belted out every show tune we knew. The
musical program started with the song from *Annie* about the sun coming out tomorrow and finished up with "My Favorite Things" from *The
Sound of Music*. Some of the people around us thought we had finally lost
it and moved away, but others, like the man behind us, came up and
thanked us for keeping him so entertained during a particularly rough
time. It was a nice feeling that we somehow helped out others.

At mile twenty-two, the blister that had started out as an annoyance
became the size of a silver dollar and was causing severe distress. But I
could now see the skyline of downtown Portland and that wiped away
the pain. I was so excited I wanted to run, not walk. We picked up the
pace and by mile twenty-five I just had to break out and sprint for the
finish. I grabbed my sister's hand and with arms held high we crossed
the finish line together. Our time was seven hours.

We joined the festivities, ate some food and headed back to the hotel,
where we soaked in a Jacuzzi. By now my ribs were really smarting. I
couldn't even lie flat or take a deep breath. But I was determined to go
out dancing, so I poured my tired-but-determined body into my size
eight Levi's, down from the size twenty seven months ago, and hit the
town. In contrast, my sister went to bed. I don't get out much, so I
kicked up my heels and danced like a wild woman with every guy in
the place.

The next day we toured Portland, making fun of all the marathon
runners who walked with a waddle in contrast to our normal gait. We
were still hungry from all the energy depletion and what we wanted
more than anything in the world was the biggest, juiciest cheeseburger
we could find. I know that sounds disgusting and totally unhealthy,
but if we were ever going to indulge ourselves, that was the best time
to do it.

Running changed my life and brought it into balance. I now feel as
though my entire essence, body and soul, is centered. I've grown spiri-
tually as well, and thank God every day for what I have. This kind of
happiness can't be bought off a shelf somewhere. It took an enormous
amount of work. But now I own it and no one can take it away. I find I

am better with my patients as well. I seem to give more of myself to their healing process. As a result, they are the indirect beneficiaries of the new me.

My children have also benefited from my walking and exercise program. My younger son is a senior in high school and when he leaves for college, the nest will be empty. I'm grieving already at the prospect of his departure. But we still have time to spend and we plan to do a half marathon together in April, which I will run, not walk. It will be our swan song. He is a very gifted runner and I'm sure he will accomplish great things in his life. My older son is in the army and when he comes home on leave in December, he is taking me on a twelve-mile double-time march with a thirty-five-pound pack strapped to my back. He's already teaching me his platoon cadences to sing while we hike.

In fact, I got a call from his drill sergeant wanting to acknowledge my efforts in raising such a fine young man. It seems that one day, while the drill sergeant was screaming in my son's face, which is what drill sergeants are supposed to do, my son told him he wasn't so tough compared to his mom, who was a night-shift nurse. Now that's tough!

My life has changed so much. I have races to run, races to walk, places to go. People notice the change in me, not only the physical change, but there is a calmer more positive side to me. I find that I am more secure in my role as a woman and I know that if it is meant to be, someday I'll find the right man. This time around, I'll be ready to make it last. It has been an incredible year for me. I can sum it up in one word: YES!

A NUN ON THE RUN

SISTER MARION IRVINE
RESIDENCE: SANTA ROSA, CALIFORNIA
OCCUPATION: SCHOOL ADMINISTRATOR
RESIDENCE: SANTA ROSA, CALIFORNIA
FIRST MARATHON: 1980 AVENUE OF THE GIANTS MARATHON,
EUREKA, CALIFORNIA
D.O.B.: 10-19-29
AGE AT FIRST MARATHON: 50

In 1994, Sister Marion Irvine was inducted into the Road Runners Club of America Hall of Fame. She came on the running scene late in life, but made up for it in a fast way. In 1985 she was invited to Rome to run the World Veterans Games and won one gold and three silver medals. In 1989 she set American and world records in the 3,000 meters. Everywhere she went, the media and crowds adored her. Sports Illustrated *covered her events. And finally, to add to all the winning records, her crowning career achievement was qualifying for the Olympic Trials marathon in December of 1983 with a time of 2:51, at the age of fifty-four.*

IN 1978 I WAS TWO HUNDRED POUNDS, SMOKING two and a half packs of cigarettes a day, forty-seven years old with a perfect Type-A personality and most likely on my way to a heart attack. Jill, a close friend of mine, suggested I take up jogging, this new running thing that people were doing to lose weight. She had already been jogging for about a year and was getting in great shape. I, unfortunately, was in very bad shape and, as a religious woman, completely sedentary. Nuns aren't big on sports: no hiking, no swimming, no anything. But even my ankle-length habit couldn't hide just how out of shape I was. Jill kept after me to start exercising, but it was out of the question, an outrageous idea.

In May I went on an eight-day religious retreat to our convent in San Rafael. It was a pretty time of year and soon I developed cabin fever so thought I might as well go out and try jogging and when I failed miserably at it, I could tell Jill to get off my back. At the school gym I found a pair of men's red shorts that fit, so armed with the shorts and my red beach shoes I snuck out of the convent to go for a run. Clocking one mile on the car odometer, I then drove back to the convent gate and started to run a two-mile loop. I made it ten steps before my head was spinning and I was out of breath. But determination was the order of the week, so despite the boiling heat I managed to half walk half run the distance by the end of the eighth day. It wasn't easy, to say the least.

Later on while cooling off in the shower, I realized how great I felt. It was the most exercise I had done since I was seventeen and it actually felt good. I did that two mile run every day for eight days. When I called Jill to let her know of my amazing feat, she was very encouraging. Running topics started to dominate our conversations. She was already planning to do her first marathon but I had no idea what she was talking about so asked her what a marathon was. When she told me a 26-mile, 385-yard race, I said I never heard of anything so ridiculous. No one can do that. Well, before I knew it, I was training with her. By September I was already entering local fun runs sponsored by a running club in San Francisco. The running boom was just beginning and we were all touting Frank Shorter as our Olympic hero. I turned forty-eight that October and was winning all the races for my age group. But let's face it, there wasn't a lot of competition. Everyone was telling me how talented I was, a natural-born runner. The media started to take notice, dubbed me the "Running Nun" and started to cover my races. People got such a kick out of it. Soon I was invited to enter races in new places. The newspapers couldn't get enough of this new human interest story. They wanted to see the nun who could run.

Anyway, Jill had gone on to finish her first marathon, which only made me more determined to do the same. The very next day I went out and ran twelve miles, my longest distance to date. I bought a book by the New Zealand coach Arthur Lydiard who believed in long, slow distance training. There were two marathon training sections, one for beginners and one for elite runners. Having been an English major and not knowing any running terms at all, I thought *elite* referred to a refined, well-mannered person. So I followed that schedule! It seemed awfully strenuous, but that actually appealed to me. Besides, I had no goal in mind, no sense of how I would finish. My longest run was twenty miles and I had no clue what would happen to me when I embarked on twenty-one miles.

I wasn't nervous because I had trained very hard, running several twenties. I also didn't have any expectations—no goal, no idea of when I would finish. I had to put an estimated finishing time on the application, so I asked Jill what I should put down. She suggested 3:30 and I questioned her as to whether I could do that. It sounded so fast. She said it didn't really matter what I wrote.

The day of the marathon was beautiful and clear. The field of two thousand people was ready to go. Unlike many first- timers who just want to finish, I started out in front. I didn't see any reason to run one more step than I had to. Besides, I had confidence and actually thought I could win. So there I was, up with all the guys. I started out fast, about a 6:10 pace per mile. After a few miles the man next to me said, "How long do you expect to hold this pace?" Along with the pace I'm sure he was taking into account my gray hair. I told him I expected to hold it the whole distance. A while later he said, "You're not Rosie Ruiz, are you?" He was making reference to the woman who had "won" Boston that year, later to be found an impostor. Her infamous publicity stunt was still the talk of the race circuit. When I told him I wasn't, he was determined to find out more about me. Finally I told him my name, and he replied, "*Sister,* as in *nun?*" Now, remember I was in a cluster of men, who were laughing as our dialogue unfolded. "Well, in that case, I'm sticking with you, because we all intend to run a sub-three-hour marathon." Being a gray- haired nun, and running as fast as I was became the running joke for the next several miles until they pulled ahead.

The course is absolutely beautiful. The route goes out and back seven miles, so at mile fourteen you pass the starting line spectators waiting there to cheer you on. I was among the first group of women to pass and their screams of "Go, Grandma!" still echo in my ears. They were a great bunch, doing what crowds do best.

I continued to run strong and steady, maintaining about six- and- a- half minute pace. I worried about hitting the wall, since I'd never run farther than twenty miles in my training. I thought, "Oh my God, what's going to happen to me?" But nothing happened. I continued past twenty miles still strong and steady. I don't remember stopping at any aid station for water. I did once but spilled it all down my front. These were the days before hydration became such an important part of conditioning. Back then we ran the race raw.

Then, by twenty-three miles, I started to lose it. Tiredness set in and the next mile marker never seemed to come. By now I was just holding on. Although I wasn't in pain, I was dead tired. At twenty-five miles the race goes over the Dyerville Bridge, which is basically flat with a small incline. It was so close to the end, but that slight incline may as well have been Mount Everest. My legs were so heavy I felt as if I were carrying around two tree trunks. I was in agony. There were some teenage boys sitting on the bridge, saying, "Lookin' great. It's almost over." But I knew I looked like shit. I had to struggle across that bridge with every ounce left.

Once over the bridge, the finish line lay ahead and I crossed in 3:01, winning my age division. The roar of the crowds became Novocain for the pain and somehow before long all you remember are the euphoric moments.

That was really the first time I put myself to the test and was amazed at just how fast I was. So I ran another one thinking I would better my time, but I didn't. In fact, it took me several more marathons before I broke that time. After my first one, every other marathon was overridden with calculating times and splits, thinking about where I should be at what time, taking notes on the back of my hands. It became more of a chore.

There's nothing quite like your first marathon. The adrenaline just flows. With no expectations, I ran pure and simple. Somehow it just all came together.

Running was beginning to change my life. The weight just poured off and the smoking habit was long gone. Some of the older nuns were not too enthusiastic about my new image; they complained about the brief running shorts. But most of the nuns were supportive. After all, I was fit and healthy so they were delighted with my transformation. And they had always viewed me as a maverick, so here was just another thing they had to take in stride. They thought it would pass!

Looking back on the stages of my running career, I realize I didn't have a beginning. I was never a novice, never paced myself. When you begin a career at fifty, there is no time for a slow start. Some people labeled me a speed freak, but that's the only way I knew how to run. Every day I was training for a new race, a new world-class event. I trained rigorously and my religious occupation as administrator of our congregation's school system afforded me the flexibility to train every day. Right after breakfast, which is quite early in a convent, I would be out there running my routine. Then I would shower and go to work. I was juggling two careers but enjoying every moment. There were times when my priorities were put to the test and I had trouble keeping them straight. My religious commitment was always at the top, then came my professional responsibilities as school administrator, and then this newfound athletic career. And it was a career, not just an activity. I even had a coach. It was difficult and I wasn't always able to keep my priorities straight. Sometimes I actually questioned my own identity. Was I this media celeb called the Running Nun? Was I giving enough time to my administrative responsibilities? It wasn't always fun and games, there was definitely a stressful mental side to the picture as well as lots of painful physical stress. I was always injuring myself, due to overtraining and never stopping to adequately rest my body.

The highlight of my career was the Olympic Trials in May of 1984. Actually, I should step back to the Qualifier for the Olympic Trials, which was held in December of '83 in California. That was truly an awakening moment. I qualified on my first attempt with a time of 2:51:01. After I finished I went back to the hotel and took a bath. It slowly started to dawn on me that I had just qualified for the Olympic Trials. I couldn't believe it. I felt like a different person from the one who woke up that day. Here I was, a fifty-four-year old nun with the opportunity to compete with the fastest female marathoners in the United States. I ran to the phone and called my brothers. I was in shock. Five months later I was in the Olympic Village in Olympia, Washington, living out my dream. My six-year journey that started with an impossible two-mile run had brought me this close to being an Olympic contender for my country. I didn't make the actual team, as my time for the trials was twenty minutes slower than the winners. But it still stands out as a highlight in my life.

At this point in time, marathoning was the runner's-choice sport, the media's darling event. There weren't that many of us, but we were fast! The race was very different back then, not the people's sport it is today. If you couldn't finish the event in under four hours, and most of us were finishing in under three, well, you just didn't compete. In fact, the race officials would literally dismantle the finish line and clear the course after four hours, because we'd all be done! There was no waiting around for stragglers. But Marathon Mania wasn't going to last. America's running stars were being dethroned by the international invasion from Mexico, Africa, and Europe. The media lost interest and corporate sponsorships were dropped like hot potatoes. I lost my Nike contract as soon as the company went international, in 1984, and my star started to fade. Actually, they reduced my contract gradually. First they cut me down to shoes and clothes, taking away the travel money. Then they cut me down to just shoes, and then it was all over! America's runners were being outclassed by the international competition and no one stepped forward to resuscitate us. There were no more heroes to read about or look up to and very few development programs for the young kids. Even the postcollegiate running programs dried up. There was no place for a twenty-year-old hotshot to go. Distance runners are just coming into their prime at twenty-two and we were losing them. The media hightailed it after the '84 Olympic frenzy died down. No one wanted to watch running on TV so they put their big bucks toward basketball and football. And in our society you can't survive as a runner without sponsorship money to get to the meets, to get the publicity, to hire a coach. Eventually, our promising next generation of runners reached a saturation point of frustration.

My last competitive running event was in 1991, at the Swiss International Track Championships in Baden, Switzerland, winning a gold medal for the 5K and a silver for the 800 meters. I was sixty-one years old and starting to feel it. I had so many injuries my body didn't know how to recuperate anymore. When the doctors advised six weeks rest, I'd take six days. I ran through injuries, was always battling fatigue and constantly putting my health in jeopardy. There comes a point when you can't cheat your body any longer and I guess I reached that point.

Someone once did a computer analysis of my running times and factored age into the equation. Basically, they were trying to determine just how much better a runner I would have been if I had started in my twenties instead of my fifties. Of course, the computer had me winning every Olympic distance event for the next century! But I never look at my career as starting late and I have never regretted the choices I made in life. If I had started running earlier, chances are I wouldn't be a nun today, and I have never regretted my religious life. My running career came at the perfect time. It was a reawakening for me. I truly believe God created us to be fully alive, to experience life. Prior to running, I wasn't experiencing life, wasn't alive inside. Running gave me that opportunity. It changed my life in ways I never expected. When I'm outside doing a dawn run on the Oregon beaches, I look around and thank our creator for the breathtaking scenery. I've had incredible out-of-body experiences running the Washington Cascades, admiring God's canvas of natural beauty. I've seen bears in the river catching salmon for their lunch, beautiful mountain wildflowers that dazzle the landscape. It gives a new meaning to the word *spiritual*. I'm not talking about organized religion here, I am describing the spiritual process of getting in touch with one's self, i.e. our spirit, our inner self, our person. You don't have to go to church to experience spirituality. Running can bring you to that place.

I'm a more compassionate person than I was. Prior to running, I had little patience with people's frailties and shortcomings, never having experienced my own physical limitations. But now that I've been battered and bruised and stressed to the test, it's as if I've finally joined the human race, reached a level of humanity where I feel compassion for my fellow person. I know what it's like to suffer and hurt. My life before running was too insular to understand and feel those things. Most people say I've achieved everything I strived for, broken every record, won every race. Well, I say, so can you! I truly believe we all have the capacity to reach our goals if they are within our grasps and we are willing to make the sacrifices.

I have so many wonderful moments and memories throughout my career. Who knows, maybe I have one more marathon to go!

ONE FOOT IN THE GRAVE

ROGER JONES
RESIDENCE: LAS VEGAS, NEVADA
OCCUPATION: RETIRED AIR FORCE BRIGADIER GENERAL
FIRST MARATHON: 1990 LAS VEGAS MARATHON
D.O.B.: 9-12-38
AGE AT FIRST MARATHON: 51

When Roger turned forty and reported for his annual military medical checkup, his blood pressure was so high he was put on medication. Maybe it had something to do with the four packs of cigarettes a day he had been smoking since he was sixteen or the constant traveling and heavy casework he did as a lawyer for the air force. Whatever the cause, the grim prognosis was a strong incentive to quit smoking cold turkey and take up running. Content with logging twenty miles a week for a few years, Roger never thought of running twenty-six miles until he saw the New York City Marathon on television and decided to give it a try. However, stationed in Nebraska, infamous for brutal winters and cold, cutting winds, he almost put it off until his superior stepped in and offered him an assignment he couldn't refuse. Being a good airman, Roger followed his unconventional orders and won the battle of his first marathon.

IN HIGH SCHOOL, I WAS THE SPORTS REPORTER for our high school paper and covered all the games instead of participating in them. After high school I attended the University of Illinois and again, sports were not part of my program. I majored in history and political science and was also enrolled in the air force ROTC program. I had an older brother who was a pilot in World War II and although I was only seven when he returned from the war, he was my hero. I admired him a great deal and from the time I was a small boy, I guess I knew I wanted to be in the air force. He was a tail gunner in B-29s and heavily involved in aerial combat. When he came home the effects of the war were apparent. He certainly didn't encourage me to join the military; in fact, he tried to talk me out of it. But I had great respect for the uniform, was deeply patriotic and wanted to make the air force my career.

Commissioned in the air force as a second lieutenant upon graduation from college, I was allowed a temporary leave to attend law school. After being awarded my law degree, my first assignment with the Air Force was four years in Alaska. At first, I was not pleased and neither was my wife, who was pregnant with our second child. I never expected to fall in love with Alaska, but I did. It was beautiful. I ended up extending my assignment there for another year. Looking back, I wish I had been a runner then. Everywhere you looked there was another incredible vista. At that point in my life, though, I thought runners were crazy. Who would want to do that?

After Alaska, I volunteered for duty in Saigon for a year, and then I was stationed in Washington, D.C. I then spent three years in England, near Oxford. Again, I wish I was a runner back then because the countryside is just beautiful. Then I was transferred to Florida, where my second life began.

I reported for my annual dental checkup in 1978 and a routine blood pressure check revealed my blood pressure was high and the dentist became alarmed. I became alarmed as well. I had just turned forty and my brother had his first stroke at forty-five. My dad had his first heart attack at fifty, an uncle had a heart attack and died at fifty, and my grandfather had his first heart attack at sixty, and never recovered. Mine was not a healthy family and I didn't want to become the next statistic. My mother was also a smoker, although I never knew it. She hid her smoking from me as I hid my smoking from her. I later found out that she smoked in the basement at the same time I was hiding out in the garage. She finally quit after being diagnosed with colon cancer. Ironically, we both stopped smoking at just about the same time.

I went on the blood pressure medication, but continued to smoke for another year. On June 17, 1980, at nine o'clock in the morning, I gagged on my cigarette so badly I couldn't catch my breath. That was it. I stopped cold turkey.

My weight had always been steady, but in anticipation of a weight gain, I dieted and lost ten pounds, then gained twenty, then lost it again. I was yo-yoing and the doctors were none too pleased. It was getting close to the annual 1.5-mile fitness run and I must admit, back then the air force lost people during this medical test to heart attacks and I didn't want to be one of them. I started reading about running and exercise in general and liked what I read.

A year later I was still on the blood pressure meds, but the pressure wasn't coming down as fast or as low as expected. I was desperate, so I started running at the base track in November of 1981. It took me six months to be able to run two miles. Obviously, after smoking for over twenty-five years, I had no endurance, no wind, no air, and lots of coughing fits. But I kept at it and in a few more months could run at a regular pace with no stopping or coughing. By 1982 I was running fifteen miles a week and keeping my weight steady. I may have been staying in shape, but I felt awful. I was sluggish, tired, and cranky. It took a young, female noncommissioned officer on my staff, who had previously worked in the medical career field, to speak up and tell me something was wrong. She spoke on behalf of all my staff members, who were worried for me. I wasn't myself. She urged me to go back to the doctors, which I did. It seems my blood pressure had now dropped too low, in fact critically low. The medication, combined with my exercise and diet regime was too much of a good thing. The doctors were shocked. They couldn't believe my running program and weight stabilization had brought the pressure down on its own and that the medication was now forcing it past normal levels.

Now that I was finally healthy, I started getting more serious about my running. I am a typical Type-A personality, which means I always overdo things. I upped my miles to twenty a week and ventured off the track and onto the road. In the spring of '82 I ran my first 10K, and died. I went home to bed and thought about not getting up. In the fall of '82 I ran a half marathon, and died again. My problem was my total ignorance of training. I was a solo runner and had no idea how to train, how to race, what clothes to wear, nothing that would have better prepared me for what I was getting myself into. I didn't know about

hydrating or anything. Soon afterward, I started to talk to other runners, solicited advice, and subscribed to *Runner's World* magazine.

Now that I was running smart, I got myself in the best shape of my
life during '82 to '84. Running also helped my sanity as during that
period, I moved five times in two years. I participated in local races and
continued my twenty miles a week. Then in 1986 I watched the New
York City Marathon on television in awe. I wondered if I could do such
a thing as run a marathon.

I was transferred to Omaha, Nebraska, in 1988. My assigned deputy,
Colonel Jim Frampton, was a marathoner and he had a lot of advice on
running. On top of that, another member of my staff was a marathoner.
I was surrounded by runners. Now I was really getting bugged by
marathon madness. By 1990, after listening to these coworkers talk
about how great it was, and reading *Runner's World* articles with an
obsession, I had to go for it.

I chose the Las Vegas Marathon because I had been stationed there
and knew it would be dry, cool, and flat. Also, it gave me four months
to train. I didn't tell anyone about my intentions in case I failed or got
scared, or got hurt and had to drop out. I had always succeeded in
everything I had ever done, but I wasn't so sure about this marathon
thing. It seemed so hard. And never having been an athlete, I wasn't
sure I could do it. I had to know if I could succeed, if I could play in
that arena, and here was my chance. And I knew if I were successful, it
would be a highlight in my life.

I followed the *Runner's World* first-time marathon schedule religiously.
The one thing I didn't count on was training during Omaha winters.
They are brutal. When it got too cold to run outdoors, I started train-
ing on the treadmill, but that was boring and tedious. Then my boss,
John T. Chain, a four-star general commander and commander of
Strategic Air Command, who had run two marathons and was totally
committed to the health and fitness of his troops, stepped in to save me.
He was so concerned about the health of his commanders and staff, he
would have the military doctors report their cholesterol levels to him.
He would then write strong letters about lowering their levels. He
started one staff meeting by saying, "I just had my cholesterol tested
and it is 138. Can anyone beat that?" He also forbid smoking among
his commanders and general officers.

General Chain was my angel of mercy. He turned an old abandoned airplane hangar into a training center, with an indoor swimming pool, tennis courts, racquetball courts, basketball court, and a running track constructed of a rubberized material. Everyone enjoyed it, especially me. Although my training consisted of running around in circles, it sure beat running outside in subzero cold and wind. My wife would come by with water and snacks occasionally, but I thought I'd go crazy if I had to run one more lap. I started to wear headphones just to break up the monotony. The songs from *Dirty Dancing* got me through many laps.

I flew to Las Vegas the day before the race. Just before landing in Vegas, the pilot announced there were strong winds. I got really nervous. This was unusual for that time of year and certainly not weather I wanted to run in. In the meantime my wife, Lin, drove to Vegas from Omaha and picked me up at the airport. We drove the course so I'd be familiar with it. That night, I couldn't sleep. I was nervous, filled with apprehension, excitement, and fear of failure. I woke up at two in the morning and said, "I'm going now. I can't wait." She calmed me down, and somehow I managed a few hours of sleep. She was very supportive. I was lucky to have her by my side.

The morning of February 3, 1990, was beautiful—thirty-five degrees at the start of the race. The Las Vegas Marathon is not particularly a scenic course. It runs parallel to Interstate 15 most of the time and is nothing but flat blacktop as far as you can see. And there's nothing to look at as everything is flat and brown. Occasionally a sagebrush will blow by, but that's about it. My wife was to meet me along planned exit stops on I-15 to give me water, take my extra clothing as the day got warmer, and administer pep talks. I was feeling great at the start, couldn't wait to get going, and naturally went out too fast. The first ten miles or so are rolling hills, nothing big, but I knew if I could get through the hills, I'd make it. Approximately half way, the course went into a steady, straight decline into the city. The first half, I ran with a guy who told awful jokes. They just weren't funny, but I needed a pacer so I put up with his humor. The worst part of the Vegas marathon is the lack of toilets, and the lack of trees or bushes to compensate for the lack of toilets. I kept wondering, "Where will people make those sudden, necessary pit-stops?" It was barren out there, no place to hide. Well, the men just turned their backs to the course and did what they had to do, but I wondered how the women would fare. Well, they fared just fine, doing the same thing. I was a little too embarrassed to brave the natural setting at first and waited till I found the only toilet on the course.

Early in the race, I remembered seeing a very attractive female runner. She was faster than me so I eventually lost her. By mile sixteen I was running on my own and trying to concentrate. My mind was starting to go numb when I caught sight of that pretty girl again. I thought I was hallucinating because I kept seeing her again and again. I knew my mind wasn't working anymore, but heck, how could I be seeing double? Turns out I was following identical twins.

In preparation for the marathon, I had called ahead to our base in Vegas and asked for a "rabbit," to run the last six miles with me. My request was answered by a young officer who was a runner and agreed to pace me. Turns out he grew up in Alaska, so we talked about our experiences there and it made a world of difference in my running. I never felt pain. Talking with him was such a wonderful distraction, I almost forgot I was running in a marathon. My wife says I have a high threshold of pain, and yes, my legs were tired and hurt, but I distinguish discomfort from real pain. There was no burning, no blisters, no dragging sensation.

My "rabbit" carried a stopwatch with him and kept track of my time. "Well, General, that was an 8:45 mile," and so on. Then I stopped to go to the bathroom, and by God, he said, "Well, General, that was a ten-minute mile." At mile twenty-three, I knew I would meet my time of under four hours, so I slowed down. I actually thought of walking the last three miles. He got very disgusted with me and was about to say something when another runner passed me. That upset me and got me running again. Then—talk about being egotistical and silly all in the same moment—I realized that if I hustled, I could beat the finishing time of a friend of mine who had completed the Marine Corps Marathon a few months earlier, so I started to sprint. I ran so hard to beat the clock that two volunteers had to catch me at the finish line before I collapsed from exhaustion. I ended up finishing at 3:50. I had a good laugh at myself for the sheer folly of it all.

The only thing I regret about that marathon was that my wife, who followed me all along the way, never made it to the finish line. She got stuck in traffic and missed the grand finale. If I had to do it all over again, I'd make sure she was there. Her life had been turned upside down by my training schedule, sometimes not having dinner till nine at night, and I felt a part of that medal belonged to her.

When I returned to the hotel, the first call I made was to General

Chain to tell him I had completed my mission. When I returned to Omaha, he called me down to his office and had me recount the entire race. He wanted to know all the details. When I told him I stopped at twenty-three miles, he became upset with me. I had to quickly cover my backside and say, "Well, sir, it was only for a few seconds." He made a big announcement to the rest of the staff about my accomplishment. I couldn't believe he was still so supportive and inspiring.

After the announcement, two other officers decided to run a marathon and enlisted the other two marathoners in the office to join them at the Lincoln, Nebraska, Marathon, ninety days later. They asked me to join them and at first I thought they were kidding, but I ended up doing it. Then in 1992 we enlisted some more officers to join us in a marathon and we had a total of four air force attorneys running the marathon and two more running the half marathon. I was very proud of them. We reached a point where one-third of the office staff were marathoners.

I retired from the air force shortly after that and have not run a marathon since, although I keep up with fifteen miles a week and enter local 5K and 10K races. Another goal I set for myself was to run in all fifty states and I have only Oregon remaining.

Running changed my life. In fact, it was the single most significant factor in my life. Completing a marathon was the culmination of all that running has to offer. That is not an overstatement; I am alive and in good health today because of it. In fact, I could have ended up worse than dead, like my brother did. He lived out the last four years of his life in a nursing home, unable to speak or walk. I don't ever want to end up that way, and running has given me that insurance.

One of my most precious pieces of running memorabilia is an auto-graphed copy of George Sheehan's book *Personal Best*. He wrote, "To Roger Jones, I hope this will help you pursue your own Personal Best and become what the Athenians desired to be: good citizens and soldiers. Happy running."

THE RUNNING LIFE

JOHN JOSEPH KELLEY
RESIDENCE: MYSTIC, CONNECTICUT
OCCUPATION: FORMER ENGLISH TEACHER; SPORTS COLUMNIST
FIRST MARATHON: 1949 BOSTON MARATHON
D.O.B.: 12-14-30
AGE AT FIRST MARATHON: 18

Kelley is a two-time Olympian who ran the Boston Marathon thirty-five times, winning in 1957. He came in second in '56, '58, '59, '61, and '63. Fond of quoting Shakespeare and Jack Kerouac, Kelley is not only a gifted runner, respected English teacher, mentor to other acclaimed runners, and the most eloquent pacer around, but just about the nicest person you could meet. A twelve-mile race in New London, Connecticut, is named in his honor and it is one of the few remaining road races with no entry fee. John starts the race each year with a short speech and a gunshot and stays till the last runner crosses the finish line.

Photo by Andy Yelenak

WHAT I AM ABOUT TO SAY IS KIND OF EMBARRASSING for me, a retired high school English teacher, but as a kid my favorite school subject was hooky. My parents couldn't keep me in school. I wasn't a bad kid, but I just loved to fish. It was a chronic case of tunnel vision. I couldn't think to do anything else. Instead of going to school, I'd grab my fishing pole, head into the woods to my favorite pond, and spend the day fishing. It frustrated my parents and I was in and out of three high schools before I landed at Bulkeley School in New London, which was known for producing some of the best runners in southeastern Connecticut. I had never run before, except from the truant officers, but I befriended a group of guys who were already setting fire to the track. George Terry, a schoolmate, became my new buddy and introduced me to running. My parents were thrilled that I was staying in school. I remember my mother saying, "Well, Johnny, I guess it's something people have done for centuries, and if it helps you to stay in school, I think it's a good thing."

The same tunnel vision that kept me out of school fishing also kept me on the track. I finally found something I liked and as an added bonus I was good at it. The coach, Malcolm Greenaway, took me under his wing and brought out the best in me. He would take action photos of the track team and place them in the lobby of the school for all to see. At a time when football was the be-all and the runners were the weirdos, Greenaway made us feel like stars. This was 1947 and I was sixteen years old. The running scene back then was a mere microcosm of what it is now. Only twenty schools in the entire state of Connecticut had cross-country teams. We were looked on with a mixture of awe and mystique. It was a very antithetical place to be. But we were so proud of the fact that we were runners, and we were extraordinary runners. George took me under his wing and would come over my house every night to run with me. I thought this was pure dedication, but later found out he was secretly dating my sister and this was their way of seeing each other! They ended up married so I guess my interest in running paid off in a big way for her.

My first major distance race was in Littleton, Massachusetts. It took all day traveling by bus from New London to just outside Boston, then catching a coal-burning local train that stopped every four miles on the route to Littleton. The smell and the heat from the engine didn't do much to cheer up our moods on this auspicious day of ninety-seven-degree heat, our first distance road race. My father accompanied me because he wanted to meet John A. Kelley the Elder, another famous runner out of New England. I had never done ten miles before but I thought I was ready. In those days we didn't have specialized running shoes so I had on my Keds. The race proved to be so grueling, and it was so hot, that I never finished; I dropped out, totally demoralized. My feet were bloody pulps and I just collapsed on the side of the road. I had to hitch a ride with the wagon that came by to pick up the stragglers. I found my father in the crowd talking with John A. Kelley, who had won the race. I was too embarrassed to meet him, but my father pulled me along, saying I couldn't give up, couldn't just quit. He was such a lover of sports and so supportive of me. It was probably the best thing I ever did because I got a great pep talk from the elder John A. Kelley; it was like a resurrection of my hopes. I decided to give distance racing another try. Three months later my dad unexpectedly passed away. He had a violent bout with pneumonia and in those days there was no cure. Now I felt like I had to keep running to honor his memory.

Back at high school, George and I started talking about doing the Boston Marathon. We had gotten the bug for road racing and started distance training with Clayton "Bud" Farrar, another southeastern running phenomenon. Bud ran strong in the 1945 Boston Marathon, leading the entire way until the twentieth mile, when he couldn't hold Kelley off. Actually historians now relate how close Bud came to winning that race because of a medical mishap with Kelley. As with many champion runners of that time, we became the experimental victims of medical researchers over at Harvard. This time around, a team of doctors were researching the effects of glucose on the body and asked Kelley to substitute glucose pills during the marathon instead of taking his usual sips of honey for added energy. Kelley agreed and throughout the race whenever he felt tired he'd take a glucose pill. I don't know how many he took but by the twentieth mile he had severe stomach cramps and didn't think he would finish but continued on, passing Bud. But the stomach pains persisted and within one mile of the finish he thought he'd have to drop out due to stomach ingestion. Out of sheer desperation he stuck his finger down his throat to induce vomiting and threw up all the glucose pills on the side of the road. Then he went on to win the race. So here I was, training with someone who was a legend to us.

This was in 1949 and Coach Greenaway was totally against me running the marathon for a number of reasons. First of all, I was underage. Second, he felt I wasn't properly trained, which was true, and most of all, the day after the marathon we had a very important state track meet and he wanted me in peak condition. But George and I were determined to do it. This time around I wanted the right shoes so I spent the worldly sum of twenty dollars to have a pair custom made. I had to outline my foot on tracing paper and send it to the only person around who was doing this sort of thing, Osborn K. Winslow. The shoes were wonderful and I treasured them like prized possessions. I only wore them for the big races. Didn't even train in them for fear of wearing them out. Anyway, training back then was really hit or miss. I remember doing wind sprints down on the boardwalk of Ocean Beach Park. One day I felt a twinge in my knee but disregarded it. Nothing was going to keep George and me from Boston. However, the knee problem persisted. Not only was I secretly training for the marathon but doing the daily track drills as well. I was definitely overworked but kept going.

The day of the marathon arrived and we were very excited to be part of a group of runners who treated each other like family. We all either knew each other or had heard of each other. Boston was the giant of visibility and popularity in those days. Still is as far as I'm concerned. I was actually an illegal runner as I was underage, but no one cared. The entry fee was one dollar, as opposed to the seventy-five dollars it is now, but even that was double the normal entry fee for those events. There were about a hundred and eighty of us ready to go. Everyone was a character, an oddball. One guy named Jake used to run with a stick to chase away the dogs that would follow us, nipping at our heels. Cars were allowed on the course, but respected us and gave us a wide berth. The fumes were a problem, though, and cars were finally banned from the course in 1947. There were no organized water stands but kids would follow the runners on bikes handing out water and oranges. But even this got to be a problem later on in years as the race became more popular and finally bikes were also banned from the route.

Anyway, I was torn between excitement to be there and anxiety over my knee, which was causing constant pain that just kept escalating in its intensity. I ended up limping and walking more than running, feeling worse with every step. I kept falling farther and farther behind all the runners. Finally, I had to quit. I remember sitting on a curb outside Boston College in the late afternoon, physically impossible to take another step. I sat there for the longest time wondering how I would get back because I had never been in Boston before. And there weren't the crowds for the marathon that there are now. I was all alone out there sitting on the curb, cold, hurt, and miserable. I must have been there quite a while, pondering my major disappointment and deciding how in hell I would get back. I thought I was a failure. How could I ever have imagined I could run a marathon! How stupid and full of myself I must have been. The mind plays tricks on us, especially when we are at our most vulnerable, and we have to be strong enough to realize that after all we are just human and we will recuperate and try again. But sitting there that afternoon I didn't think I would ever run another marathon. After many hours pondering my proverbial fall from grace, a Studebaker pulled alongside and an elderly couple, seeing my distress, offered to drive me back to Boston. I remember the woman saying, "Why on earth would they allow a boy to run in such a race!" As I got out of the car in downtown Boston, a paperboy passed by with the news headlines announcing the winner of the marathon. I didn't know at the time that even elite runners have their bad days and suffer the slings and arrows of outrageous fortune when it comes to career running.

I gave up road racing for a number of years after that and concentrated on staying in school and doing well with my track events. I was attending Boston University on a track scholarship and the coach took this very seriously. He banned me from even thinking about distance racing. But here I was in Boston, the road racing mecca of the world. The pull to start doing distance again was very strong. I would sneak out on weekends and run with the Boston Athletic Association, under the supervision of Jock Semple. Jock wanted me to run officially with the club and represent them in the 1953 Boston Marathon, but my B.U. coach was dead set against it. So every weekend I'd leave my dormitory in Kenmore Square, meet up with the B.A.A. and run out to Jamaica Plains, putting in about twenty miles. I loved it. It was actually like living two lives, or having two lovers. I couldn't mention one coach to the other. They were fighting over me and what team would ultimately win my loyalty.

Finally, I just had to give the Boston Marathon another try. Jock was thrilled and assumed I'd run with the B.A.A., but I couldn't antagonize my college coach and risk the scholarship money, so we came up with a compromise. My B.U. coach allowed me to run the marathon, which appeased Semple, but only under the condition that I wear a Boston University shirt. This time I was prepared. It was a very fast race and I finished in fifth place with 2:28. I stayed neck and neck with the eventual winner for the first thirteen miles until he pulled away and won in 2:18. But I felt good about my time, was pleased with my performance, and I was still wearing that same pair of customized shoes from 1949.

So I continued running marathons. There was strong competition in the field, especially from the foreign runners. But no matter how many marathons I ran, the night before a race I was edgy, couldn't sleep. I'd pace the floor, thinking I can't do this, I'm not ready. I would want to drop out, not race at all. The focus was so intense. It meant so much to me. To understand the significance of the marathon back then and my obsession with it is to step back in history. During the late forties and fifties, marathon running took on a new dimension. World War II created a chasm for runners. The high school and college runners who were drafted and fortunate to survive came back from the war and resumed their running, but with a different drive. They took their running more seriously. It's as if because they survived this terrible, horrible ordeal, they were going to make the most of their life and what they loved about life. If it was running, well then they were going to take it to the next level. Training became more structured. Finishing times became faster. Foreign runners started to test their skills against ours. There was a new zest, a renewed zeal for running and ultimately making a business out of it. You can't even begin to compare the prewar marathon event with what is going on today. The social times we live in have dulled our senses to what greatness really is. The marathon now deals with meganumbers and mass-produced champions. An entire country team will be hired to go on a corporate advertising-sponsored racing circuit. Next thing you know, they'll be on a Hallmark card.

I juggled my entire life just so that I could run: My jobs, school, marriage, my teaching position, everything was just a hurdle to cross and overcome so that I could run. No one was paid to run back then, there was no prize money or endorsements or lucrative contracts. We did it because we loved it, because we had the tunnel vision that blocked every other aspect of life from view. So winning was everything. The sacrifices we made to get there were too great not to want to win.

That era of marathoning seems so antediluvian now, with commercialism running amok and athletes getting million-dollar contracts and the winner at Boston going home with over a hundred thousand dollars. My last marathon was in 1992 and I foolishly ran with a pulled hamstring. It took me four hours to complete the race. I don't compete anymore, but still thrill to get in my daily run. And my feet are so messed up from all those years of training and running so hard that I don't think I'd even have a chance at winning a potato sack race nowadays. But I do love the marathon. I've always said that marathoning is just another form of insanity and I cherish every insane moment of my life's experiences.

ON THE RUN TO A NEW LIFE

THOMAS KING
RESIDENCE: PORTLAND, OREGON
OCCUPATION: VICE PRESIDENT—OPERATIONS, ATHLETICA, INC.
FIRST MARATHON: 1996 PORTLAND (OR) MARATHON
D.O.B.: 12-25-53
AGE AT FIRST MARATHON: 42

Thomas King had been heavy his entire life, suffering through the verbal abuse served up every day by friends and strangers alike. When the scale tipped at over three hundred pounds and doctors started talking about strokes and heart attacks, he decided to do something. That something was run. Inspired by Oprah Winfrey's marathon, he decided to give it a try. Prior to this metamorphosis, King's biggest athletic challenge was going to the movies. Through perseverance, many miles and the will to succeed, he reached his goal and went from couch potato to marathoner. Not only did he lose the weight, but he found a new job and turned his life around. His only regret is that it took him so long to discover the real meaning of life.

BEING LARGE IS NEVER EASY in our Slim-Fast culture, but it's brutal when you're the fat kid in the neighborhood. I always felt left out. The other kids considered me a loser. No one wanted me on their team, which was understandable because I wasn't athletic at all; the best I could be was home base. And since weight was always a factor, it got in the way of everything I did. Ultimately, I lost all sense of self-esteem and a very rebellious nature took over. My modus operandi became, "If you can't join them, fight them."

My parents weren't large people, but like most Americans, they had very little knowledge or understanding of balanced meals. We ate the typical American heart attack diet: fried everything washed down with ice cream. Sometimes I would finish off an entire berry cobbler and my folks wouldn't blink an eye.

When I was ten, my Dad was involved in a near-fatal motorcycle accident and lost his leg. It created havoc in the family and my mom was overwrought. Not only did she have to care for him, she had me and my brother to contend with. To make matters worse, my Dad got pretty dependent on the pain killers and wasn't himself for a while. It was not a happy household. And since I was rebellious by nature and felt both my parents were inaccessible, I rebelled even further.

As I look back on my childhood, I was depressed so I ate. That was my life; I just accepted my fate to be fat and unhappy. I'm not a fighter by nature but I had an absolutely horrific experience in my childhood that left me scarred for life and I vowed to fight back and fend for myself the next time I was threatened. When I was nine years old, the local bullies decided to have some fun with me one day after school. Fun to them was humiliating and torturing me for no other reason than that I was fat. Among other things too painful to recount, they held a BB gun to my head and made me drink water out of their dog's bowl. It left a wound that wouldn't heal. When I complained to my parents, they didn't do anything about it. That also hurt. The bullies grew up to be alcoholics and are now the local bums.

During my senior year in high school I started to work out and dropped from 200 to 160 pounds and considered myself skinny. For the first time in my life I felt in shape and noticed that people treated me differently. I liked that. I started to work harder at school and actually made the honor roll.

Leaving high school in 1972, I attended Pacific Union College but never finished. My draft number was six and I thought I'd be the next to go so I figured why bother with school. I went for the physical, had all the forms filled out, and then Nixon cut the draft. I was right down to the wire, but eventually saved. Now I had my future back in my own hands, but I had spent all my college tuition money thinking I'd be drafted. Looking back, I was in the best shape of my life that one year of college. I started running three to four miles a day and considered going out for track. I was doing a hundred sit-ups and push-ups daily. If the threat of the draft hadn't interrupted my first year of college, my life may have taken a different turn. I really believe sports would have changed my life. Instead, I went wild.

With no place to go, no plans, and no money, I started to put on weight. I spent my free time picking up chicks and riding my motorcycle. That alone should tell you where my head was: My dad loses his leg in a motorcycle accident and a few years later I buy one and spend my time cruising. Ultimately, fate caught up with me and I crashed at high speed, lying unconscious and partially paralyzed for ten days. I now use another name for motorcycles: "donor cycles," the greatest source of organ donations. Fortunately, I recovered fully.

Afterward, I started another college but still didn't learn much, as I continued my wild streak. My parents were pressuring me to quit college and come home to a nice, secure job in the lumber mill. They told me I was wasting my time. Since I was wasting my time, I decided to take action—which resulted in two big mistakes. Mistake number one was getting married, followed up with mistake number two, taking the job at the lumber mill. I was a crane operator, which meant I wasn't physically active and started to put on the weight. And to really help screw things up, I'd hang out at the bars after work with my buddies. For ten long years, I lead a blah, goalless life. I was depressed, unhappy, and had no ambition to change it. Not to anyone's surprise, my marriage ended in divorce. It was rough times. I started drinking heavily and the weight poured on just as fast as the drinks.

I got into the car business, which did me more harm. It was a very demanding dealership and we weren't allowed to leave the floor for very long, even for a lunch break. I lived on junk food. My biggest decision of the day was whether to order from McDonald's or Wendy's. I was over three hundred pounds with high blood pressure and basically, wrote myself off. I ceased to care about anything.

Then, in 1994, I went to a training event that was the first step in changing my life. It was an Outward Bound–type experiment for car dealerships run by Larry Wilson at the Pecos River Learning Center. His motto is: "Do the best you can with what you've got." Well, I gave them a lot to deal with. The second day of the retreat, I found myself in a group that was challenged to climb to the top of a telephone pole. The idea was to take us outside our comfort zone, and they couldn't have found anything more intimidating for me than to climb a skinny pole to the top platform, stand up, and shout. "No way," I said, as I kept inching to the back of the line until I was the last person. The group gave me incredible support and twenty minutes later I was at the top, crying my eyes out with exhilaration and joy that I could accomplish such an unbelievable task. The entire pole shook. It was the first time anyone cheered for me. I now knew I could change my life.

The first thing I did was get a physical, but I was scared. So to soften the blow I knew would be coming, I ate a bag of potato chips on my way to the doctor's office. Sure enough, I was put on high blood pressure pills and other medicines to help avoid the inevitable stroke due to obesity. I was advised to start an exercise program so I joined a gym, which turned out to be the most expensive shower I ever took, as that's all I did whenever I got the incentive to go. Slowly, I lost some weight and began to feel comfortable on the treadmill. I was very self-conscious in my gym outfit, sure that everyone was making fun of me.

Then Oprah Winfrey ran the 1995 Marine Corps Marathon and she inspired me. I knew her story and felt, "Heck, if she can do it so can I." Right after reading about her marathon experience, I started a steady routine of walking on the treadmill and walked straight through April. I walked so much I developed shin splints and had to ice my legs every night. Then someone suggested I see a podiatrist, who told me I needed orthotics as I was a pronator. I thought he was describing a gardening tool; do I weed with it?

I had no idea about these things. A whole new world was opening up and it felt good. By June I progressed from a walk to a steady jog and decided to tackle the local Starlight 5K. It's a fun run, a costume event, so I wore a runner's outfit as my costume. To my surprise I was able to finish in a respectable time of 43:38. While I was out there, it seemed like an eternity because I had to walk parts of the course. Again, my old fears surfaced, and I thought I could hear the bystanders making fun of me: "There goes the fat guy. What's he doing out there?" My wife, who was waiting at the start with me, said I reminded her of the look on kindergartners' faces when they are left at the door the first morning: "Don't leave me here."

I get very emotional when I think about that accomplishment. For weeks, I proudly wore my Starlight race shirt everywhere I went. I even framed my number. In forty-four minutes, I went from thinking people were laughing at me to feeling the most accomplished in my entire life. It was an amazing journey of self-discovery. All those years of believing I was a failure were erased with the race. I didn't want to go back to the old Tom. I was hooked and started entering races all over. I truly believe the triumphs of the back-of-the-packers are the most significant.

Since I had now crossed into a new life, I needed an extraordinary goal, so I fixed my sight on the marathon. I knew that event would test every part of my body and soul. I started running every day, obsessed with making up for lost years. Realizing I needed some help to take on this challenge, I joined the Oregon Road Runners Club. Out went the junk food and in came the veggies and healthy carbos.

I became fixated on the marathon. I have never been so focused, so consumed, so driven toward a single goal. There was no doubt in my mind that I would succeed. Nothing was going to stop me, whether I had to walk or crawl my way to the finish line. During training I did a couple of 5Ks and 10Ks and with three weeks to go, I ran with Team Oregon, a marathon pacing group, for sixteen miles. I was thrilled.

The night prior to the race, I couldn't sleep. I knew come morning that I was facing the culmination of my efforts. To keep the nerve shaking in check, I went back to that telephone pole and visualized that I was standing on top all over again. It helped to calm me.

The day of the race, I did everything wrong. First, I went out faster than I should and second, I didn't pee enough prior to the race and had to go again in the first mile. This particular marathon has a rather strange tradition called the Peeing Wall. All the runners form a wall and have their last pee together. I was too embarrassed to participate, so I had to hold it until I found the first-aid station three miles later. And since I was so worried about hydrating, I overhydrated and ended up stopping at every Port-a-Potty along the route.

At eight miles I wanted to walk, but kept myself amused by the volunteers, who were dressed in all sorts of costumes. Some of the volunteers were in tuxedos or Hawaiian shirts; some men dressed as women and women dressed as men. It's a great show, but nonetheless, I did resort to walking at mile nine, realizing the fun part was now over.

I alternated a run-walk pattern from mile fourteen to twenty. After that, my mind went into survival mode and I ate everything in sight. I gorged bananas, Gatorade, gels, you name it—if it was offered at a station, I took it. During one of my walking segments, I was accompanied by a sixty-five-year-old woman from Rockford, Illinois, who was doing her thirty-fifth marathon. She was a great inspiration to keep going.

Then I hit the wall at twenty-two miles. Everything hurt, I was completely drained of energy and was still hungry. I started asking other runners for their leftovers. If someone took a bite of a Power Bar, I'd ask for the rest. Miles twenty-two to twenty-four were pure hell; I was reduced to a crawl. My only motivation was to keep moving so the vultures wouldn't get me. By mile twenty-five, I could taste the finish, but what I couldn't taste was the stiff Power Bar I was gnawing on.

By now I was in familiar territory. I was also with other runners experiencing the same pain as I. We were the walking wounded, supporting and caring for each other. It didn't matter that we were last. We knew we were finishing, that we would endure to the end. Tears streamed down my face as I crossed the finish line. I was in total disbelief. All those wasted years, all the suffering, all the humiliation just poured out of me, never to be felt again. I was a new person, a runner.

After the finish line, I could hardly move, but I had to force myself to the awards table to collect my finisher's shirt. I kept muttering over and over, "I want my damn shirt!" Afterward, a friend of mine drove me to her house and I soaked in her hot tub. It stung at first because my entire body was chafed from the running. That night, I crawled into bed wearing my marathon finisher's shirt and my medal. I don't think I took them off for a week. The next day I sat down and wrote a letter to Oprah Winfrey, thanking her for being my inspiration.

A few days later I went into postmarathon depression. What do I do next? I was listless for months. I kept running, but slowed down. Finally, I entered a half marathon to break the blahs. I continued to do a half marathon every month just to keep in form.

My first marathon changed my life. First of all, I no longer shop at the "big and fat" store. I lost a total of seventy pounds and can't even relate to my former fat self. I accomplished an eighty-two-mile bike ride and started volunteering as a co–race director at local races. I decided that involving myself in the running community would be insurance that I stay the course. It keeps me energized.

Now that I have more of a can-do attitude, I quit car sales and joined forces with another running friend, forming a new company, Athletica, a distribution house for various sports products, nutritional bars, things like that. We've already built it up to a full-time business.

This has been an incredible two years for me. I ran three marathons, participated in three two-hundred-mile relays, and helped start a business. And I still believe the best is yet to come.

RUNNING ON EMPTY

GAIL WAESCHE KISLEVITZ
RESIDENCE: RIDGEWOOD, NJ
OCCUPATION: WRITER
FIRST MARATHON: 1993 OCEAN STATE MARATHON, WARWICK, RI
D.O.B.: 9-29-51
AGE AT FIRST MARATHON: 42

I GREW UP IN NEW JERSEY, where Dad did the commuter trek into New York City for a career that sent him traveling all over the world and sent the four of us kids to bed many nights without seeing him. However, in summer he blossomed, making himself available for all the wit and wisdom we missed during his travels. It was in August that the six of us participated in the yearly summer sail, leaving all creature comforts behind and venturing forth into the waters of New England. Let me make one thing clear: This was not yachting. It was four kids from age five through twelve, Captain Bly, and First Mate Mom. Home for two weeks was a leaky, chartered sailboat where we all worked the deck and manned the sails in order to make it to the next port before our dog, Tina, heaved-ho in the cockpit due to the ever-constant swells of New England's waters. Poor thing, she was always the first one off the boat.

What does all this have to do with running? Everything. On those summer sails, my parents instilled within us principles of life that became our foundation: a strong commitment to our goals, the discipline to work through those goals, and the responsibility to live up to those goals. We all had our tasks to do and if the knots weren't tight, the sails not stowed properly, the sheets not secured, the ropes not coiled correctly, we were all at risk. These same lessons apply to a marathon. I had to be committed to running it in order to have the discipline to train for it and the responsibility to take care of myself throughout the journey. My parents worked hard to raise us that way and most of the time I try to follow their example. Sometimes I find myself in troubled waters, but I always manage to find my sea legs, even at the twenty-mile marker.

My very first run was inspired by my two older brothers, who ran cross country for River Dell High School. I loved the idea of just getting out there and running through streets, fields, backyards, anywhere and everywhere. It seemed like such freedom, something girls didn't have. One night I pulled on my trusty white Keds and headed out the door with the dog in tow, in the cover of darkness, and ran around the block. I loved it. That was the beginning. I kept running around the block, slowly increasing the distance and finally coming out of the closet with my desires to run in the daylight.

During college, with no women's track team, I played lacrosse as a close second but kept up the running. I don't remember when I first hear the word *marathon,* but I'm sure it seemed like another language to me, something totally unattainable.

I continued my running after college and looked forward to coming home from work, stripping off the stockings, and pulling on the running shoes. I ran through both pregnancies, but now when I'd come home from work, there were mouths to feed, more laundry to do, and getting out the door wasn't so easy. Although I had been running for more than twenty years, I kept steadily plugging away at four or five miles a day. A marathon was a pipe dream for me; it seemed out of reach, something other people did, a race for dedicated, talented athletes. I never shared this dream with anyone, fearing they would laugh at my lofty ambitions or mock my attempts at such a physical and mental challenge. My excuses were common ones. Working full time in New York City and raising two children, when would I have the time to commit to training? As it was, my husband and I would fight to see who got out the door to run first after coming home from work. There were never enough minutes left after rationing time for the kids, the office work, the housework, and each other. No way, no time, no marathon.

When my son was about to enter the horror house of middle school years, I decided to quit work and stay home. I wanted to be there to chauffeur the car pool, go to the soccer games, and conduct extensive background checks on the next generation of friends my kids were bonding with.

So now, excuse number one for finally running that marathon, the big time commitment, flew out the door. Now I had to face the more deeply rooted excuse, the psychological head trip: What if I attempted to run the Big One, and failed? That excuse, that fear, kept me off the battlefield for a few more years.

What finally kicked in? What was the impetus that broke through all the excuses and years of denying myself the challenge? My very controlled, orderly life was suddenly taking a deep spiraling plunge downward. Factors beyond my control invaded my life and sand traps seemed to be everywhere. I was still in denial over the death of my mother a few years back; the world I knew ended with her passing. Part of me died with her; I was empty inside, depleted of humor, drive, and ambition. Just getting through the day was a goal. I was desperately trying to learn to live my life without her, and I was failing miserably. And if that wasn't enough to deal with, I was diagnosed with skin cancer. The scar on my back is a constant reminder that my hedonistic days in the sun are gone. I had to do something to shake up my life and get back some sense of control and trust in the world and along the way fill the hollow space. I needed to rebel against these negative forces, to scream so loud and for so long that the anger living inside me would evacuate forever. But instead of screaming, I ran. Running was the only thing in my life I could count on day in and day out to make me feel better, in control, and satisfied with myself.

I decided to take running to the next level and entered my first race. I needed to focus on a goal and it seemed logical to tie it in to running. The training and discipline required were an instant addiction for me. I started to keep training logs, read all the books, went on route expeditions tracking miles with the car odometer. I should add that this big event in my life was my town's annual Memorial Day 10K race. I was moving up from a daily five-mile jaunt to a six-mile challenge. So what? Big deal? It was to me. A race is a breed apart from the daily run. I had to perform. I never tested myself against other runners and although I didn't expect to place, I didn't want to come in last, either. It made me nervous and anxious. For the first time in my life, I would be asked that gut-wrenching question, "What was your time?"

I can't say I loved the competition of racing, but it did get me back in control of myself. I'm very goal oriented, and the race became a personal challenge. My daily run is a routine, not a challenge. It is automatic, something I do without thinking. There are times on my regular route that I can't remember having run past familiar landmarks. It becomes a blur as my thoughts take over and I am brought into another dimension. Nothing else seems to work for me. I'm not great in team sports because I don't want others to rely on me.

That summer, a woman I was just getting close with told me she had run two marathons. I was in awe. She encouraged me to train with her during the summer and we would run a September marathon together. I couldn't resist the call this time. It was fate. I had my own personal trainer, it was the best months to train and the marathon was a particularly good course for first-timers. We started the training with a ten mile run in June. Never having run with anyone else, I was worried about keeping up with her, not disappointing her. To both our amazement we talked the entire ten miles. A bond was formed through our running.

I kept my marathon commitment a secret, knowing full well my family would not support me in this quest. They were worried about the health factors, as I never seem to eat enough to keep any substantial weight on my bones. My diet and exercise routines were always being scrutinized. But as my runs got longer and my weekly distance tripled, it was hard to keep my marathon secret any longer. As predicted, it was not welcome news. My sister was the toughest nut to crack. Our telephone conversation still echoes in my ear. "If you drop dead of a heart attack while running this stupid race, I'll never talk to you again." I had to take an oath that I would not jeopardize my health to train for the race. So after much arbitration, I received a reluctant go-ahead.

I loved the discipline of training, but was plagued with constant toenail problems. They would turn black and eventually fall off. I went to a podiatrist, who warned me against running a marathon. "Worst thing you can do to your body," he'd say as he pulled off another nail. But I was determined. A pair of expensive orthotics later, I was cured of my toenail trauma. Training continued. During the week, I would put in my basic miles, but the weekends were saved for long runs. My friend and I developed a Saturday-morning ritual. Rising at 6 A.M, while the rest of the house slept, I'd creep downstairs to a cup of coffee, a bagel, and the newspaper. After stretching, lathering on the sunscreen and grabbing a visor, my friend and I would hit the road at about seven. It was exhilarating to be out in the warm summer air, running along the water, and talking all sorts of topics. It's amazing how much two people can blab during a sixteen-mile run. Water was a problem as neither of us liked to carry bottles around for that distance. So we had to get creative. If we passed a fire station, we'd stop in for a quick fountain drink. Fast-food stands could be counted on for a cold cup, and parks usually have a fountain somewhere. And when desperate, there's always someone watering the lawn. When we finished the requisite miles, we'd head back to the beach and dunk in the water to cool down. After swimming a few laps I'd head back to the house around 9:30, in time to prepare breakfast for my sleepy-eyed family just emerging. In September, I did a twenty-mile run in three hours flat and thought I was a winged-foot goddess. Nothing was going to hold me back now.

The day before the event, I packed all the necessary paraphernalia. Picking out the most appropriate T-shirt was a major prerace predicament. I started with a pile of ten. On the first go-round I eliminated five. Then it was down to three, then two. Now I was starting to sweat and get really nervous. The marathon T-shirt is so important. It's a statement. It will be featured in all the photos. It is a big decision. After much pondering, trying on and pacing about, I selected the one with a picture of my friend Jane and me sitting at a bar on the beach in Anguilla. The night before the race we gathered for a big pasta diner, no wine, and early to bed, but no sleep came.

Then, talk about unpredictable variables, we woke up on race day to torrential rain. I mean buckets thrown from the skies, streets already clogged and choked from leaf-filled drains. And adding to all that rain were my own tears of disappointment. This is not how I wanted to run my first marathon. This was not just a normal rain, it was time to start building the Ark. We went to the race hoping it would be canceled, but no such luck. Severe wind, snow, or rain will never cancel a marathon. We drove home heartbroken, but still determined. It takes courage to walk away from a marathon, but we had to do what was best for us. Luckily, the most convenient marathon was just three weeks away. We would just keep doing our basic training, maybe one more ten. There was the fear of overtraining at this point, so we really had to hold in the reins.

On race day, the premarathon rituals were in full swing as we registered and headed to the gym to stow our gear. Everyone was stretching, doing their routines, and saying last good-byes. For the umpteenth time, we went to the bathroom. All the women were discussing what to wear as it was partly rainy, partly sunny with a nip in the air. One woman opted to wear shorts and was rubbing olive oil on her exposed skin. I thought it looked kind of kinky, but when offered I gobbed some on. Then the herd headed out to the starting line. I was so psyched, I could hardly contain myself. We started midpack and kept a nice steady pace for the first half. Of course, my friend and I talked the entire way. Part of the race went by the ocean and it reminded us of our training route. Running through the scenic New England towns with the white picket fences was charming and occupied my thoughts for a few miles. Every once in a while a runner would come by and spend a few miles chatting with us. Runners are always willing to share their experiences and personal tips. An instant bond is formed during those twenty-six miles that is unlike anything else I have experienced in any other sport. I was having so much fun I couldn't believe I was actually running in a marathon.

When I approached the twenty-mile marker I totally lost it and started jumping up and down, pounding my friend on the back. "It's almost over," I exuberantly cried. Having been there before, she quickly grabbed my arm and pulled me close. "Now you just settle down. This is going to be the longest six miles you've ever run and you will need every bit of strength and focus to get you through." I was shocked at her seriousness. We had been laughing it up for twenty miles and now she totally withdrew inside herself to find that last bit of energy somewhere. I tried to do the same, but couldn't focus. At twenty-two miles, I suddenly lost my euphoric high and tiredness set in. At this point the course went uphill on a busy road and it wasn't fun anymore. I wanted to cry and to make matters worse, my Achilles heel was acting up, causing me pain, but I wouldn't stop. Not me. I was going to run every step of the way. At twenty-four miles I wondered how I would get through.

I started to think about my mom and what she would have thought of the marathon. I had to laugh out loud as I imagined the heated discussion. Her Irish temper would have had a field day. As I thought of her, my steps and my mind-set became lighter, more determined, more focused. I swear I felt the wind at my back, pushing me to move on, closer and closer to the finish line. Was she there beside me? Sitting on my shoulder? Above me? All I know is that she was somewhere out there with me. She gave me the strength to finish the race in a last-minute frenzy of joy.

Ellen and I finished back to back and then I had to face the three-hour drive home alone, and I wondered if I would make it but I wore a smile on my face the entire two hundred or so miles. I envisioned the gala homecoming Andy and the kids had waiting for me, their marathon queen: a glass of champagne atop a silver tray, a screen of Mylar floating balloons and streamers, and my adoring and proud family surrounding me with outstretched arms. Instead, I got a hello and no dinner. Oh well. That's why dreams were invented.

The high I felt from finishing the marathon lasted for weeks. I was so proud of myself. It was the adventure of a lifetime, rating right up there with childbirth. It was something I did all by myself, a dream come true. I would tell anyone who is thinking about a marathon to go for it and not fall into the "I can't" syndrome. For that matter, I would tell anyone to follow their dream. Life is too short. Every day we should reach out as far we can to bring that dream into focus and grab it for all it's worth. I am a true believer in *carpe diem*—seize the day, squeeze every ounce out of it.

At night, I roam through the house like a specter making vespers, checking on the kids for the umpteenth time, listening for their breathing, and memorizing the sight of their sleeping bodies in bed: Anna curled up and cozy, Eli sprawled with every limb floundering around. Then I look up at the night sky, search for the brightest star, say good night to my mother, and surrender the day.

I plan to keep running until I physically can't drag my body to the starting line. The discipline, motivation, and personal challenge to train and perform for 26 miles and 385 yards have helped me pick up the pieces of my life. Once again I have a sense of myself, and just the right amount of order and harmony to make life fun again.

BREAKING DOWN BARRIERS

NINA KUSCSIK
RESIDENCE: HUNTINGTON, NEW YORK
OCCUPATION: HEALTH PROFESSIONAL
FIRST MARATHON: 1969 BOSTON MARATHON
AGE AT FIRST MARATHON: 30

To understand why Nina Kuscsik is called one of the pioneers of women's running, a brief history is necessary. In 1896, a woman named Melpomene scandalized race officials at the first Olympics by disregarding their decree that women could not run that event. She finished in four-and-a-half hours, the first woman known to have unofficially run a marathon. Women did not compete in the Olympic Marathon event again until 1984. In the 1928 Olympics, several women collapsed after completing the 800 meters and it was decreed that women could not run any race over 200 meters for health reasons. The ruling held until the 1960 Olympics. The Boston Marathon barred women until 1972. Nina was the first official woman to win Boston in 1972, although she and a handful of other women had run unofficially since 1966, jumping out of bushes, and almost getting thrown out. She also won the New York City Marathon in 1972 and 1973. An outspoken advocate for women's sports, she is a board member of the New York Road Runners Club and a sought-after speaker and motivator. More importantly, she is a delightful person, warm, congenial, and with a great sense of humor.

I GREW UP IN THE FLATBUSH SECTION of Brooklyn playing street games like stoop ball, punch ball, ring-a-levio, and of course biking and roller skating. With two sisters and one brother, there was always someone to play with, plus we all had our own gangs. Everyone belonged to a gang in Flatbush. We played in the street all day long. My favorite sport became basketball, which I started playing when I was thirteen for the YMCA. I absolutely loved it. It was the only organized sport I knew and I was good at it. I was a bit of a reckless player, not careless, but I knew no limitations. At sixteen I had to quit due to repeated dislocated shoulders and forcing myself into body casts. I have shallow ball-and-socket joints and eventually required surgery. I tried to play with less abandon, but it wasn't fun, so I quit altogether.

After basketball, I took up speed skating and was soon a member of a speed skating team at the Eastern Parkway Roller Rink. I also tried freestyle skating, but after taking a jump and landing incorrectly I dislocated my shoulder again. That was it for the freestyle; I stuck with speed skating.

Around that time, I read in the sports section about Roger Bannister breaking the four-minute mile. I couldn't comprehend the speed of a four-minute mile so I got on my bike, rode to Wingate Field which had a track, climbed over the three-tier cyclone fence, and ran around the track once as fast as I could and timed myself at 1:25. Of course he ran much faster than I had, but I was very impressed with how fast he had to be moving to set the new world record. I admired his speed. It was incredible. But I still hadn't thought about running as a sport.

Sports were very important to me, something I looked forward to doing every day. While the other teenagers were hanging out, I couldn't just stand around all day and talk; it seemed like a waste of time. I wanted to be active and I liked the discipline of knowing every day I could account for something. I needed that sense of accomplishment.

In 1955, my speed skating team went to the National Championships. One of our members had just run the Yonkers Marathon and I remember thinking that was a fantastic accomplishment. I was about to graduate Midwood High School and thought that I had learned everything I needed to know in life. That's what school was for. My guidance counselor asked me what my plans were and I thought about nursing, which meant two more years of school. He told me to clean my dirty fingernails or I would never get into college. I wanted to remind him that I was working mornings and afternoons at a cookie factory and that was my midmorning snack, but I didn't, and I did go on to nursing school.

Along with speed skating, I decided to try out bike racing, but I didn't own a bike so the German Bicycle Sports Club gave me one. It was a "track" bike, which meant it had no coasting and braking was controlled only by backpedaling. I used to ride my bike to the bike races at the Queens Worlds Fair grounds. One night I fell into a manhole grate and wrecked the bike and had to buy a new one. I do have one favorite memory of a bike race in Central Park back in the fifties. It was a twenty-three mile handicap race and I beat this older German guy and I think he was upset about being beaten by a woman. Just then, a pigeon flew by and excreted on his head. Then he really had something to be angry about.

In 1960 I was the New York State champion for roller speed skating, ice speed skating, and bike racing. I don't know if I considered myself an athlete, but I certainly was. I didn't think in terms of defining myself in any way.

In nursing school we were learning about heart disease and it seemed from the point of the medical books that life was over after forty. Diseases would suddenly take over our middle-aged bodies so we better slow down and take it easy. I didn't buy any of it. Even back then I knew that exercising was important. My daily routine was to bike to the rink, do my speed skating workout, then bike home and go to school. During exam week, I would take a break from studying and bike twenty-three miles. As a full-time nurse, I would ride to work in Manhattan from Brooklyn.

When I became a mother, I decided it was time to be a woman, which meant not participating in sports events. I was going to accept the role of wife and mother as defined in the sixties. My husband would go out to play softball and I would sit with the baby carriage and cheer him on. But I hated it. I couldn't adapt to being a spectator, not a player. It didn't make sense to me that family time was put aside for men's sports but not mine. Then President Kennedy took office and promoted physical exercise. I figured if our president could take time away from his responsibilities as an adult and hike fifty miles, than it was acceptable for me to continue to exercise. So I went back to skating and biking. Right before our vacation I got a flat tire and in those days, you just couldn't go to a neighborhood bike shop and get it fixed. I had to send away for a mail-order replacement. Without a bike to ride for exercise, I started to jog. Bill Bowerman had just written a book called *Jogging* which cost a dollar, so I bought it. This was 1965, the first time the word *jogging* was used in print. Bill also went on to develop the waffle running sole for Nike.

So I started running. I went to the track and ran a mile in 7:05 and thought I was pretty good. At the time I didn't know I was pregnant with my third child. The doctor told me I could continue to run and I did so for a few more months until it became too uncomfortable. Six weeks after the baby was born I participated in a twenty-four-hour out-door track relay. I ran a total of eleven miles over the twenty-four hours and met some more runners. I was given a magazine called *Long Distance Log,* which profiled the 1968 Boston Marathon. A woman named Elaine Pederson from San Francisco had jumped into the race from the sideline right after the official start and completed the route. I was very impressed with that. Then with two speed skating buddies, Bob Mueller and Charlie Blum, along with my husband, we talked about running the Boston Marathon. I started to train more seriously, following Bill Bowerman's theory of alternating workouts. One of my favorite ten-mile runs became a 1.5-mile warm-up to the track, then five miles of quarters with 110-yard jogs in between, and a 1.5-mile cool-down run home. It was a great routine that I still use today. I par-ticularly remember one September morning when the track was empty and I had just put in a hard session. Afterward, I stood there in the still silence, feeling the sweat and the humidity on my skin, looking out across the deep green leaves that formed a canopy circling the track which was engulfed in the eerie morning fog. It was a special moment, as if everything was one.

Another training method I use is visualization, which is a catchy term to mean when I am on a long run, I imagine I am anywhere I want to be. During one marathon, my hip was hurting so I decided to drop to a eight-minute pace and to take my mind off the pain, I visualized that I was at Fire Island. I imagined the feel of the ocean breeze on my face and it refreshed me. I tried to figure out if it was high or low tide at the beach so I could imagine playing in the tidal pools. When I got tired, I brought my pace down even further and imagined that I was taking a nap on the beach, in the warm sand. Then I pretended to see seagulls flying above and worried that they'd shit on my head. The other run-ners around me thought I was crazy, mumbling about ocean breezes, seagulls, and tidal pools.

During some solitary runs, I would observe when and where in my body fatigue would strike. As an example, during a marathon training run, I would lose some of my spring between twenty and twenty-four miles. I believe the body needs to experience things so that it has a memory of all the different variables it will have to endure under extreme marathon conditions. If everything is going smoothly, at the end of the test run nothing will significantly hurt, it just won't be as elastic as it was three hours ago.

By January 1969, I decided to run Boston, which did not officially allow women to run. But in 1966, after twenty-three-year-old Roberta "Bobbi" Gibb was declined an entry number based on her sex, she decided to run it anyway and slipped in shortly after the official start. The officials never noticed her and the male runners welcomed her. Her unofficial time was 3:21 and she made history. She went back to Boston again in '67 and was joined by another woman, Kathrine Switzer. This time Kathrine was noticed by the officials, who tried to throw her off the course, unsuccessfully. Now there were two women who had run Boston and in '68 Elaine Pederson was added to the growing roster of women unofficially running Boston.

Training during the winter months for the '69 marathon was a bit rough. People thought I was a weirdo. Actually, my neighbors already thought I was crazy and now that I was running in the dark, in the snow, in the rain, they really thought I had lost it. Every time I ran in the rain I got picked up by the police, who thought I had escaped from some institution. I was the only woman running the streets. There were no jogging clothes or running outfits to identify what I was doing. There was no such thing as a woman running just because she liked to. In 1973 I was interviewed for a documentary on women's sports and I told them I had a fantasy that someday two women would be seen running together on East Seventy-Second Street in pastel jogging outfits and no one would bother them, that it would be normal.

I worked up to thirty miles a week and completed one twenty-miler. I also started taking yoga classes in February because I thought it would be interesting, but I stretched the ligaments that are important in shoulder stability so I was back in a cast. My arm was so sore I couldn't even close the diaper pin for the baby and had to get my neighbor to do it, as my husband was traveling. It was a very tough time. Actually, I have learned to love yoga and think it is very valuable for runners. But at that time, it was new and I tried to accomplish too much too soon.

In March, two weeks prior to the marathon, on the Saturday before Easter, I decided to do a twenty-miler. Rain was in the forecast, so my husband told me to stay on the Northern Parkway and in the event of rain he would come pick me up so the body cast wouldn't get wet. I was wearing a pair of sweats and a St. John's sweatshirt. I went out ten miles, turned around to come back and then it started to rain and get cold. As I was running home, the police came by and started yelling at me for running on the side of the parkway. It seems they had gotten a report of a one-armed woman running and covered with blood, and I was that woman. The so-called blood was the red St. John's lettering. The police were not amused, and to add insult to injury, told me to call my loverboy for a ride home. I was humiliated by their attitude toward me.

Two weeks later I was in Boston for my first running race and my first marathon. My arm was still sore, but out of the cast. I knew it would tire early in the race, so I cut a little hole in the front of my shirt so I could rest my arm by hanging my thumb on my bra. We had gone over the course the day before and wrote down mile markers because there weren't any on the course. They also didn't have regular water stations, so I had to rely on the spectators for fluids. I didn't see any other women on the course, although two others ran. Another runner noticed I was from New York and told me I should run the Yonkers Marathon next month. I said, "No, why would I want to run another marathon? I came here to run Boston and that's it." It was a very hard race, a tough run. I didn't walk at all, but when I got tired, I picked up the pace to alter the stride. There was never a sense of quitting and I stayed on target with my pace the entire race. Women officials from the B.A.A. timed me, but it was off the record and never announced. To find out what my time was, I needed to know the male runner next to me and look up his time. I finished in 3:46, twenty-four minutes behind the first unofficial woman winner and eight minutes ahead of my goal.

My first Boston marathon was not a woman's issue for me; I didn't go to set an agenda or prove anything. It was a wonderful human accomplishment to run the marathon. And as much as the Boston Boys didn't want females in their race and would not recognize us as official runners, we were provided with our own changing area and showers and New England clam chowder in the runner's cafeteria. We were treated with respect because we were athletes.

The next day at home, I thought I was going back to a normal life, my three kids (all under the age of six), and fixing the washing machine. I had developed a running program for the women in my neighborhood to get them out exercising, an outgrowth of the CYO track team I coached for the kids. I got them running a quarter mile and they thought it was great, an incredible accomplishment. They had heard about my marathon and came by to congratulate me.

I didn't run another marathon until March of 1970, when I did the Cherry Tree Marathon in the Bronx. They used to give out liquor at the water stops. Then I decided to do Boston again in 1970 to improve on my time and finished in 3:12, thirty-four minutes faster than the last one. The next month I did the Yonkers Marathon. That sounds like a lot of marathons, but I paced myself. I would pick a pace, say eight-minute miles, and stick to it. Then I joined a women's running club in Long Island called Cinderbelles. I was more than twice the age of the next oldest member. This was before Title IX, so all the girls who had no access to high school and college running teams were members.

In June of 1970 I went to compete in a two-mile race in Van Cortland Park, but was turned away because it was only for men. I was shocked. It was an epiphanal moment for me, the awakening of my outrage and outburst at being denied to run a race just because I was a woman. I was even a member of the A.A.U., which sponsored the race. There was nothing on the entry blank that said no women allowed. I remember arguing with the race director and saying, "I know the race isn't for horses because the A.A.U. doesn't allow horses as members, but I am a member. How can you keep me out of a race sponsored by an organization that I am a member of?" I was angry. If the race is just for men, it should say so.

I immediately became an advocate to change the rules and started attending A.A.U. meetings, studying the rule book, and challenging entries such as women were not allowed to run more than five miles and must be accompanied by a chaperon on overnight trips. In the spring of 1971, channeling all my angry energy to ensure equality for female runners, I contacted two other women runners, Kathrine Switzer and Pat Tarnawsky, to rally the cause. We started off big, tackling the Olympic Marathon event, and aiming to challenge the Olympic committee to change the name to the Men's Marathon event, or to include women. In order to effect these changes, we knew we had to promote women's running in this country and abroad so that females everywhere would

unite and rally around the changes we were fighting for. Kathrine went
the corporate route, and got Avon to sponsor a women's running program which was one of the best-organized and attended programs ever.
I went to the A.A.U. convention in 1971 and fought to have women
officially allowed to run the marathon distance. They did not want to
recognize our demands, but ultimately gave in with the caveat that only
"selective" women could run marathons. The term came to mean
women who had already proved they could run the distance without
collapsing. Sexual biases in sports were still running rampant and for
the official "leaders" of our sport, the image of a tired, sweaty woman
running competitively was still not a pretty picture, whereas for men it
was accepted as part of athletic prowess.

We decided to make the 1971 Boston Marathon our platform for
progress and wrote to the directors to officially include us. Boston
accepted us with open arms and in 1972, women could officially run
Boston.

Eight women ran in that Boston Marathon. We were allowed to start
at the same time, but in a different starting point, according to the
A.A.U., so we drew a line on the sidewalk. But at the gun, we were in
the street anyway, never intending to start on the sidewalk. It was a
history-making day and I was hoping for good results from all of us. I
had everything going for me: I was in good shape, and I had fought
hard for women to get to this place. There was only one woman with a
better marathon time than me, Beth Bonner, and she didn't show. I
wanted to win and decided that I deserved to win. I also knew this was
going to be a world of opportunity for women and all eyes were going
to be on us. This was our shot for all women runners.

At the start, I ate a chocolate bar. I didn't think much of it, as I was
hungry. Another time I ate waffles before Boston and it was fine. But
around Wellesley, my intestines began to growl and I looked for a bathroom but there weren't any. I was running well and thought I had a
great chance to win. I didn't want to take the time to stop, but would
have had I seen a bathroom. Soon I realized one stop would not have
been enough. I remembered reading that Frank Shorter had a bout of
diarrhea at the Pan American Games and ran through it, so I decided if
that was going to be my fate, I would run through it also. The only difference was he was a man and that sort of thing would be accepted, and
I was running the first official race for women and didn't want to make

this the focal point, to read the next morning's headline and see something like: WOMEN ALLOWED TO RUN MARATHON, BUT WINNER GETS SICK WITH DIARRHEA.

If this was any other marathon, I would have stopped, but I wanted to win this. I was really getting uncomfortable, but I kept going and finally let the diarrhea out and down my legs. I was more concerned with the media playing on my troubles and making this a big issue than I was about the humiliation of this physical expenditure.

At the twenty-mile mark, my friend was waiting with the tea I had asked for. I figured she would think I was crazy, but since there were no water stations en route to count on, I took the tea and poured it down my back, hoping to clean my legs a bit. I was very self-conscious and imagined that everyone knew of my condition. In retrospect, my anxiety over the medical mishap was far worse than reality. I thought the crowds really knew what was going on. I was so sensitive to my problem that I listened as the crowd cheered for me as I approached, but stopped as I past, and I imagined they stopped because they saw the brown streaks on my legs.

When I knew I was going to win, I conceived a plan to avoid the press photographing me in this condition. I decided I would just sit down after crossing the finish line and wait till I could get a blanket to cover myself. I knew reporters would be out in force to capture the first official women's running of Boston and I was determined to make it a proud moment. As it turned out, as soon as I crossed the finish line I was wrapped in the ceremonial winner's blanket, which covered just about all of me. My secret was safe and it never came out in the press until years later when I chose to recant the story during an interview. I do remember one of my quotes to the press that day: "This race proves that I have guts."

I received my winner's trophy, but not the accompanying diamond-studded medal that the men also received. I didn't even realize this until twenty-four years later when Boston made up for that in 1996, and Sara Berman, Bobbi Gibb, and I were presented with the medals at the Hundredth Boston ceremonies.

We continued to press for women's rights at the running tables. Pat handled a lot of the public relations, calling the press and media to cover any big event where women would be participating. Part of all our jobs was educating women on their rights. In 1974 the A.A.U.

allowed women to compete in all distances and have their own National Championships, just as the men did. And in 1977 they asked the International Running Federation to pursue our Olympic goal. In February of 1981, the International Olympic Committee announced that there would be a women's marathon in the 1984 games. Joan Benoit Samuelson won the first women's marathon event ever in the Olympics. The breakthrough for women was now complete.

In 1976, I was invited to speak at the New York Academy of Sciences Symposium on marathon running. I spoke about the history of women's running and delved into tons of fascinating research. One interesting fact I discovered was that Lewis Carroll included a women's race in his *Alice's Adventures in Wonderland*.

When I am asked to reflect on the fact that women today take for granted what I fought so hard to attain, I don't view it as taken for granted. Women are running more marathons today then ever and their best times equal and in some cases surpass the best men's times of the fifties and sixties. In 1994, Uta Pippig collected ninety-five thousand dollars at the Boston Marathon for winning in three separate categories, and in 1996 went on to win a hundred thousand dollars. I feel honored to be one of the facilitators who made it happen.

I have such great memories of my racing days. One time I won a lamp at a bike race, but since I rode my bike to the race, I couldn't get it home. Another great day was running the Yonkers Marathon, when I was the first and only woman. There was no trophy for me so the Millrose Road Racing Team turned around and gave me their trophy. I always had wonderful support from the male runners. I never obsessed about my running, it was just something I was good at. If I was having a bad day, I'd go home. In 1970, Fred Lebow asked me to announce to the press that I would break the three-hour finish at the first New York City Marathon. I knew I couldn't, it would have been silly of me to say so. I ended up quitting that race because I wasn't feeling well. I started to walk, thinking I could recover, but decided to just go home. I didn't have to prove anything; I had already run six marathons. Why should I kill myself? When I ran the hundredth Boston in 1996, I hadn't been training so I just took my time. It was a wonderful day. I stopped along the side and spoke with the spectators, had a piece of marathon birthday cake someone offered me, walked a bit and just enjoyed the beautiful day. I finished in over five hours, but I didn't care. There was no pressure. If someone beat me, it's because they trained harder. A male friend once told me he overheard another guy in the shower bragging about how he had beaten me that day. I took it as a compliment. I've always done everything at my own pace. It's a great way to live and enjoy life.

I've raised three kids, ran over eighty marathons, winning fifteen, and completed at least five ultramarathons, set an American record at fifty miles, biked across Iowa, and still work in the health care field. I run shorter distances now and still speak on women's sports issues. Occasionally you can find me at the New York City Road Runners Club giving a seminar or conducting a workout.

And I'm still learning with my mind and my body.

KENYAN KINETICS

PAUL MBUGUA
RESIDENCE: KIAMBU, KENYA
OCCUPATION: ELITE RUNNER
FIRST MARATHON: 1995 TORONTO MARATHON
D.O.B. 12-15-62
AGE AT FIRST MARATHON: 32

Kenya's world-class runners seem to be crossing the finish line in first place at every major marathon in the United States and abroad. Everyone wants to know what makes them so fast. Teams of sport researchers and coaches have traveled to Kenya to get a better understanding of their practices and techniques. They are a running phenomenon. Paul Mbugua is one of Kenya's elite runners, growing up and running on a farm just outside Nairobi. He was picked up by an agent and put on the European circuit for almost ten years before coming to America in 1994 to start the rigorous pursuit of the fame and fortune provided by the United States marathons. In 1997 he placed third in the Las Vegas Marathon and has his hopes set for winning one or two before going back to Kenya a very prosperous man.

BACK IN KENYA, WE START RUNNING at a very early age as a form of transportation. I had to run three miles to school, then back home for lunch, then back to school. During recess we run some more, maybe four miles, combined with some calisthenics. Our schools don't have gymnasium facilities; in fact we don't even change into gym shorts. Some of the kids don't even have what you here in America would call running shoes; they run in whatever shoe they can afford to buy and wear it every day for every other purpose. After school I had to run home. That's a total of sixteen miles a day just to get back and forth to school, plus gym. And I'm lucky, I wasn't too far from school. Some kids in the northeastern part of our country, what we call up-country, can be at least six miles from school. And after school we don't go home and watch TV or hang out in the village sipping Cokes. We have to do chores. I live on a farm, so I have to feed the cattle and the chickens, maybe gather wood or other things. When I was still a young boy, my father died and left me in charge. That was a big responsibility at an early age.

In Kenya, every company, every agency, the post office, Kenya Power and Light, even the military, has a running team that competes against each other. Sometimes an employee is hired not based on his working skills but on his running skills. We take it very seriously. Our sports heroes are our runners. All the kids want to be like them when they grow up. We pick nicknames based on our famous runners. I wanted to be Henry Rono when I was a kid. My friend wanted to be called Kip Keino, our '68 and '72 Olympian gold medalist. Some kids wanted to be Ibrahim Hussein, who won Boston consecutively in 1991 and '92, and Cosmos Ndeti, who followed Hussein's career, winning Boston in 1993, '94, and '95. They all came back to Kenya with fame, fortune, and a Mercedes Benz. They were our heroes like American kids want to be Michael Jordan or Tiger Woods. Our elite runners return home with a nice car, able to buy a nice house, and the neighborhood kids say, "Hey, there's Kip, he did well in America. I want to be like him."

All the store owners and restaurant owners know who I am. I like that. Kenya has so many good runners we could put together teams, send them all over the world to compete, and win every time. The Olympic team we sent to Atlanta in 1996 was probably not even our best runners; they were on the circuit making money. The coaches know so much about training and how to make us the best runners. Their knowledge is incredible. Everyone respects them because they make us the best. Runners in Kenya do not have jobs. We run all day, we train all the time. I don't know how Americans can work and train at the same time and expect to be world-class runners. Training is a full-time job.

I always wanted to be one of Kenya's elite runners and get discovered by an agent. When we studied geography in school and I learned about the countries and cities around the world, I would say to myself, "Paul, someday you will visit there if you are fast enough." I wanted to be rich and be treated nice by others. Some of the elite runners can make as much in one or two races as some Kenyans make in a year. But when I started running after high school, the money wasn't that good. I won a lot of trophies and certificates but the money didn't happen until the eighties, when the Kenyans started winning the Boston Marathon and other important world-class track events. Then we were taken seriously.

I was a national champion at the high school level, which is very good. I needed that recognition to get an invitation to the National Championships in Nairobi, where the agents hang out looking for the best runners. I spent time talking to other runners who were on the circuit and learned as much as I could about agents, prize money, appearance money, whatever I could that would help my career. Some runners come back totally burned out without any money and I didn't want to become one of them. I wanted to do it smart.

In 1985 when I was twenty-three and running the Nationals, I was approached by an agent. Most runners are members of the Kenyan Athletic Association (K.A.A.), which is the equivalent of the U.S. Track and Field Association. We call it the Federation for short. Agents have to register with the K.A.A., pay some kind of yearly fee and then can recruit runners. They show up at the Nationals with bags of money and airline tickets. The usual agent fee is 10 percent of winnings, but if you get appearance money it can go up to 20 percent. It's a risk to go with an agent unless you know his reputation. Unless there is an opportunity to talk with other runners about their agents and begin to develop a feeling for who is good and who isn't, you can lose a lot of money; you can really get burned. Agents show up offering thousands of dollars in cash, right there on the spot. You must realize, we never see that kind of money, not in our entire lives. They wave it under our noses and it is so close, we can touch it, grab it, it's ours if we just go with the agent. It is so tempting.

Personally, I was better off waiting until I was in my twenties. I had learned a lot talking to the other runners. Some kids, especially if they are from a very remote area of the country, really get burned. They travel hundreds of miles to get to Nairobi and it is the first time they have seen a city. It is very overwhelming. Then an agent offers free shoes and thousands of dollars. Of course they will go with him. But what they don't know is in some cases the agent has requested appearance money from certain races and doesn't tell them and pockets it. That happens a lot. That's why I am glad I waited and learned all these things. I know of some of the younger kids who are approached by agents who give them cash, and that very night they are on a plane to Europe and don't come home for months. I didn't want to start out that way.

After watching the Nationals, an agent I knew I could trust selected me and another runner to go to Japan to complete a team he was putting together. The other four members of the team had already been out on the circuit and joined us to train for a relay marathon in Japan. We worked together for three weeks at a training camp and then flew to Japan. We received shoes, warm-ups, free food and lodging. I will never forget that day as long as I live. It was very exciting for me. I had been to the Nairobi airport to pick up people but never to fly. I was so excited to be on a plane that I had to go over and touch the plane before I entered the cabin. I was so happy. If I died that night I would have considered myself a happy guy. I wasn't even thinking of the money, I just wanted to experience flying in a plane. I thought I was going to another world. It was a night flight and we flew eight hours to Paris and spent the night there. I couldn't believe I was in Paris! I had a king-size bed. I never saw a king size bed before.

If I knew traveling was going to be this exciting, I would have run faster to get onto the circuit sooner. The next day we flew thirteen and a half hours to Japan. At the relay, we came in third place. We each received appearance money and place running. So in the ten days that I left Kenya, I came back with more money than I had ever had in my life.

One month later the agent sent me to Europe, where I raced in every country, sometimes running a race a week. I stayed in Europe for two months accumulating appearance money and prize money. Sometimes I won, sometimes I didn't. We were traveling with a group of ten Kenyans. Everything was paid for. My life was race, train, sleep, eat, travel, and race again. The only sight-seeing I got to do was if I was running through the city.

I am a runner. That is what I do. That is what gets me money and gets me to travel all over the world. I don't think I could be anything else. I don't think I could wake up in the morning and go to a job, working for someone. Sometimes I think about that when I am running and it makes me run faster and train harder. I don't want to give up this life. I have already made more money than most Kenyans.

I stayed on the European circuit from 1985 till 1993. During those eight years I was never home more than two months at a time. I loved what I was doing. I was sponsored by a shoe company and everything was going along fine. In 1993 I met a Kenyan during one of the few times I was home, who lived in America. He was looking to recruit Kenyans to go on the United States marathon circuit. I wasn't sure I wanted to do it because the prize money in America is less than I was making in Europe and it is also harder to obtain appearance money. I thought about it for a long time and decided my European running was mostly track work, and although I was fast and still winning, I was thirty-two years old and much younger Kenyans were coming on the circuit, reducing my chances of winning. I listened to my body and decided to go to America and try my luck at the marathon where the field was more my age.

Eighteen of us flew to Albany, where a friend of the agent offered us housing. I felt like I was starting a new life. The following day, we flew to Tampa, Florida, and entered our first race. It was a 5K and we did miserably. I finished twentieth. We were tired from the travel, which was prolonged by some visa problems, and just didn't perform well. Our new agent understood this and said not to worry. From that point on, we flew all over America racing every weekend. I covered thirty-three states in three months, with Albany as our home base. At first I was making less money than I ever did in Europe. Some of the guys complained that we had made a mistake by coming to America. We weren't getting appearance money and the competition was greater among our own people. Kenyans were winning everywhere. We had to run harder and faster to beat our own countrymen. I was still running shorter-distance races, mostly as trainers before tackling the marathon. I concentrated on 5Ks, 10Ks, and 15Ks. One weekend I won a 5K and the next morning won a 10K in 29:10. I knew it was time to leave the short distance races behind and let the younger guys have them.

After being in Albany for a while, I made another big decision in my life and split from my agent. They are getting too tough to deal with. They take more money than they give to the runners and the race directors are getting tired of their arrogant attitude. Besides, I had built a decent reputation for myself and was a familiar name with the race directors. I really didn't need an agent to book races anymore. Now when I see a race I want to enter, I send my résumé and get an invitation with travel and accommodations paid for. I always ask for appearance money and in most cases I get it. Since I have been handling my own entries, I have found that most race directors would rather deal with me on a one-to-one basis than go through an agent. In fact they seem almost relieved that I don't have one. I think the Kenyan factor is beginning to work against agents, as some are getting very greedy and demanding.

I knew it was time to try the marathon, despite that people told me it would be hard, that I would die at twenty miles. It scared me. Two hours is too long. I did not want to die. I decided when I got to twenty miles I'd just close my eyes and hope for the best. This was May of 1995 and I picked the very next marathon I could get to, which was in Canada. I didn't get appearance money but they paid my travel, hotel, and food. There were three other Kenyans running, members of my European team. I didn't get any special marathon coaching, which was a mistake on my part. Not knowing any better, I ran in my racing flats, which offered no cushioning. It was not a good race for me: finishing in eighth place with 2:19. And I did die at twenty miles. I was tired and thought, "I will never do this again. This is crazy. Even Kenyans get tired after running that far."

I returned to Kenya and signed up to train with a highly ranked marathon coach. I trained only for the marathon, concentrating on distance. One day was dedicated to a long run, the next day was hill work, then a day doing track work, then interval work. Then the coach said, "Go out for an hour, turn around, and come back." He knows that as far as I run out, I have to come back even if I am tired. No one comes around to pick me up. The coach is very smart.

When I returned to the states I ran the Walt Disney World Marathon in January of 1996 and came in fourth with a time of 2:17. Then came Cleveland in May, which I finished in 2:14 and won a very big cash prize. My efforts were starting to pay off. I was pacing myself better and not starting out too fast. In February of 1997 I ran the Las Vegas Marathon and placed third with a time of 2:16. I am sure I could have done better but my feet were swollen from the flight the night before and my shoes didn't fit properly.

My plan is to run three marathons a year and in five years when I become a master I will even be better and make more money. Right now I spend about two months back in Kenya training. The training camps are very focused, very disciplined. It's like being in the army. We live there anywhere from three weeks to two months, training as a team. We have a different training routine for every type of race. Don't forget, running is what we are used to doing every day just to get around, so the camps take running to a much higher level, something even we are not accustomed to. The team concept is very important to us. I think it is the number one difference that makes us better than other countries. We associate only with runners. And once there, you do not leave. There are no distractions from daily life such as phone calls, kids, spouses, whatever. In other words, there are no excuses. When you wake up in the morning, and maybe you don't feel like running, you have to. Your team is making you. You cannot hide. The team gives you the support to get through the training. We rely on each other. It doesn't matter if you are married or anything. You still go the camps. And most of the elite runners are married because they want a wife to stay home and protect their money. Most of them want to build big homes and it can't get built unless someone is there to supervise. One win, which could be as much as twenty-thousand dollars, can get you a very, very big house. Men who are not married usually end up spending their money foolishly, but a good wife will take care of it while they are running marathons back in the States. We are very desirable husbands. Women wait at the airport for us when we come home to train. I could get married anytime I want. Women have their way of letting us know they want to marry us. They have their own devices.

Our diet is not much different from what you eat here in the States, but we eat more red meat. And we never worry about getting fat. That's all I hear in the States. Everyone is worried about getting fat. They think so much about their weight. Just run like we do and you can eat whatever you want and never get fat.

I would love to bring my mother over to America for a visit. I told her in the year 2000 I will take her to the top of the Empire State Building and put New York City at her feet. I think she will like that.

SUFFERING THE SINS OF NEGLECT

JIM MILLER
RESIDENCE: DUXBURY, MASSACHUSETTS
OCCUPATION: DIRECTOR OF FINANCIAL AID, HARVARD UNIVERSITY
FIRST MARATHON: 1985 CHICAGO MARATHON
D.O.B.: 3-25-51
AGE AT FIRST MARATHON: 34

What happens when an all-star college athlete faces the hard facts that he's hit his thirties, his corporate job has wreaked havoc on his once-fit body, and he has lost that edge, that natural ability to stay in shape regardless of diet and an exercise routine? What do you do when you realize you're out of shape and you miss that adrenaline high of a competitive sport, and the over-thirty soccer league and recreational basketball just don't do it for you? If you're Jim Miller, you look around for the biggest sports-related challenge available and you decide to run a marathon.

I CAN'T REMEMBER A TIME IN MY LIFE when I wasn't playing a sport. Whether it was a pick-up basketball game, high school swim team, or college athletics, I was always involved in something. I played varsity soccer and lacrosse for Brown University and really worked my tail off for both teams. Brown recruited the best players from around the world and it was a rude awakening to go from king of the high school team to a mere mortal. It was extremely competitive and you either played well or sat on the bench. Running was a major conditioning exercise for both sports, and I have to say, I hated it. I would have gladly sacrificed a body part not to have to run the football stadium stairs every day after practice. I could justify running after a ball, but running for the sake of running? No way. I never understood the track guys. What's the point?

Four years after college I went out to play a pick-up game of soccer with some guys from the office and I couldn't do it, just died out there. For the first time in my life I was winded, out of shape. I couldn't believe it. Ever since grade school I played some sort of sport season after season, and now only a few years down the road I had lost it, lost that magic touch to just go out and do it. I took it for granted and paid the price. So I started running. From my college days of training and discipline, as much as I hate to admit it, running was the foundation for getting into shape. Whatever the sport, running was the first discipline. Two and a half miles was all I could do for the first week or so, but I did it every day. It wasn't easy for me; in fact it was a real struggle. I still hated running, but my desire to get back in shape overruled my personal preferences. The other reason I stuck with it was because I knew it would enable me to build up endurance for the sports I loved, soccer and basketball. I am definitely a product of the seventies mentality of fitness: No pain, no gain. I had to punish myself, physically and mentally hurt myself, in order to see improvement. And since I was also guilty of the sin of neglect, I had to doubly punish myself. In the Jim Miller School of Guilt-Ridden Exercise Dropouts, rule number one is beat yourself up. It would have been easier to go to confession, but I'd still be out of shape.

So I ran from a sense of duty. My schedule at Harvard allowed me to run in the afternoons either around the campus or indoors if I had to. One of the things I miss most about college athletics is the adrenaline high, that rush, of competition. Having spent most of my life playing competitive sports, that excitement and that desire to win at all cost was now gone. I joined an over-thirty soccer league to try and capture that feeling, but the games were played at 9:30 A.M. on Saturday mornings and I wasn't always motivated to jump out of bed early on my weekend morning and rush to the game. So here I was, turning thirty something and in search of whatever holy grail would ignite my passion for competitive sports.

In March of 1985, I was on a fund-raising assignment in Chicago and met with a colleague who was also a runner. He was a real runner, not a fake one like myself. He had done a marathon so I knew he was one of the crazies. Running a marathon back in the eighties was something only a few insane runners aspired to, weirdos with a death wish. It was totally out of my league, but even I knew that anyone who could run twenty-six miles was an incredible athlete. He asked me to run the next Chicago Marathon with him and suddenly the light went on in my head. It hit me like a ton of bricks, like a rude awakening. Staring me right in the face was the ultimate challenge I was looking for. I would run a marathon. It was different enough to be a unique experience, it was athletically challenging, and since team sports were now out of the question, it was also the most accessible challenge for me. It was a way to recapture that feeling of being an athlete again. At the time of this revelation, I was doing 10Ks, which I thought was the farthest distance humans were programmed to run. I also knew from my college days that I would have to train rigorously for this event if I wanted to do well. The next day I bought a running magazine that had a training article, something about eleven weeks to your next marathon. I had a base of twenty five miles a week, so I fit the profile. And I have to say that somewhere down the road I crossed over from hating running and doing it out of a sense of obligation to my body to actually liking it and looking forward to my afternoon run. It became my daily religious retreat, my private escape from the world of financial aid to whatever I wanted the next hour to be. Church never worked for me, but running gave me that sense of spiritual well-being, of finding an inner calm. My thoughts wander, digging up the unsolved problems taking refuge in the crevices of my brain. Sometimes I find the hidden solution to that day's crisis; other times I engage in some serious soul-searching. I became known as "Jim the Runner" by my office colleagues. I've had a lot of reputations in my day, but this one was respectable! I had become a runner, and I liked it. I was the only one out there every day, all by myself. I have to admit, I liked the attention, the notoriety of being the Runner. Call it vanity, but I liked being in shape again, having the stamina and the dedication to run every day. And I look great in those shorts.

The first thing I did was tell everyone I knew that I was training for a marathon. This was my way of guaranteeing that I would run it and not back down. After I made such a bragging fool of myself, I had to run! It was my personal security tool. I designed my own training shirt that said I WILL RUN CHICAGO and wore it every day. I cranked up the mileage, which was the first big hurdle. I considered myself the undisputed god of the five-miler and now I was just a mere mortal, huffing and puffing and experiencing aches and pains. But I stuck with it. I remembered a conversation I had back at Brown with my friend Dick McEvoy, discussing the parameters of being in top physical shape. We thought we were hot stuff and decided we were the defining example of fitness. Since we had to run four miles for soccer practice, we determined that was all it took, we never had to go any farther. I had to laugh at our macho naïveté as I attempted my first ten-miler. I started to train with a vengeance, which was not smart. I should have rested more, cut down on some of the miles, because I was always in pain. I also never drank water, another thing I did wrong. But remember, to my perverse way of thinking, pain was gain.

November came all too soon and I boarded my flight to Chicago. I was worried about the weather, but race day was fifty degrees and beautiful. I met my friend and we were doing the prerace stuff together and he asked me if I was hydrated. I didn't know what he was talking about. He insisted I start drinking gallons of water, which only made me have to whizz about a hundred times before the race even started. I remember standing in line at the Port-o-Sans when the race countdown started. The noise of the stall doors opening, slamming, opening, slamming was intense. Everyone was rushing to squeeze out the last drop. I started to panic, banging on the blue stall doors, yelling, "Hurry up!" to whoever was in there. I didn't want to miss the start of my first marathon and be caught on the can when the gun went off, but that's exactly what happened. Five of us were caught with our drawers down when the gun sounded. We hurried out of the stalls, ran across Daley Plaza, jumped the barricade and landed smack in the middle of the elite runners. I didn't realize this at first; all I knew was that they were running faster than I ever did. I kept thinking, "This marathon business is really tough." I was having real trouble keeping up with them, but that's what I thought I was supposed to do! By the second mile, they all passed me as if I was a beached whale. These were the elite runners and no way did I resemble them in form, shape, or dress. By the third mile I was finally running at my own pace and could catch my breath.

My early attempts at fluid intake continued to haunt me throughout the day. Having never run a race before and never attempted to drink while running, I was in for a real experience. I grabbed water at the first station and damn near drowned myself trying to drink the entire cup at once while running. I didn't get the knack of it until the middle of the race, but by that time I was soaked. When I started to sweat and heat up, I got the great idea to grab a Gatorade with one hand and a cup of water with the other and use that to pour over my head. Well, in my haste and confusion I poured the Gatorade over my head and drank the water. The sticky liquid combined with my sweat as it dripped down my face, and soon my eyelids were stuck together and all the gnats were sticking to my face. I felt like a giant fly strip. At fifteen miles I was still feeling good, running strong, high as a kite. But then things began to fall apart. While dressing for the race, I thought I'd play it smart and wore two new pairs of socks, brand-new shorts, and two new shirts. And believe it or, I almost wore new shoes. I was reading a running magazine on the plane that featured the new shoes and if I had the time, I would have bought a pair for the race. I also didn't know about wearing Band-Aids on nipples and other areas where chafing can occur, so I was somewhat surprised when I started bleeding like a stuck pig and blisters the size of potholes formed where my feet had been. It was awful.

At eighteen miles, the carnage of worn-out runners became increasingly noticeable. Chicago is famous for the amount of runners who drop out of the race. Only about 50 percent of the field actually finishes. The course began to resemble a war scene out of *Ben-Hur*, with bodies strewn across the road, people cramping, crying, yelling, vomiting. It was not a pretty sight. I was feeling very lucky not be among the wreckage, but at twenty miles, I hit The Wall. I crashed so hard, this mythical wall literally collapsed and landed on top of me. I felt as if someone had pulled the plug from the base of my spine, letting all my body fluids leak out, leaving me shriveled and empty. I staggered around for a while trying to remember my name and why I was there. I was finally able to jump-start my brain, but not my body. I wanted to quit so badly, but I could never go home a quitter and face all those people I had bragged to. Dying right there on the course was an easier way out. Someone ran by and made a comment about only having a 10K left. Well, that may work for some people, but for me it was devastating news. I didn't want to run a 10K, I wanted the race to be over.

One of the thoughts that occupied my mind during the run was the difference between playing a team sport and running a marathon. There were twelve thousand runners in Chicago that day, all doing the same thing but doing it individually. It is a totally different concept than the dynamics of team sports. Back in college, if I was having a bad day there was always a team member to pick me up. It struck me that in that huge crowd I was alone, responsible only for myself. There wasn't a team member to pick up the slack and make up for my lack of energy. This thought didn't do much for my morale, as I was thoroughly exhausted and would have welcomed the camaraderie of a teammate. I actually resorted to walking, which destroyed the last vestige of machismo I had forever. I was humiliated, swore I would never tell anyone I walked. At twenty-three miles I was dragging the remains of my body along with three other guys who were in similar trouble when a very pretty woman sprinted by wearing very brief shorts and a tank top. We all thought we were hallucinating, but the sight of her woke us from our stupor as we tried to catch up with her. I guess I owe my last attempt at a strong finish to her. At twenty-four miles there was a guy dressed in a gorilla suit handing out bananas. Not just slices, but whole bananas. People were actually eating them, thinking it would be a great source of last-minute potassium. There was banana peel all over the road. And just one mile later there was a lineup of the same people throwing up banana pulp. It was the strangest sight, totally insane.

The last two miles of the course is a loop, so even though I could finally see the finish line I had to run past it to complete the loop. That was a real mind tease. When I finally ran across the finish line, I started to cry. Physically I was a mess, and that embarrassed me. I thought I was going to have a stronger finish. I totally underestimated the destruction that a marathon causes on the body and mind. I kept thinking of that famous line from all the bad grade-B war movies, "We take no prisoners." That should be the tag line of marathons. However, as badly as I thought I had done, I finished in 3:40. I was shocked. But I couldn't help thinking that because I walked, I cheated. I know that's ridiculous but that's the way I was programmed. That day I made the decision to do another marathon so I could make up for my wimping out and dedicate myself to running the entire distance. I entered the New York Marathon two years later and finished in 3:35, running the entire race. Only then did I feel entitled to say I ran a marathon.

I've run three marathons so far and consistently do about twenty-five miles a week. The big event didn't change my life, make me more goal oriented or any of the things other first-time marathoners claim. I'm sure they are true, it just didn't do it for me. But there is one thing running does for me: It makes me more creative. My job is based on numbers and facts, with very little gray area for mental creativity. However, the part of my job I love the most is traveling around the country giving speeches to alumni and other clientele. That's where the running really helps. I find that my thought processes are much more creative when I run. I'll think through my speech, what I want to say, organize it in my mind, and as soon as I get back to the office I write it all down. It's about the only time of day when I can clear my head of all the other issues clouding my cerebral membrane and concentrate on my topic.

I made it through my thirties, I'm halfway through my forties, and I am very content with the fact that I am as good an athlete as I will ever be. I don't have to live in the past and replay those Brown games over and over to make me feel like I achieved something. I know I can run a marathon—ironically, something I couldn't do in my younger years. This aging thing isn't so bad after all.

ANY IDIOT CAN RUN A MARATHON

MIKE ROAM
RESIDENCE: BROOKLYN, NEW YORK
OCCUPATION: CHAIRMAN, COMPUTER DEPT.,
SAINT ANN'S SCHOOL, BROOKLYN
FIRST MARATHON: 1974 COLORADO MARATHON
D.O.B.: 8-25-61
AGE AT FIRST MARATHON: 13

Mike Roam ran his first marathon when he was thirteen years old. His dad, who was both inspirator and instigator, was at his side. A year later they run another one together just for the fun of it. Then Mike took a twenty-year hiatus from running. When he picked up again, most of his friends thought he was a novice, but when he told them the story of his first marathon, they were shocked and surprised. Mike credits his father for giving him a gift: a shared adventure and a demonstration of determination and confidence. And recently, Mike was able to return that gift to his father when he took him skydiving.

WHEN I WAS IN THE FIRST GRADE, my dad enlisted in the air force and the lives of my mom, my two brothers, and myself were changed forever. Prior to his enlistment he was a forester and developed a deep sense of pride for his country. He loved the outdoors and wanted to give something back to his country so off he went. My brothers and I spent our time playing kick-the-can and little league football. Dad had been a runner and before he left he used to tell us exciting stories of his high school cross-country days. You could say I grew up listening to his glory days of track tales.

During his air force years we were in transit most of the time, setting up temporary roots in cities and towns all over the country, sometimes moving twice in the same year. I was always smaller than the rest of the kids my age by a good six inches. I was also very shy, an introvert. Maybe that was due to always being the new kid on the block, but for whatever reason, I tended to hang back, be a loner.

While my dad was stationed overseas, he resumed running with his air force buddies. When he returned home we moved to Denver, Colorado, and he took it upon himself to teach us all to run. At first, I followed alongside on my trusty bike while he ran. I can remember thinking he wouldn't be able to keep up with me as I pedaled away, but it was I who couldn't keep up with him. We went around a lake for about two miles and I struggled the entire way. But as much as I appreciated the art of running, I still saw it as boring and tedious. Dad persevered through all my excuses: "Not today, my ankle hurts; not today, I don't feel like it," and soon we were all members of the Rocky Mountain Road Runners Club, my brothers and I becoming among the youngest members. Dad wasn't being a drill sergeant or forcing this on us, he just loved to run and thought it was a wonderful sport, something he wanted to share with us.

My brothers and I wore matching purple and white striped tank tops and called ourselves "Team Roam." Mom ran a little, too, and carried the stopwatch. We must have been quite a sight: three little kids, aged eight through ten, with our purple tops and pencil-thin legs sticking out of red oversize shorts.

Our first race, when I was in fifth grade, was a two-mile handicapper. Every runner was handicapped with the pace of their previous run. Winning was based on improvement instead of actual time. When I was in sixth grade, I had improved enough be in the top three out of one hundred people based on the handicap scoring system. That was very encouraging to me and I sensed a certain amount of prestige. Soon Dad had us out on distance runs and I entered my first ten-miler. Dad never made it perfunctory, he made it fun. He was reading various running books at the time and "fartlek" became a training idea and favorite word. It also didn't hurt that we lived in Denver, which is a perfect running center, surrounded by the mountains. The running trails were absolutely beautiful. We'd head up into the mountains for occasional runs and cross-country skiing. Dad was in his element out there. He was such a free spirit, so unique. I think he would rather have been a poet than a government employee.

Running was becoming more acceptable to me, more of a project with a specific goal. I didn't love running, but I appreciated it. I remember watching a little girl playing in the park one day, just aimlessly jumping, skipping, and running in circles while singing to no one in particular, concerned only with the moment at hand and how to enjoy it. I thought, "Wow, she is having more fun running than I ever do." I felt too old to frolic as she had done without being self-conscious.

In seventh grade I joined the track team, which gave me what I was looking for: a way to continue the challenge and have fun doing it. When I met the other kids on the team I was surprised at how good they were. My world up to then had been filled with adult runners where I was one of the few kids. Now I was with my own peers and they were running six-minute miles, faster than I ever dreamed of going. I was shocked. It was a revelation for me.

I lived about a mile and a half from school at the time and usually took the bus home. But I cooked up a new goal: to see if I could beat the bus home. I dashed out of the building as soon as the last bell sounded and ran as fast as I could, sometimes doing seven-minute miles. I deliberately chose the same route as the school bus and sometimes I did beat it. That's when the improvement started kicking in. I kept running faster and faster to beat the bus. There was definitely a "show-off" factor happening, and I loved it.

In the fall of 1974, Dad decided to run a marathon and I said I'd go along. It was a casual kind of statement, no big deal. We didn't even have to discuss it. I was familiar with the marathon, as one of my favorite books was profiles of Olympic heroes. Stories of Emil Zapotek, Jim Thorpe, Paavo Nurmi, Jim Ryun, and Frank Shorter were among my favorites. We wanted to share the adventure and accomplishment of running a marathon, just like them. It never dawned on us to even consider that we couldn't do it. I had already completed a March of Dimes twenty-mile walkathon, and lengthy hikes with my family and the Boy Scouts.

So that the run wouldn't be just for me, I tried to find sponsors to raise money for Honduran hurricane victims. I was very reluctant to ask publicly, but before I could outright say no, I was walked to the principal's office and handed the mike to the P.A. system and told to make my announcement. I was so nervous that I inadvertently slipped my finger off the activator button halfway though my very shaky and soft-spoken message, so no one really understood what I was saying. However, some people did pledge money, but I was too embarrassed to collect it. Mom came to my rescue and donated the thirty dollars that was pledged.

The marathon was in three months and we made casual preparation for the distance. We didn't do any fancy training techniques, just slowly increased our mileage per week. Within our community, there was no publicity regarding the marathon; in fact most people didn't even real-ize it existed. It was looked upon as a bunch of loonies running through the park. We barely laid the groundwork for the event, with a longest training run of ten miles. I didn't boast of my upcoming contest of will, just thought it was a really cool project I was sharing with my Dad. This time, there was no "show-off" factor.

We didn't do much in the way of pre-day rituals, jitters or antici-pated nervous buildup. I think I remember eating a spaghetti dinner the night before, but that could be just revisionist memories. We arrived at the park, which surrounds Sloane's Lake, one hour early but no one was there, no sign of other runners or the beginnings of a marathon anywhere in sight. It was a little strange, especially since we couldn't even find the starting line. The course was nine loops around the lake. It started to drizzle and we were anxious to start as we knew it was going to take us a long time, longer than most of the runners, to finish. We would finish, but finish "slow and steady." We had water jugs and changes of socks in the car, which we parked right alongside the path. We stretched, did some warm-up loops, and actually had to guess what direction to take since there were no markers. We decided to make the car the starting line, turned to each other, said, "Are you ready? Yeah, are you? Yeah. Well, let's go," and took off. We did the first loops in our sweats but unfortunately the drizzle turned to a downpour and the sweats got saturated.

Our routine settled in, stopping at the car after each loop to stretch, change socks, drink water, and take off again. After the sixth loop we ran out of dry socks. By now we were meeting other members of the marathon, but the only thing I remember about them was that they were running much faster than we were, actually looping past us. Every once in a while we would take a break and lie down in the grass and do bicycle stretches.

My Dad and I passed some of the time by discussing what type of treat we wanted to eat when we finished. This part of the marathon is still very vivid in my memory. My fantasy treat was homemade fried doughnuts, covered in powered sugar. They are very greasy and very sweet, and I could begin to taste them melting in my mouth as I ran. They became my carrot, my incentive to keep going. Dad promised we'd make them as soon as we got home. My family called them "Boy Scout doughnuts," as we'd make them on camping trips. The recipe is kidproof: a tube of Pillsbury dough, the pop-open kind of tube that I would smack on the corner of the counter to open. Then you punch a hole in the middle and pop them into boiling oil, then sprinkle with the powdered sugar. I don't actually remember what my dad's food fantasy was, but I certainly remember the fried donuts. There weren't any deep, heartfelt conversations taking place during the twenty-six miles; we just enjoyed each other's presence and encouragement. Dad was pleasant to be with.

Over the next few hours, we just kept plugging along with no intentions of quitting. We didn't have a time goal in mind, just kept chugging away. It's similar to building a garage or any simple structure. You nail things up, get sweaty, take a break, then resume. When the garage is built, you're done. We knew this task wasn't impossible. As a family, and with the Boy Scouts, we had already done hikes up to fifteen miles. I knew we would finish in our own good time.

There weren't any spectators along the course, but that didn't matter; we had each other. Our sweats were soaked through due to the rain and finally we had to take them off, leaving them in the car. There was usually no sight of other runners either in front of or behind us. We just kept counting our loops, as if we were the only ones in the park that morning.

Finally, we did find the officials, or should I say the one and only official. He was standing at a light post with a stopwatch, which is the only reason we knew he was the race director. There wasn't one balloon or piece of crepe paper in sight to mark the finish line. Maybe that's why he was standing at that particular light post, which indeed turned out to be the finish line. Our time was five hours and forty minutes, as best we could judge. After one more stop at the car, which by now looked like a makeshift gym, and smelled like one also, we headed over to the awards banquet. I'd like to say we walked in, but in actuality we limped in, sorefooted and hamstrung beyond belief. I just remember thinking it was nice to be done and having a big-time sense of accomplishment. Dad and I didn't get sentimental, there were no hugs or strong emotional outpourings, just a cheerful pat on the back. In retrospect, I think Dad would have liked a hug, but I wasn't into that, being only thirteen.

The next summer, 1975, Dad was back in his forestry job and we moved to Montana, right outside Billings. We kept running our regular weekly pace. Again, our longest runs were no more than ten miles. We ran with our dog Heidi, a mix of Saint Bernard and sheltie collie, a medium-size mutt, who was the official pacer. She could keep up a good, steady doggy-trot for eight-minute miles, but when we broke through to a seven-minute pace, she would have to start running. That's how we knew how to pace ourselves. We called it Heidi's pace, instead of a seven-minute mile.

I was now in eighth grade and Dad found us another marathon, the Governor's Cup in Helena. We thought it would be kind of neat to do it again. Twelve miles was our longest training run, and we felt that since we survived the first marathon, how bad could this be!

The Governor's Cup was a much better-organized marathon than we had run the year before. The twenty-five participants loaded into a big yellow school bus and were taken to a campground in the mountains. The course started out with a downhill and we were tempted to go fast but held back. This time we had a goal, to break five hours and thought of it in terms of a really rugged hike.

We were amazed that there were actually mile markers and maybe two water stations along the way. At twenty miles my dad went into someone's yard to stretch and nicked himself on an old barbed-wire fence. He was bleeding and wanted me to go on without him, but I wouldn't leave. We continued running together, although Dad was beginning to wither, due to his leg wound and just the general fatigue and strain of the event. He kept urging me to run ahead, but I wouldn't leave him. I wasn't feeling that much better myself, so both of us needed the companionship to keep going. I was relying on him as much as he was relying on me.

One aspect that was always in our favor during these events is that we were never intimidated by the distance. We knew we could walk twenty-six miles if need be, but it was actually easier to run at a steady pace. We never let the largeness of the marathon overtake us. We kept reducing it to things we could relate to, such as a hike or a walk.

This time, when we crossed the finish line, our family was there to greet us, which again was a new thrill for us. Our official time was four hours and forty minutes, an hour better than our previous marathon.

By the time I finished eighth grade I had completed two marathons. I kept running with the track team, but soon discovered gymnastics and that took over. After high school I attended Princeton University and continued with gymnastics. Once in a while I would feel a renaissance and go out for a run, but didn't continue it on a regular basis. I did ride a unicycle for awhile, which is akin to balancing on top of a basketball. It was my mode of transportation at Princeton for a year or two. Academics was a priority and it was very tough and challenging. I didn't have much free time to concentrate on anything else.

After graduating in 1984, I stayed on campus for another year and played the bass in a jazz quartet. The following year, I started teaching at Saint Ann's (a school for the gifted) in Brooklyn, and saw my first New York City Marathon. I was awestruck by the event and the size of the crowds. I had never in my life experienced such a phenomenon. The eighties decade was experiencing a pandemic outbreak of running and New York was celebrating the event in style, taking the marathon through the five boroughs and capturing the enthusiasm and hearts of all New Yorkers. It was a celebration of the entire city. As I watched it go by, I thought of my marathons and felt great empathy for all the runners. It was very emotional for me, sweet and exciting.

After three years of watching the marathon pass me by, combined with a latent tendency to become lazy and lethargic, I decided to run it and started training, finally getting up to Heidi's pace, seven-minute miles. I used the New York Road Runners Club training guide and posted a grid in my room to chart my miles. This time, I did about three twenty-milers. I trained with some friends and while we were on some long runs, they kept telling me how good I was for a novice. When I told them I had already run two marathons with very little preparation when I was a young boy, they were shocked. I told them we hadn't known any better and we persevered through the pain. If I could run a marathon at thirteen with only one long-distance run for preparation, then anyone could.

Even though my dad was now in his fifties, he was in better shape than I, as he always kept up with his running. I kept him updated on my training and our conversation brought back the memories of our marathons together. We could remember yearning for Boy Scout doughnuts and the finish line.

My first impression of the New York Marathon was the absolute canyon of spectators that form a wall for the entire twenty-six miles. That was a huge difference. The twenty-five-thousand participants was also a difference, actually intimidating and creepy, especially at the start. I felt as if I was in the middle of a cattle stampede and didn't want to lose my friends before the race began. We held on to each others' T-shirts in a line like a caterpillar getting to the start. I finished in 3:20, due to a more rigorous training, and I was quite pleased.

There is a sense of relief and joy after completing a marathon, combined with a sense of power and accomplishment. However, it takes tons of enthusiasm to keep the commitment going during the long months of training.

I would bet that most extreme sports fall into that same pattern because I found similar traits with my new sport, skydiving. You don't do it if you don't want to. No one can force you to participate in these exceptional sports. I did my first jump eight years ago on my birthday and loved it. Now I own my own parachute and jump every couple of weeks. I guess it's in my blood, growing up with a father in the air force. My brothers and I played the typical war and soldier games as kids, fantasizing about jumping out of planes. I distinctly remember as if it were yesterday, making handkerchief parachutes for our G.I. Joe toys.

There are many memories I cherish of my marathons with my dad. There was definitely a bond of togetherness that will never be forgotten. We accomplished something together, a challenge, an adventure that left us with great memories. This past spring I visited Dad in Florida and we did a skydive together. We jumped about five seconds apart and flew our canopies near each other. It was his first jump in twenty-seven years and it was spectacular. I guess we still enjoy sharing special moments in our lives together.

REBEL WITH A CAUSE

BILL RODGERS
RESIDENCE: SHERBORN, MASSACHUSETTS
OCCUPATION: ATHLETE
FIRST MARATHON: 1973 BOSTON MARATHON
D.O.B.: 12-31-47
AGE AT FIRST MARATHON: 25

It is easy to understand how Bill Rodgers captured America's heart and was a major force in causing the running boom of the late seventies. He greets you with a big smile, is friendly and warm. The press and media loved him. He was the golden boy of American running. Pictures of elite runners and other celebrities now crowd the wall of his office, along with medals, trophies, and race numbers placed haphazardly. The pair of shoes he wore for his first Boston win is there. They hold a special place in Bill's memory—not just for the win, but because they were owned by Steve Prefontaine, who sent them to him to wear for that race. Rodgers has been called a rebel, an angry young man, and an agitator for being a proponent of awarding prize money to runners without losing their amateur status. He is a four-time winner of both the Boston and New York City Marathons. Rodgers is now retired from the marathon, though not from shorter races. His weekly training is not the two hundred miles it was back in the seventies, but it is still enough to keep him race-fit and able to keep up with his two young daughters.

I WAS BORN IN HARTFORD, CONNECTICUT, but by age seven we had moved to nearby Newington. My brother, Charlie, our friend, Jason, and I were inseparable. We were very active kids, always hiking, always getting into something, always together. In high school, the three of us ran cross country on a small team, consisting of us and three other kids. The coach was a great motivator. He didn't overwork us or destroy our love for running, just enhanced it. I do think there are lots of kids out there who have the potential to be great runners if only they have the right coach, someone who shows an interest and cares. I loved cross country right from the start. I loved the open territory and going the distance. I wasn't too good at track, couldn't get that initial kick required for short distance. I received feedback about my so-called talent back in high school. I was in the local paper quite a bit and my name would be announced on the P.A. system at school, along with the football players, announcing my wins at the meets.

At Wesleyan University in Connecticut, I continued running cross country. The coach wasn't a crack-the-whip type and I enjoyed the camaraderie of the other runners. Maybe if I had a hard-nosed coach I would have run faster, but I enjoyed what I was doing and that was more important to me. I only ran during the season and never in the summer. In my junior year I slipped a bit even during the season and my roommate, Amby Burfoot, would return to our room after a weekend to find beer cans and cigarette butts scattered around. He was a more serious runner than I was, more committed to the sport. One Sunday morning, he took me out for a twenty-five-mile run, to punish me, I think. I kept up until the last few miles when he decided to pick up the pace and left me behind. Amby had been coached by John J. Kelley at Fitch High School in Groton, Connecticut, and one weekend he came up to visit and we all went for a run. John was fortyish at the time and I thought to myself, "This guy can run pretty well for an old man." Amby learned a lot from the older runners and he'd pass the information on to me. I was a firm believer in the L.S.D. method— long, slow distance, which was introduced by Emil Zapotek. I was never interested in the marathon back in college, but Amby was. He dreamed about it. He trained hard for it and won Boston in his senior year, 1968. I had never even seen the Boston Marathon so I wasn't caught up in its mysticism. And I hate to train in the heat, which is all summer, and I hate to train in the cold, which is all winter. Road racing is a tough sport and I wasn't committed to it, hadn't been caught by its lure. Training for a ten-miler was the most I wanted to do. I thought I'd die if I had to train for a marathon.

After college I stopped running and the occasional cigarette grew into a habit. There was no postcollegiate outlet for runners so there was no reason to continue. The Vietnam War was looming over our heads; I was a college graduate with barely passing grades, no job, and no real future. I applied for a Conscientious Objector status with the draft board based on my Roman Catholic beliefs and was granted one along with my brother and Jason. We still did everything together. Having a C.O. kept us out of the draft but it also limited our job opportunities, as we could only apply at nonprofit organizations. Jason and I got job at Peter Bent Brigham Hospital in Boston. My skills were put to use taking deceased bodies to the morgue. It didn't pay well and wasn't that motivating, but at least I was employed. I borrowed money to buy a motorcycle, let my hair grow long, and, basically, let life go by.

I have to say, I probably became a marathoner because I had nothing else in my life. I got fired from my job for trying to organize the non-union employees; my motorcycle was stolen so I had no form of transportation other than running everywhere; I had no money and no immediate positive outlook on life in general. The one positive thing I did was quit smoking. I wheeled too many cancer victims to the morgue.

Jason and I shared an apartment by Symphony Hall in Boston and one day in April 1971, we watched the Boston Marathon for the first time. Huge crowds were everywhere. I was amazed at the spectacle of the event. And then to my amazement and shock, I saw my former cross-country teammates crossing the finish line. I saw Jeff Galloway, my teammate from Wesleyan, and John Vitale, whom I ran against at the University of Connecticut. I thought, "Wait a minute, if they can do it, so can I."

I still had mixed feelings about running a marathon, but heck, it had to be better than doing nothing and I knew I was just as good a runner as the guys I saw. First, I needed to get back in shape, so I joined a YMCA by our apartment and started running this slanted, tiny track that was boring as hell, but I hadn't run in two years and needed to start somewhere. I went back to running because it was all I knew, all I had left. I went back to running to bring a sense of order to my life. When I got my endurance back, I started hitting some of the local road races and did well at the 5Ks and 10Ks. In February of 1973 I entered a 30K and ran in blue jeans. I didn't have any money to buy the proper shoes or clothing, and besides, it was cold. Ironically, Amby also ran that race and ultimately won it. The prize was a pair of car tires, which he had no use for so he offered them to me, but I didn't even have a car.

I felt like I was on an upswing. It was time to start making big plans and I really thought I was ready for a marathon. Frank Shorter had won the gold in the '72 Olympics and that was a huge influence on me. I started running twice a day, averaging about 130 miles a week and concentrating on endurance. I ate more because I was also hungry. I'm not a good breakfast eater, but I make up for it the rest of the day. I didn't do fast intervals like Salazar; I mainly concentrated on distance. My maximum mileage was two hundred a week, split between sixteen miles in the morning and thirteen miles in the afternoon, around Jamaica Plains pond. I could never repeat that now, but at the time I was striving for distance endurance.

By now I had made it public that I was running Boston in 1973. Amby gave me some advice, but I don't remember what it was. I do remember it was a very hot day and I never felt strong from the very start. Everyone started passing me and finally I dropped out at twenty-one miles at the top of Heartbreak Hill. I couldn't even go another five miles. I had no interest in finishing. My only thought was how to get home. As I look back to that day, I can't believe how I miscalculated the field, thinking I would place among the top five. I had no idea just how talented the runners were. I was demoralized. I had always been a winner and now I was humiliated.

The following week, as I analyzed my failed attempt, I decided that the weather had played a major factor in my poor performance because I never trained in the heat. Determined to make a strong comeback, my wife and I made the decision to move to California so I could train in a hot climate. She quit her job, and since I didn't have one, we packed what small belongings we had and drove cross country to sunny, and hot, California. That trip turned out to be a total fiasco. We stayed five days, turned around, and drove back East. I was too overwhelmed by all the cars, the people, and, yes, the weather, plus we had no money, no place to stay, no contacts, and I guess you could say it was not a well-planned itinerary.

Back in Boston, we lived on food stamps for about six months until I finally landed a job teaching behavior modification to disabled adults, and also started a graduate degree at Boston College. The running boom was beginning to explode and 1974 was a very exciting time for us. I was training hard, but something was missing. Having always been part of a team, I missed the camaraderie and support of team-mates. The Greater Boston Track Club had just formed and I became one of its first members. We were a formidable group, winning most of the titles in the area. I loved being part of a team again. We were like the Kenyans of today, practicing the concept and dynamics of team strength. Athletes motivate each other and it's a wonderful environment to be a part of. Billy Squires came on board as our coach, which was a great asset. I decided to give the Boston Marathon another try in 1974 and placed a respectable fourteenth. I held fourth position for twenty miles and then just dropped back, finishing at 2:19:34. I wanted that win badly, but my training just wasn't good enough. The top pack at Boston then usually included the same names, give or take a few newcomers: Galloway, Fleming, Vitale, Kelley, Drayton, and me. We were all very competitive, we all wanted to win. Fleming was the most serious. He never shared his training tips with us. Neither did Shorter. They kept to themselves when it came down to winning, but at the same time we were all the best of friends. Heck, we saw each other all the time at other races or training runs. We kidded each other about our wins and losses but it was never malicious. In the '77 Boston Marathon I shared my water with Drayton, who didn't have any and there were no water stations in sight. It was a very hot day and once again the heat did me in, but Drayton went on to win.

I did have a few rivals who weren't so friendly and at one road race when I lost to one of them, he won a bouquet of flowers, which he then proceeded to give to my wife, saying, "Give these to Billy. He could use them."

By 1975 I was determined to win Boston. After two failed attempts, I needed a win. Once again, the press dismissed my chances of winning. They never took me seriously, but then again, I didn't take myself seriously. I wasn't consistent, didn't have a great marathon record. What they underestimated was my desire and my recent wins. In November of '74 I won the Philadelphia Marathon and had just returned from the World Cross Country Championships in Morocco, performing exceptionally well, winning a bronze medal. My teammates knew I was poised to win Boston, but the press hadn't covered the World Championships and quite frankly, they didn't know much about the sport.

When you want to win Boston, it's not just a matter of your own training, being in the best possible shape. You had to know your com-

petition, how they ran, how they felt, how they breathed, and you had
to pray to Mother Nature for the perfect day. A tailwind or headwind
could make or break a winner. And if the field is particularly strong, the
competition can be decimating. The weather on the morning of April
19, 1975, was perfect: not too hot, not too cold, the type of morning
you pray for. I looked up into the heavens and said a soft, "Thank you,
God."

Wearing a white T-shirt with GBTC hand-painted on front in big,
bold letters and a pair of white gardening gloves for the morning chill, I
was ready. Tom Fleming gave me a headband to hold my hair out of my
eyes. I really was a rogue runner. For the first part of the race, I listened
to my competitors' breathing, trying to determine if they started out
too soon, if they were tiring or if they were saving it for a powerful
surge at the end. I talked to them, reasoning if they still had enough
breath to speak, they could still kick at the end. All of this was very
important to me because I planned to go like a bat out of hell and never
stop or look back. I did stop once to tie my shoe but only after I knew I
was far out in front with no one on my heels. There were no water stations at Boston so I relied on my brother and Jason for my fluids.
Everything worked in my favor that year and I set a Boston and an
American record of 2:09:55. I went from running a 2:19 to a 2:09. I
couldn't believe it myself, it was such a phenomenal breakthrough.

Fame came my way, but not money. I was still broke. In 1976, Fred
Lebow invited me to run his New York City Marathon. Fred was always
the promoter and thought it would be a big story having me and Frank
Shorter run the race, competing for a win, plus the fact it was the first
year his marathon was moving out of the boundaries of Central Park
and through New York City. He couldn't promise me any money but I
went anyway, traveling the back roads as I couldn't pay tolls on the
turnpike. Everyone thought Frank, the Olympian, would place first,
but I beat him for my first New York win. I didn't even know the route
as it wound its way around the city. I do remember running on the East
River Drive Promenade, passing guys fishing or just plain drunk, not
even realizing we were running a marathon. It was insane, but I loved
it. The crowds were great in New York, and I fed off their energy. I like
running for the crowds, hearing them call my name, cheering for me.
After that race, I went back to my car, which was parked on the street,
and it had been towed. Fred had to take up a collection so I could get it

back and drive home.

After my marathon successes, Nike and New Balance offered me five hundred dollars to endorse their athletic line. I thought it sounded low, so while I was thinking about it I flew to Japan for the Fukuoka Marathon and was offered three thousand dollars by Tiger/Asics for a one-year contract. I thought I was rich, had finally hit the jackpot. Things were beginning to look good.

In 1978 I was ready for another victory at Boston and trained harder than ever. I didn't want to be a one-time winner and also had my sights set on the 1980 Olympics. It was a tough field that year and I knew I had to concentrate, run hard, and not look back. I held the lead for most of the race and just when I thought I was in the clear, a motorcycle cop came alongside me and alerted me that someone was fast on my heels. I panicked, it was like a bad dream. I had been running hard and didn't have a lot of push left. I surged forward with all I could muster and won by two seconds. It was very nerve racking. The internal pressure to win was incredible. Once you taste a win, you want it again and again. If you don't win, it is very disappointing.

I won Boston again in '79 and '80. I ran to be the best and back in the seventies we were the best. Representing the United States at the Olympics and World Cross Country Championships was a highlight in my life. It was a feeling of patriotism that is missing today, as sports have become diluted with commercialism and million-dollar contracts. We didn't have that; we ran for the glory of our country. I was very proud to be a member of the U.S. team wherever I competed.

Nowadays I only run in one gear. I can't shift into surges or kicks. I think of myself as a dependable car: one steady gear and accident free. And I don't believe mile markers anymore; ten miles seems more like fifteen. In my past life as a marathoner I could never get to the start line injury-free. Now I know better. I take care of the little injuries before they turn into big ones. And once a week I get a deep muscle massage. I still love going to races and being a spokesman for the sport. It brings me in contact with lots of great people and some very interesting situations. I was invited to the state of Washington to officiate a race and was asked to hand out the prizes. Great! I love to do that. However, what the officials didn't tell me was that the prizes were fresh-caught salmon and the winners received their weight in salmon. A huge scale was at the finish and as the winners weighed in, I had to load the other half of the scale with the salmon. All morning long I pulled huge salmon out of a box of chipped ice and threw the fish on the scale. That was quite an event.

These days, I usually win my age group in the half-marathon. Sometimes I do miss the marathon, especially when I attend the big expositions such as in New York or Boston. When people tell me they are thinking of running a marathon, I tell them to go for it. I give two pieces of advice: Go to a race and watch the crowd. You can learn a lot from just being an observer. Also, when you commit to a race, check out the last two miles of the course. You'll want to know what it looks like, if there are hills, or curves, or if it's a straightaway to the finish. Look for potholes, anything that could get in your way. The last two miles is not the time to be thinking about the course.

Anyone who runs a marathon is on a mission, whether it is to win or to finish. It's a hard race and I respect anyone who runs it. It is a neat achievement, very satisfying. The medal, the T-shirt, the trophy will stay with you always. Every runner is an athlete. It's a great thrill, a way to turn your life around. Use it to achieve something positive in your life, like quitting smoking. Whatever it takes, it is worth it. It will be with you the rest of your life.

ME AND THE MARATHON

ERICH SEGAL
RESIDENCE: LONDON, ENGLAND
OCCUPATION: AUTHOR;
ADJUNCT PROFESSOR OF CLASSICS, YALE UNIVERSITY
FIRST MARATHON: 1955 BOSTON MARATHON
DATE OF BIRTH: 6-16-1937
AGE AT FIRST MARATHON: 18

Erich Segal is best known as the author of numerous books including Love Story, *the famous one published in 1971 that later became a movie. He also wrote musicals, the Beatles' film* Yellow Submarine, *and has a Presidential Commendation for his work with the Peace Corps. Erich has been a visiting professor at institutions of higher learning throughout the world. Segal is also a big sports fan, covering the Olympic Games as a commentator in '72, '76, and 80. What most people don't know about Erich Segal is his passion for running the marathon. It is his favorite topic. The Boston Athletic Association reserved his Boston Marathon number, 99, for him for years. He also won a 33-mile handicap race, his first ultramarathon effort.*

FROM EARLIEST CHILDHOOD, I KNEW what I wanted to be when I grew up: an athlete. But my first dozen years did not reveal any evidence that this goal could be achieved. I was too short for basketball, too scrawny for football. And I cannot recall any swimming pools in my area of

Brooklyn.

Thus it seemed I was destined to grow up a failure. Then fate took a hand (or should it be a foot?). When I was fifteen, I injured my leg in a canoe accident and was told by the physiotherapist to speed my rehabilitation by walking and gradually trying to jog a little.

So I tried it. First a bit, then a bit more, then a lot more. It took a bookworm like myself into the outdoors and got some (relatively) fresh air into my lungs. Sometimes I even got a "high" after a long effort.

Gradually, an increase of energy in my body began to lift my mood in general. But I had no idea that the specific talent (if that's what it was) of being able to run endlessly without tiring could be put to any sporting use.

But when I was a freshman at Harvard, I first heard the magic words "Boston Marathon." This twenty-six-mile footrace *cum* carnival that was at the time (the midfifties) all but unique on the American scene.

For the local New England ephebes, this Patriots' Day holiday was a kind of rite of passage; merely finishing the course, however slowly, was regarded as an initiation to manhood.

Meanwhile, as we mortals were cruising and fraternizing in the back of the pack, far ahead of us at the front there was a completely different activity taking place: what always turned out to be an annual race between Johnny Kelley and Everybody in the World. (How I admired that brave bridesmaid who—to Boston's great joy—actually took the whole bouquet once: when he won in 1957.)

I started to "prepare" about six months ahead. At the time, I had no idea how to train, so I just ran for about an hour, five days a week, along the Charles River or through the streets of Boston. In those days a man jogging through the city in his "underwear" was the object of drivers' ridicule and a potential snack for angry dogs.

Finally, at 10 A.M on April 19, 1955, I presented myself to the officials at the noisy Hopkinton High School gymnasium, got my three-digit number, and then lined up for the prerace physical.

It seemed that every year these skillful doctors would reject not only the obvious misfits, but also one or two stars, suddenly discovering they had "heart problems" that disqualified them from participating in the Great Run. As if to refute the judgment of medical experts, one of the *refusals,* Ted Corbitt, went on to become America's greatest ultramarathoner, to whom the fifty-two miles of the London-to-Brighton

Race was a mere warm-up.

Anyway, although my own heart was beating a mile a minute, I passed, and soon found myself shivering at the starting line with a few hundred other runners, half of whom I already knew from the shorter races that led up to the Patriot's Day extravaganza. The camaraderie was wonderful.

Never having played a team sport—or any sport for that matter—this kind of fraternity (no girls back then) was a new and welcome experience for me. As we began to pass the first sparse cluster of spectators waving American flags and clapping, I was thrilled to be cheered by name. "Who could possibly know me way out here in rural Hopkinton?" I wondered. Then a runner next to me explained that the *Boston Globe* had published the names and numbers of all the competitors.

The first hour was bracing; a continuous exchange of salutations with the spectators, many of whom would offer you a slice of orange to nourish you along the way. This euphoric phase culminated at the halfway mark, where the pretty young ladies of Wellesley College emitted frenzied shrieks at the sight of HARVARD on my shirt. Suddenly, I felt important, heroic, studly. Not long after, all I felt was tired.

Then came the hills. When I had driven over them they seemed like gentle slopes. Now they were dauntingly alpine. My legs were hurting with the kind of pain I have never felt before or since. My thighs were on fire. I began to ask myself some very existential questions, like what the hell was I doing there? There were no rational answers.

When I finally reached the dreaded Heartbreak Hill it was like Mount Everest. I could not muster the strength to run up it—*I walked* (The Shame!). The worst of it all was that I was inflicting this agony on myself. It was definitely a masochist's delight.

Mercifully, the course after Heartbreak was—like my mood—all downhill. Somehow as it declined into Cleveland Circle I began to plod again and entered the city of Boston semicomatose, but determined to reach the finish at Exeter Street. The last mile seemed endless. The one indelible memory: In Kenmore Square stood the baseball immortal Ted Williams (the race was run in between the games of a Red Sox double header). He was clapping with admiration for all who passed. A friend of mine actually heard him say, "Now *those* guys are real athletes."

Now, I had known that if I ever succeeded in achieving this feat no one would believe me, so I had a classmate, one Larry Ambush, wait at the finish line with his camera to record my achievement for posterity. At long last, I stumbled across the line on two wooden legs and was unable to walk for a week.

This caused a bit of a problem back in school as I was playing King Creon in the Greek club's production of *Oedipus at Colonus* and I was supposed to storm angrily on stage, leading my soldiers and assert my authority. But I was rigid and could scarcely move my legs to shuffle. And so the director had to change the staging and have my troops carry me in. I am sure many of the scholars present that day thought it was a new artistic interpretation.

I ran my first Boston in 3:40, which made me seventy-ninth. (Those were the days!) I had originally thought that if I actually finished the entire marathon it would be the peak of my "career," and I could retire a winner. After all, had I not achieved something athletic? And I'd have the photo to prove it.

Except that Larry Ambush's picture did not come out! It showed nothing but an unrecognizable blur. Now I would have to do it again and find a better photographer.

By the next year I was hooked. I now set myself a genuinely impressive target: to break three hours for the distance. Which I finally did in 1960.

In all, I ran twenty consecutive Bostons and became such a regular that Will Clooney, the race director, reserved the number 99 for me every year. My best performance was almost a full hour faster than the first. Most of the others hovered on either side of the three-hour mark —the most frustrating: 3:00:19!

In the twentieth year I had a bout of pneumonia a month prior to the race and was strictly forbidden by my own doctor to run. I disobeyed. I felt by then that my feet knew every step of the way and would do it for me. And they did.

The serious training I did in those years changed my life forevermore. It is one thing to be scrawny, but it is another to be scrawny and *fit*. The strength I acquired through long, hard running energized my entire life, mentally as well as physically.

I would often come back from a run with the idea for a plot of a story or the words of a song, which would come to me as if the mind had been refreshed with more oxygen and inspiration lubricated by the perspiration from my efforts.

No day—no matter how stressful—ever ended on a sour note. A ten-mile run beats Prozac anytime.

During my less-than-brilliant career, I ran another twenty marathons in places as distant as Belgium and England. And wherever I went the feeling of mutual support and camaraderie made instant friendships.

I also picked up some tips along the way, one of which is worth passing on. Every marathon runner has a favorite song to which he sings in his head to keep the cadence of his stride. My most effective tune was "Hello Dolly," which underscored literally thousands of miles. Try it—it'll take you a long way. That is all the wisdom I have to impart on this matter.

Oh yes, for the record, I do deserve a tiny footnote in the history books—for having been Frank Shorter's teacher at Yale. I would like to take this opportunity to report a hitherto unknown incident.

One afternoon I was chugging around the college track, timing myself for a ten-miler. Frank watched me reel off lap after lap and could not keep from remarking to his teammates, loud enough for me to hear, "A guy would have to be *crazy* to run a marathon."

A few years later, I reminded him of this when he won the gold medal at the Olympics in 1972 and I was interviewing him for ABC-TV.

Frank smiled. It didn't seem crazy then.

Alas, an unexpected injury—unrelated to running—spoiled my intention to keep running until I was at least a hundred.

I miss it.

Some people dream of becoming president, winning the Nobel Prize, or flying to the moon. My own fantasy is to be running once again in my short pants through the streets of Boston being cheered by that knowing, loving crowd.

So listen, the next time you are due for a workout and it is raining, windy, and freezing, and you are thinking of putting it off, count yourself lucky.

Get out there and enjoy the best feeling life can give.

BEETHOVEN'S TWENTY-SIXTH

MATTHEW SHAFNER
RESIDENCE: GROTON, CT
OCCUPATION: LAWYER
FIRST MARATHON: 1980 EAST LYME MARATHON
D.O.B.: 2-23-35
AGE AT FIRST MARATHON: 45

After putting in long hours all week at his law firm, Matt looks forward to his weekend runs with friends, catching up on current events. A frequent face at local road races, the few times he doesn't compete he and his wife Denise go anyway to cheer their friends, take snap shots along the way and stage a two-person greeting party at the finish. Getting a running start late in the game and despite a childhood recurring case of severe asthma, he is proud to distinguish himself as "one of those weirdos who run all the time." Matt quotes the classics, hums a few bars of classical music and theorizes about life in general. He's the real thing: a gentleman, a scholar and a runner.

MY ATHLETIC BACKGROUND HAS A SHORT beginning and an even shorter ending. In 1949, a freshman at Bulkeley School in New London, I looked upon running as boring and viewed the track guys as somewhat weird. They tended to keep to themselves and their idea of a good time was to run up and down the coast all day long. However, I was desperate to be one of the high school athletes, so without much thought, I decided to be a high jumper. The first day of practice, the track coach told us to warm up with a run. We lined up and he said, "Okay, every-body follow Kelley." Johnny Kelley was a senior and already racking up awards for his running abilities. By the time I made it to the first block, Kelley was two blocks ahead. By the time I made it two blocks, he was out of sight. That was it for me. I quit, turned around, and went home.

Moving ahead twelve years, with no athletic endeavors since my failed run at Bulkeley, I made the decision to quit smoking, a bad habit that followed me around since high school. I was able to quit cold turkey, but in the process put on forty pounds. So once again I tried my feet at running to try and drop those extended love handles, and once again failed. I remember getting up early all set to run, putting on my old college sweatshirt, and just not having the drive or desire. I was lonely, it was cold and dark, and the only companions I had were the neighborhood dogs, who kept barking at me. My attempted routine lasted for about a week.

Move ahead another ten years or so and now I'm in my thirties, sin-gle but looking, working hard, and I meet Denise. She and a group of faculty from Connecticut College would run together and after watch-ing them from afar, I made the big move and joined them one day to socialize and impress Denise. I didn't make such a great impression, as one lap around the Coast Guard Academy track and I was wheezing so hard I had to stop. But I still wanted to impress Denise so I kept at it and after about a week I could finish one mile.

In 1970, I finally caught up with Denise and we were married. Ten years later, we ran our first race together, a fun run with thirty or forty runners. I loved the thrill of the race; it brought running to a new dimension for me.

One Friday night while we were doing a Groton Long Point loop, my buddy Bernard suggested we do the Rose Arts 10.5-mile race up in Norwich, which was the following day. At first I said "No way," but Saturday morning I was in the car with Bernard heading up to Norwich. We ran the race but it was a terrible experience. I only did it because Bernard and some of my other friends said it would be fun! Well, it wasn't. Afterward, I was hurting badly and couldn't walk. I was in my forties but felt like an old man. But on the positive side, my asthma was keeping itself at bay; I didn't experience any breathing or wheezing problems.

Later that summer we heard rumors that a new marathon course was being formed nearby in East Lyme. In my circle of running buddies, no one had considered it. But here was a new one being created in our own backyard so naturally we got interested. The local YMCA sponsored a program in support of the marathon. They offered body-fat testing, conducted lectures by Amby Burfoot of *Runner's World* and Dr. Ken Kirstein, and handed out information about the race and how to train for it. I remember some of their tips were about not changing your socks or your shoes or even your favorite shirt right before the race because the least little change may seem harmless at first, but multiplied by twenty-six miles could cause some physical injury. I thought the whole idea was ridiculous but Bernard wanted to do it so I agreed to train with him. In August we started training for the September marathon and the first day of our routine he tore his Achilles tendon. That was the end for him. But for some reason I kept going, kept training. I figured, "What the heck, if I can run ten miles I can run twenty-six." So I did a twelve-mile race and that wasn't too bad either. I began to believe that maybe now, after all these years, I really was an athlete. As a kid, my dream was to play for the New York Knickerbockers basketball team. I went to visit my brother at Columbia University and he took me to a Knicks game at the old Madison Square Garden. I sat there mesmerized and fantasized about playing on the team. But destiny has a strange way of dealing out athletic skills. I was only 5'3" during my high school years and couldn't even qualify for the junior varsity basketball team. No matter how much I loved the game, I would never play on a team. I was tormented with this unfulfilled passion, this drive to be an athlete, but had no outlet in sight. But now I was a runner. I felt such a sense of power. I had real stamina, my asthma seemed to disappear, and I felt invincible.

The race was big news for us local runners and training groups sprouted up everywhere. I had a morning group that allowed me to get in some basic miles before work, and weekend groups where we concentrated on distance. We took our training very seriously and wanted to be prepared for our debut marathon. My longest run was twenty miles. The day of the race dawned bright and beautiful. Three hundred of us showed up for the first official East Lyme Marathon. I was nervous and excited at the same time. Someone suggested rubbing Vaseline between parts of the body to prevent chafing so I rubbed it in my armpits, between my toes, everywhere I could think of to avoid chafing or blis-

tering. I was one squishy mess. Planning my run, I set a goal to finish in
three and a half hours. I didn't use any scientific formula or measure, I
just thought I could do it. I started out strong and felt great. As usual, I
socialized with whomever passed me or, more accurately, left me in the
dust. I was conscious of drinking water at all the stops, but that just
meant making bathroom stops. Right around the sixteen-mile marker,
coming out of Rocky Neck State Park, I started to get tired. Then to
make matters worse, the course started to go uphill. Just when I was
about out of breath, the course rounded a bend into Black Point and I
came upon the house of my good friend Harry. He knew I was running
that day and there he was, standing on his front porch that overlooks
the reeded tidal marsh with a glass of cold water stretched out to greet
me. It was so refreshing, and so like Harry to be there for me. I needed
that lift, not only the physical refreshment of the cold water but the
acknowledgment from an old high school friend that I was running my
heart out. He added new life to my dwindling stride.

Farther down the course, I thought I'd die going through Black
Point. I had reached total fatigue and for the first time the idea of quitting actually seemed feasible. My legs had become giant oak trees, inca-
pable of moving on their own. They felt thick, stiff, a burden to me. I
literally had to drag them along by sheer willpower. By twenty miles,
almost everyone had passed me by and there was no one to talk to, no
one to help distract me and get through the last six miles. So I started
singing. I thought Beethoven's Ninth was an appropriate melody and
did that for a while. Then I started to make up jokes about running. I
can't remember them now, but they had to be pretty bad because even I
couldn't laugh at them. I was desperate for distraction. During the last
four miles I passed a woman familiar to me who'd just had a baby and
that made me feel better. I don't want that to sound mean, but at least
I knew I wouldn't be last! Then a friend passed me on his bike. He was
out there cheering the stragglers such as myself. By this time, I couldn't
even run, or walk, in a straight line. I was weaving from side to side, my
gait resembling a very drunken stagger. The last four miles of the
course is a straightaway on a busy road and my friend cautioned me to
stop zigzagging or risk getting hit by a car. I remember my response
being something along the lines that at this point, being hit by a car
would be the best thing that could happen to me.

The last half mile, I staggered toward the finish line, a half lap around the East Lyme High School track. There was no way I was going to enter the track looking like I felt, which was half dead. Everyone sprints the track, no matter how exhausted or wrecked they feel.

I don't know where the energy came from, whether it was pure adrenaline or the last burning embers of the passionate fire that fueled the soul four hours ago, but I sprinted onto that track, past the two people left in the stands, and received my medal, yelling "Free at Last!"

After I showered and cleaned up, a reception was being staged at the Travelodge sponsored by the folks who put on the race. I remember entering the room and seeing some of the running legends who came to christen this new marathon and feeling, "Wow, I am now one of them. I ran a marathon. I am finally an athlete." It didn't matter that I almost came in last and others finished hours before me, we were all one in that room. A bond was formed that continues today. I went home to a party Denise had put together, complete with a Carvel ice cream cake that I dug into with careless abandon. I told my friends I would never, ever do this again. For days I couldn't walk, was totally fatigued. I remember having to appear in court for a case I was working on and I tried to sit the entire time. But at some point the judge asked me to approach the bench. I slowly pulled myself out of the chair and ever-so-painfully hobbled up to the judge. He watched me with some curiosity and said, "Is something wrong Mr. Shafner?" I explained that I had just run a marathon and my legs weren't working so well. He rebuked me with, "Well, don't think you'll get any sympathy from this court."

About a week after the race I began to analyze my performance and played the event over and over in my mind. How could I improve my time? How could I develop more stamina? Perhaps if I ate more pasta and trained with more long runs I could do better. Before I was even conscious of it, my subconscious was already preparing for the next marathon.

I've since run eight marathons and continue my Friday-night loops with my friends. But I have noticed recently that my asthma is coming back. In fact I blacked out after my last marathon, so I don't know what's in store for me. I can't imagine a life without running. It has had such a positive impact on me. On a physical level, I feel I can do anything I set my mind to, that I have the endurance to accomplish the task. Also, I have a great respect for what the body can accomplish when trained and maintained, so I practice a reasonably healthy diet and exercise regimen. Finally, the discipline it took to train has entered all facets of my life. I am more focused, get more done during the day. It's all about setting goals; I view life as a series of training events building up to the big race and final finish line and I am always in training, always in the process of reaching the final goal.

On a good day, it all blends. I feel a part of a private universe where everything comes together and feels great. I once wrote down what running means to me, why I do it. I am not sure that I can describe what has been called the "runner's high" but like poetry and beauty, I know it when I experience it. When it does set in, usually around three or four miles, my body flows into a smooth rhythm and my mind is no longer conscious of how far or how long I've run or how much farther to go. The mind is not aware of the physical activity taking place, the miles logged. The feet seem to barely touch the ground. My entire being seems to be one with the environment—a form of unity and total harmony takes over. Sometimes fragments of poetry come to me, a mantra for better or verse, you might say. One recurring line is from Kipling's "If." It begins, "If you can fill the unforgiving minute/With sixty seconds' worth of distance run. . . ."

Running has filled many unforgiving minutes for me. And of course there is Housman's "To an Athlete Dying Young," full of memorable lines for runners. At some point, we'll all become "Townsmen of a stiller town . . . and silence sounds no worse than cheers, after earth has stopped the ears." I wonder, was Housman a runner himself?

I didn't have running heroes growing up, so perhaps I looked to the classics for my heroes. Literature abounds with famous trackmen. Perhaps it's because they get a closer look at the world that surrounds them every day. One of the things I love about the East Lyme Marathon is the natural beauty of the course. I've seen herons and egrets nesting on the ponds. And the golden reeds of the tidal marshes always seem to catch the sun's rays as I'm passing, a rare sight that stimulates all my senses. The orchards are just getting ready to burst with ripe red apples. For a few moments I can forget about the pain and breathe in the serene surroundings.

Through running I experience my own epiphany, a manifestation of the essential nature of who I am, the man I want to be.

THE MOTHER OF ALL MARATHONS

LARRY SMITH
RESIDENCE: MANHATTAN, NEW YORK
OCCUPATION: MANAGEMENT CONSULTANT
FIRST MARATHON: 1978 ATHENS MARATHON, GREECE
D.O.B.: 3-20-38
AGE AT FIRST MARATHON: 50

Given the hundreds of possible marathon courses to choose from for the all-important first one, the Marathon to Athens course, which commemorates the legendary run of a foot soldier named Philippides in the Persian War against Greece back in 490 b.c., has got to rank right at the top. During his tenure as an international banker for Citibank, Larry Smith was able to make this dream a reality. It is a run he will never forget, and he still treasures the now-withered laurel wreath presented to him by a young Athenian girl during the race as a memento of his day in the land of the gods.

I GREW UP IN WHAT WOULD NOW BE CALLED inner-city Washington, D.C., five blocks from the Capitol Building. My two brothers and I thought the rectangular shape of the side lawn was just perfect for playing touch football. All our neighborhood friends played the typical playground sports like baseball and basketball in our asphalt-surfaced school yard. Basketball was my favorite; indeed, my passion. One year, I played on four different teams: my high school freshman team, CYO,

Boys Club, and the Chinese Merchants League. The Chinese team was allowed to pick two Caucasians and since I was 6'2", I was chosen to play center. It was the only time I ever played that coveted position.

Running as a sport did not exist in my growing-up world. My high school didn't have a track, much less a track team. I knew there were athletes who ran because I saw the newsreels and read the magazine articles, but that had as much relevance in my life as men riding ponies at a polo match.

I was an above-average but not exceptional athlete; never chosen first, but never last, either. I made the varsity basketball team in high school but when I moved on to Harvard, I only made the junior varsity. As a lark, I went out for the freshman lacrosse team and qualified as a third-string midfielder, a position that requires more running than anywhere else on the field. I was in the best shape of my entire life during those college years. I would follow the seasons, moving from one sport to another. After lacrosse, I decided to see what track was all about, so I entered the freshman intramural track meet for the half-mile and mile races. It was the very first time I ran a race. I knew nothing about times or strategy but, knowing from the movies that underdogs do win and storm to the finish with a burst of thunderous applause, I ran hard but finished fifth in the half mile. Later in the afternoon came the mile race. Only when we are young and carefree would we ever consider running two such races with an hour's rest at best. To my pleasure, I indeed won the freshman intramural mile at Harvard in the spring of 1956.

I remember this so well because I have never yet won another race. I have won trophies for various placements in age-group categories, but never even a first-place age-group award. I guess I peaked early. As I look back on my collegiate athletic career, I loved every minute of it, wouldn't give up one second of endless basketball practice. I do wish I had more exposure to competitive running, but even after winning that mile race I never thought to join track. I was just one of many eighteen-year-old active males in great shape who could run pretty fast.

Years later, I started running as an adult for the same reasons many do: I got fat, felt heavy and missed the pleasure of feeling like an athlete. By 1970, fourteen years after my heroic mile run at Harvard, I had put on forty pounds and had not played basketball or done anything more athletic than fishing in the last ten years. Furthermore, I was living and working in Europe, frequently taking customers to lunch and dinner. I simply had to do something about my weight and conditioning. So one day I put on a pair of sneakers and went out the door of our house in Antwerp, Belgium, and ran around the block. It took forever. It was just under one mile.

In the early 1970s, Kenneth Cooper's word *aerobics* was just coming into use. Since I like keeping tallies and records I bought his book and began tracking my "aerobic points" for each week. I actually began to enjoy the running. To celebrate my newfound sport I bought a pair of red running shoes. One of the pleasures of exercise is getting to buy all the neat gear, and for me that meant a good pair of shoes. As I kept running, the weight started to come off. I also started taking long hot baths, really hot baths that caused lots of sweating. I convinced myself that the sweating each night contributed to my weight loss. Experts will probably disagree, but when something seems to work, you don't look for statistical validity.

I came to enjoy running for its own sake and not just for its ability to help me lose weight. At this point, I was transferred to Rio de Janeiro and for the next three years joined the hundreds of Brazilians every morning putting in three miles along the famous Copacabana Beach.

Two years later I was brought back to New York City. Now I could run in my hometown! I joined the New York Road Runners Club and planned to join their organized races in Central Park. I discovered that as much as I liked running, I liked racing even more. For me running was no longer just running. I divided it into racing and training. Despite this newfound love for racing, I only entered one race between 1976 and 1978. I think getting divorced from my first wife, getting transferred to Bahrain, getting remarried, and moving to London as a base while traveling to and from Bahrain might have had something to do with it.

I continued running while in Bahrain but there were no organized racing events. I did run a few times with the Hash House Harriers and learned the meaning of "On ON!"

While attending a Citibank conference in Istanbul I met a fellow banker named Cedric Grant who just happened to live near me in London. We got on the topic of trying to stay in shape, losing weight, and the conversation led to discussions about running. It turned out we were both born on the same day, four years apart. Other than that, we were direct opposites: I am tall, he is short. I was lean, Cedric is built like a rugby player—broad shoulders, a powerful chest. He lifts weights, treks across deserts, and in general defies gravity in all sorts of ways. We agreed to do some runs together when we got back to London.

On Saturdays we would meet in Surrey and do a five-mile run with a local pub as the finish line. We decided that Guinness was the perfect fluid replacement drink for our training. We got so good at our training, we moved the distance up to more than ten miles, which meant we needed another pub somewhere in the middle for our fluid replacement program.

I don't remember what made us choose a May 1978 marathon in Athens as our first marathon; I am not even sure what made us think we could run a marathon. At the time, neither one of us was logging more than thirty miles a week and neither one of us had run more than twelve miles at one go. Perhaps someone challenged us by saying we couldn't do it. Perhaps I wanted to because my older brother had done it. Perhaps we just thought it would be a lark. Whatever the reason, we couldn't have chosen a more symbolic course.

My training back then was very unscientific. Precious little training advice was available in 1978. Now I have several shelves full of running books but then I was on my own. Even the celebrated Kenneth Cooper didn't factor in a marathon in his aerobics books. I did wear good shoes and concentrated on hill work—actually the hills were sand dunes. But most of all, I figured if I could run thirteen miles, I could run twenty-six. I also didn't set a time goal for my first marathon; just to finish would be fine. But I did wear a huge stainless-steel Omega chronometer and it didn't take long before I got interested in timing myself. According to my calculations, I could finish in four hours.

The day before the marathon, my wife, Cedric, and I traveled to Glyfada, a beach resort just outside of Athens. None of us slept well because the travel agent forgot to mention the hotel was on the approach path for planes coming into Athens airport. We had been advised to rent a cab for the next morning to take us to the starting line. The three of us went together to the start so my wife could capture the moment on her eight-millimeter movie camera (this was way before the advent of camcorders) and then take the cab to the finish line, where she would also record that moment for posterity. Everything was planned with precision, but what we didn't count on was the cab driver getting lost.

The cabby didn't know the streets of Marathon very well and despite the fact that we had a map he could not find the starting point. We were getting very nervous as the time approached and we were still lost. The cabby was actually stopping people in the street and asking for directions. When we finally got there we could see the starter's upraised hand with the pistol about to go off. As we jumped out of the cab, the gun went off and I regretted not having time to kiss my wife good-bye for good luck.

We rushed to the check-in table, registered, grabbed our numbers, and headed into the pack. We pinned our numbers on as we joined the other runners already in progress. The first part of the course loops around the presumed site of the tombs of the warriors of the battle of Marathon. As I went past the site, a young Greek girl of about eight years old handed me a sprig of laurel from one of the trees at the tomb's site. I carried that sprig with me for the entire race and kept it with me years afterward. Most athletes are superstitious and I thought it a most favorable omen that a Greek girl gave me a laurel sprig from Marathon at the beginning of my very first marathon. This, I thought, is my event.

The ten-mile marker remains in my memory because I had read that you should not let feeling good fool you. And I felt, if not good, at least normal. But by the time I hit mile fifteen I was definitely tired and my legs were beginning to weaken. And I was very aware there was still a long way to go. Every road looked endless to me. At this point the pain was both physical and mental. Marathon pain differs from other kinds of pain in that it is all-encompassing toward a single goal, finishing. It is not a sharp or acute pain. Assuming there is no serious injury such as a sprained ankle, marathon pain is simply total fatigue, muscle soreness, an inability to maintain your normal gait and posture. Actually, I think marathon pain is overrated, not because it doesn't exist, but simply because it is extreme overexertion that begins to diminish as soon as you stop running.

The rest of the race is a blur, a rising crest of a gradual hill and a descent into Athens. I relied on self-talk to get me through most of the difficult times, such as the last six miles. I told myself I was lucky to still be alive and running and that I could still do the multiplication tables in my head. The thought that I might break four hours also kept me going. Other thoughts that occupied my brain for the last six miles included a cold beer at the finish line and how embarrassing it would be to quit and have to ask for help.

I do remember the twenty-five-mile marker because it was on a main street in Athens in which the middle lane was blocked off for the runners but cars were on either side belching so much exhaust that I felt nauseous.

And finally, there was the exquisite feeling of crossing the finish line, which was situated in the lovely elongated marble stadium built for the first modern Olympics in 1896. When I saw the stadium I almost cried but could not because what I really wanted to do was throw up. I had read that Frank Shorter drank defizzed Coca-Cola during races and I had been drinking Cokes that I shook to defizz throughout the race. Looking back, I realize I did not drink enough and what I was drinking was too sweet. All I knew as I approached the stadium was I wanted to barf. I saw my wife and some friends from the office as I entered the stadium, crossed the finish line in 3:59, hugged my wife, and ran for the bathroom.

Cedric came in thirty minutes behind me and by then I could stand up without throwing up. We all headed to a party at the apartment of mutual friends living in Athens. There was plenty of food but since I kept throwing up in the gutters on the way to the apartment, I was in no shape to eat. All I wanted was a bath, which was provided. That seemed to soothe me but I still had no appetite. However, I did drink bottles and bottles of beer, which finally seemed to hydrate me and calm my stomach.

I was so stiff the next day I felt like a cartoon character. I got tired of hearing the jokes about how you can tell a marathon runner by the way he walks downstairs backward. I couldn't walk at all. I spent the next couple of days doing nothing but sitting on a beach.

Finishing that first marathon helped me internalize the thought, the self-image, that "I am a runner." I got more serious about doing better and then I became compulsive, having since run about twenty-six marathons. Cedric has outpaced me with 103. Even when my mileage and weight reversed themselves later on (mileage down and weight up), I still thought of myself as a runner and kept running. And since life moves in cycles, not straight lines, I eventually began to bring the mileage up and weight down. I don't view running as a commitment; it has become a part of my life. Eating is not a commitment, it is just something you do. That's what running is to me. It pervades my life. I wouldn't go so far as to say it has crept into other parts of my life; I would rather say it has become its own part of my life. I love hanging out at the prerace expositions, looking at all the gear, feeling the camaraderie of the runners at the start of a race, the congratulations of other runners when they find out you've done it and the amazement of non-runners when they hear you've done it, the fun of wearing your race shirt later on and knowing you've earned it, unlike some others who buy it for a fashion statement. And then there's the memory of the actual race, forever stored in my mind. I have even cried once or twice when I crossed the finish line, out of a fullness of feeling that can't be expressed in words.

And I have my own set of running rituals. What runner doesn't? Often I wear a USA cap, especially in overseas races. Sometimes I wear a PENNSYLVANIA RAILROAD cap in honor of my father, who worked fifty years for the Pennsylvania Railroad. I always wear the same Celtic cross on a chain and I pin two medals to my shorts or singlet: St. Christopher and St. Michael. Anyone who has gone through Catholic school knows the significance of these saints, but for those who don't I'll explain. St. Christopher carried a child on his shoulders across a river and the child grew mysteriously heavier in midstream. The child was the Christ-child and his mysterious weight was the sins of the world. St. Christopher became the patron saint of travelers. I pray to him when my legs won't move and I start to feel heavier and heavier myself and would he please carry me safely to the finish line. St. Michael is God's number one soldier. The standard prayer to St. Michael is, "St. Michael the Archangel, defend us on the day of battle, be our protection against the wickedness and snares of the devil." For me, marathon day is a battle and the last six miles are where the devil lays his snares and I ask St. Michael to help me out.

My final and favorite ritual is the one I perform when I finish. As soon as I get home I take a long hot bath and drink cold beer in the tub. Then I lie on the bed and drink more beer, eat pretzels, and watch a videotape of the race. The combined feeling of exhaustion, euphoria and accomplishment is luxurious.

I have a favorite quote, actually it is a speech, that sometimes Cedric and I will chant if we are running together. It's Shakespeare's famous

"We band of brothers" speech from *Henry V.* It came to mind while he and I were waiting for the cannon to go off at the start of a New York Marathon. I started to recite, "We few, we happy few, we band of brothers; For he today that sheds his blood with me shall be my brother . . . And gentlemen in England now abed shall think themselves accursed they were not here. . . . "

I feel that way whenever I reach the start of a marathon. God knows I have caused myself enough discomfort to get there and thoughts of why I should not be doing it yet again enter my brain too late to do anything about it. And I know its going to hurt a lot before I get my cold beer and pretzels, but at that moment I would not be anywhere else for anything else on earth. All those "gentlemen still abed" everywhere should indeed feel cursed they are not here with me.

MY NEW PASSION

RAY STEFFEN
RESIDENCE: WESTPORT, CONNECTICUT
OCCUPATION: STUDENT, THE COLLEGE OF WILLIAM AND MARY
FIRST MARATHON: 1996 MARINE CORPS MARATHON
D.O.B.: 10-7-75
AGE AT FIRST MARATHON: 19

Ray played soccer in high school and loved the game. For him, it was the perfect combination of running and dexterity. His team was very talented and they played a fast, hard game. But an injury put Ray on the sidelines for a while, healing his hamstring. While he was recuperating, his soccer coach had him work with the track coach in order to keep up his endurance. This twist of fate turned Ray into a runner. But it wasn't love at first sight.

I DIDN'T ENJOY RUNNING AT FIRST. I thought it was boring. Running in soccer was part of the game so it was okay, but not running for the sake of running. I wasn't crazy about the idea of working with the track coach, but I wanted to get back into the game, and besides, when coach says go, you go. But after a few days I realized the track coach was terrific. He taught me how to run, something I took for granted. He worked on my form and took me through techniques such as fartleks and interval training. By the time my injury healed, I had changed my attitude toward running and joined the team, becoming captain my senior year.

The track guys were a great group, a lot of fun to be with, and I enjoyed their camaraderie. Most people think of soccer as a team sport and running as an individual, but I found as much team play in track as on the soccer field. Also, in track there is more time to think about your strategy. Soccer is all reaction. You've got a few seconds to decide what you want to do with the ball and your moment is over. In the eight hundred meters, which was my event, I had two laps to think about my strategy, to plan my move. It's still not a lot of time, but I could think through my positioning better. Another unknown bonus about running was the way it helped me through some tough times my senior year. There's an incredible amount of stress and anxiety to deal with regarding college, leaving home, the future, all that stuff. It's quite nerve racking. Running helped to clear my head and got me out of the senior slump.

In September of 1994 I started college, not knowing a soul on campus. I kept up my running and found it was an easy way to meet people. At William and Mary, students can be seen running through the campus at all hours. In fact, I've been out there burning off a few miles at one in the morning. It's not unusual. We also have some amazing courses, such as the requirement that all students take two credits in the field of kinesiology, the study of human movement. Class offerings range from tai chi to rock climbing, but I set my sights for the triathlon course. Although strenuous, I thoroughly enjoyed it and couldn't believe I was getting credit for running! The final exam was completing an eight-hundred-meter swim, 5K run, and twelve miles on the bike. I met a lot of new friends through that course and started running with a group of them.

Running actually helps with my studies. If I go out and run to the point of depletion and fatigue, all the gunk floating around in my head gets released, so I concentrate better when it's time to hit the books. Other times when I'm running, I'll review material on a book I'm reading or try and memorize dates or formulas. Repetition is good for running.

In February of my sophomore year, a group of us entered the Colonial Half Marathon in Williamsburg, Virginia. Basically, our decision to do the race was a social thing, something different to do on a weekend. We trained a little bit, but no one was taking it seriously. Eight miles was my longest run. Right before the race, though, I started to get really nervous, thinking I hadn't prepared enough. What if I hurt myself, reinjured my hamstring? This was a very popular race and I had never run something like it before. It was also billed as a tough half-marathon course. That really got me shaking. The race turned out to be as tough as predicted, but I pushed myself to keep going. Finally, the adrenaline kicked in, overriding the nervousness, and I actually started to enjoy it. I know this may sound very unsportsmanlike, but the thrill of passing people was awesome. I wanted to pass everyone! But at ten miles, never having run that far ever, my body started to react and I was in trouble: tired, achy, and my feet were killing me. The last mile was terrible and I swore I would never race again. At the finish, we were dead tired. But when I finally caught my breath and began to feel normal again, it was a great sensation. I was on a high. The reality that I actually finished and in a decent time (1:30) was fabulous.

The competition of racing changed everything for me. I became more regimented, followed a running schedule instead of just randomly throwing on my Adidas and doing a few miles around the campus. I was now a running convert. The marathon was the next hurdle and I found a friend named Aaron who was willing to run it with me. We chose the Marine Corps because it's billed as the People's Marathon and has a nice flat course. Our plan was to train through the summer, which would leave us with time in the fall if we needed it. Also, it was only two hours from school, so the logistics of traveling wouldn't be a problem.

When September rolled around and we were back on campus, I definitely needed to do more serious training, having slacked off during the summer. With six weeks to go, I had to kick in. I didn't want to be unprepared for the event. We concentrated on textbook training: fartleks, speed work, hills, you name it, if it was in the book we did it. The one thing we didn't do was morning runs. I knew I should have done a few, but I'm not geared that way. We did our training mostly at night as it was the only time Aaron and I had open schedules. We read somewhere that runners who train in the afternoon have less endurance when the race is in the morning, but sacrificing sleep was not part of the package.

Three weeks before the race, we did a twenty-one-miler and I felt like a machine. I could have run forever that day. But on the downside, I noticed a slight irritation building in my hamstring. All that constant pounding wasn't doing it any good, but I chose to ignore it; nothing was going to stop me from doing the marathon. Two days before the race we borrowed a car, drove to D.C., and stayed with Aaron's relatives. The race preregistration was so intense it made me even more nervous. There were thousands of people. In the back of my mind, I was getting concerned about my hamstring. In retrospect I shouldn't have run, but I was committed. I had come too far not to compete.

Anyway, the day of the race we got an early start to the Pentagon parking lot, but the traffic was intense. Even at six in the morning, the access roads to the Pentagon resembled one big parking lot. You'd think the entire world was going to the marathon. At the Pentagon, the procedure is to board a transfer bus to the starting line, about a fifteen-minute ride away. Because of the traffic, we were late getting to the transfer bus and barely made the last one out. Talk about fate taking a bad turn, we couldn't believe what happened next: The bus driver got lost and all hell broke loose; as late as we already were, now there was no way to make it to the start on time. Everyone was constantly checking their watches, getting more nervous by the minute. Some of the runners were really ticked off and I thought a huge fight was going to break out. Aaron and I just laughed at our predicament along with some others who found the situation more amusing than irksome. It actually helped take some of the pressure off. Anyway, we were still on the bus when we heard the marines fire their howitzers to officially start the race. The driver finally just stopped and pulled over and we all ran out of the bus, charged across a field, and ran for the starting line, fifteen minutes late.

For the first five miles, we just enjoyed being there, taking in the festive atmosphere of the race. We ran with a character who juggled six balls in the air while keeping his pace. He was amazing. Since we were still at the back of the pack due to our late start, we decided to pick up the pace and began passing people. That is such an incredible feeling, like picking off duck decoys at a shooting gallery or mentally eliminating one more competitor. At the ten-mile marker we were cruising at an eight-minute pace, feeling good and thoroughly enjoying ourselves. The marathon was everything we had hoped it would be. There was always something going on in the crowds to keep us amused, and passing the monuments is a real special feeling, very patriotic. One runner jumped rope the whole race and another carried a boom box and was doing dance steps. And of course, you see a lot of marines pass by carrying their platoon flags and chanting their marching songs. Some of them run in full battle gear, right down to the big heavy black boots. It's an awesome sight. The atmosphere was so festive it didn't even feel like we were in a race.

However, at seventeen miles we approached Haines Point and then the reality of the marathon hit us. It is desolate out there, and the wind cut right through us. The crowds are not allowed on that part of the course and I felt a real sense of isolation. Plus it started to turn cold and to make things worse, Aaron developed a bad knee and had to stop and rest it. He eventually fought through the pain and finished the race, but now I was alone at the worst part of the race and my hamstring was beginning to hurt. I was so tired and fatigued, I just wanted the race to be over. At nineteen miles hunger pains struck, so I grabbed a handful of Power Bars from a food stand but forgot to eat them! I just held them in my fist until they molded into one big gob of coagulated goo.

I was struggling hard at this point. I had to keep moving because if I stopped to rest or walk I wouldn't have the energy to get going again. I tried to run on grass when possible because the pain in my thighs from pounding the pavement was unbearable. It was a throbbing, nagging, annoying pain that gradually grew worse, like a tightly wound rubber band that could snap at any moment. But I was almost finished, only had three more miles to go, so I kept the pain at bay. At this point, a lot of runners had quit. I was passing people who couldn't walk, no less run anymore. I didn't want to be a race dropout; finishing the marathon meant too much to me and I truly believed that my drive and ambition would see me through it. I was feeling very light headed and my mind started to wander. It was if I entered a dream state where all sorts of visualizations danced through my head. I thought about my family, about my plans after graduation, I even itemized what I'd eaten for the last three days, remembering every meal and how good it tasted! Then at times my mind went completely blank and I felt like a machine that was running on automatic pilot and I wasn't a part of it, wasn't conscious of making it move.

The last two miles were the toughest. I actually got angry with the crowds who kept saying, "The finish is right around the bend, you can make it." But the finish wasn't around the bend, or the next bend. I know they thought they were helping, but when you want the end to be in sight so badly, I felt deceived instead of encouraged. I was so exhausted because I kept running faster, thinking it was over. I did my "final sprint" three times. Finally, the finish was in sight, and all my months of planning and training had become a reality. I was so dizzy I couldn't hear anything or feel my body; I was floating, detached. At the end of the finish line chute, marines are lined up in full combat gear handing out the medals, space blankets, and bags of food. I lay down on my space blanket in the middle of the crowd and fell asleep.

When I awoke, the commotion around me resembled the battlefield scene in *Gone with the Wind* with stretcher bearers walking through, carrying the wounded to the hospital tents. Only this was real. The guy lying next to me started to throw up and I just barely rolled out of the way. Finally, I got up and started to stretch and try to walk when I noticed blood all down the front of my shirt. My nipples were bleeding! My shirt, which I specifically selected because it said WILLIAM AND MARY across the front, was very coarse and had been irritating my skin the entire race. But I never felt it or noticed it till then. And it's funny, because all through the race whenever we passed an aid station, volunteers were handing out sticks smeared with Vaseline. Aaron and I shared a few good jokes about the Vaseline, but I guess the joke was on me. I should have used it to coat my skin. Oh well, next time I'll know better. I suddenly felt incredibly hungry but couldn't move to get food. I gobbled down all the melted Power Bars in my hand, which at the time tasted better than anything I've ever eaten.

My finish time was 3:30 and that was fine with me. I definitely plan to run another marathon and there are so many great places to run them, like New York and hopefully someday qualify for Boston. I also plan to get better acquainted with my new passion. I really don't know anything about the running scene in the United States, past or present. I didn't even know who Frank Shorter or Billy Rodgers were until now. I feel like I've discovered a whole new world out there and I want to know everything about it. I think I'll be running for a long, long time. In twenty years I can see myself doing yet another marathon, probably finishing around 4:00 and having my wife and kids meet me at the finish line. Wait a minute, did I really say that?

WHO WANTS STEINFELD?

ALLAN STEINFELD
RESIDENCE: MANHATTAN, NEW YORK
OCCUPATION: PRESIDENT AND CEO., N. Y. ROAD RUNNERS CLUB
FIRST MARATHON: 1979 HONOLULU MARATHON
D.O.B.: 6-7-46
AGE AT FIRST MARATHON: 33

Allan Steinfeld is the man responsible for ensuring that every November approximately thirty-thousand people run together in a smooth and orderly fashion. Not only does he orchestrate the New York City Marathon and over a hundred of other road races sponsored by his running club, he is also a sports administrator whose talent for finances, organization, and marketing make him a sought-after consultant. So what does he think of the New York Marathon? He has never run it. In fact, Allan has only completed one marathon. Growing up, he went from the skinny kid no one wanted on their team to one of the fastest runners on the track. Along the way, he received a masters degree in astronomy and physics, started on his doctorate, and finally met the man who would have the greatest impact on his life, Fred Lebow. Allan has what many of us would consider the greatest job: working with runners all day, just one block away from Central Park—where he can at any moment choose to go out for a run.

GROWING UP IS NEVER EASY, BUT it can be damn hard if you are a skinny little kid in the Bronx and have to get up at five-thirty in the morning to travel to Brooklyn for school. While all my friends were attending Bronx Science, I had to travel down to Brooklyn due to an antiquated and now-obsolete ruling about entrance applications to schools. I was becoming an outsider in my own neighborhood. To make matters worse, I wasn't very good at sports. Any game that required eye and hand coordination was my downfall. I couldn't catch a baseball or sink a basketball, although I was great at defense and rebounds. In football, the all-American pastime for everyone but me, I could run a good defense, but again, couldn't catch the ball. I was the cartoon character kid who gets sand kicked in the face and the reality of it was, no one wanted me on their team. It was tough growing up in a city neighborhood, being the guy who was uncoordinated, couldn't participate in sports. Of course it bothered me; I was the last one chosen. I can still hear the big shots calling out, "Who wants Steinfeld?"

The irony of it all was that I knew I was fast, could beat all those other kids in any race, but no one raced. Our games were played on the streets and neighborhood empty lots. If you couldn't play baseball, you were a nobody. And with such a long commute from school, I couldn't join the track team at Brooklyn Tech and still get back home in time to get all my studying done. It's funny how life decisions, even at such an early age, form us for the future. I hated the fact that I was viewed as an outsider in my own town and I had no friends at Brooklyn Tech because there was no time to socialize. I didn't really come of age with myself and friends until college. That's when running saved me and changed my life forever.

My metamorphosis from the neighborhood nobody to a track star started at Hunter College and continued when I transferred to City College. I was running the two hundred meters and quarter mile and all of a sudden I had lots of friends who just happened to be athletes. I was no longer observing life from the sidelines, waiting for the moment when a school-yard friend who was out on the field would wave or say hello. The days of being snubbed by the other kids were over. I finally made it to the other side and running brought me there. I was now an athlete.

My family of running friends began to grow. Not only was I best friends with the college track team, but as we competed with other schools, I met new people who became part of the circle. In fact, the captain of my track team at Hunter is still a good friend that I see often. This became my rallying point, the beginning of a new life where I saw myself differently. I started doing weight training, running faster and training harder. At 5'8" and 117 pounds, I was a very fast sprinter, but also strong, doing two-hundred-pound squats and carrying a hundred pounds on my back while running the giant, concrete stadium steps. We had a great coach, which was a double blessing for me as I tend to have a problem with authority figures. There is a rebel hiding inside me that gets me in trouble every now and then.

I also tended to view running in a different way than most of my teammates, focusing more on the cerebral side of the sport. It's not all about speed. It's viewed as boring because it's not necessarily a fun thing, but it is very intense and involves more of the body than any other sport. I've run sprints so fast I throw up, but go back for more. I've run till I can't breathe, yet go back for more. You can't put it all out at once and at the same time you can't go too slow. There's much more strategy than people realize. It's not just running fast; it's cerebral.

I'll tell you my personal secret to successful running, which I discovered during a critical track meet that we were doomed to lose. Even the coach anticipated a loss. My personal goal at the time was to do the quarter mile in better than fifty-seven seconds, but I was having trouble breaking it, a block of some kind. I decided at the meet to go out relaxed, with an "I don't care" attitude. My attitude also tends to get me in trouble, but this day it did the opposite. Before I knew it, I was running neck and neck for first place, drawing even, and somehow, somewhere out of me, I pulled ahead to win and broke fifty-three seconds. I'll never forget that day.

I guess it was also my cocky attitude that brought me to Boston, in hopes of running the 1966 Boston Marathon. I was coming off a high from winning my first New York Road Runners Club race, a handicapped race, keeping a steady six-minute pace for eight miles. I figured if I could keep that pace for eight miles I could keep a seven-minute pace for twenty-six miles. I must have been really full of myself, because I didn't prepare, didn't even read a book about marathon training. Deep down inside I think every serious runner aspires to do Boston and this was my shot. There was no qualifying time requirement, so I just went. It was a lark, I'll admit, but I was young, wild, and crazy. I held my seven-minute pace for ten miles and then started to slowly fall apart. I got slower, and slower, then started to jog, then walk, then came to a complete stop and couldn't move. I had to lean against a telephone pole to hold my body upright. One lane of cars was allowed on the course back then and out of desperation I flagged down a driver for a ride. A man with two kids in the car picked me up, put me in the backseat, covered me with a blanket, and drove me to the finish. I felt badly, but I certainly wasn't devastated. As I said, it was a lark and I blew it. End of story.

After college I attended graduate school at Cornell in astronomy and physics. I kept running, training with the track team. Actually, my running was one of the main reasons I went to Cornell. One of the interviewing department heads was a previous all-Ivy two-mile champion and shared my love of the sport. After my masters, I wasn't quite ready to work yet but it was also the time when Nixon was escalating the draft for Vietnam and most of my graduate school friends were heading for Canada. I decided to continue my schooling and went to Alaska for my doctorate, working on a thesis involving the northern lights. While in Fairbanks, I put in five to ten miles a day running cross country in one of the most beautiful settings in the world, in full view of Mount McKinley. It was a real trip to look out and see that mountain range. I stayed for about one year and realized I was in the doctoral world of publish or perish, so my team produced over two dozen papers of which I was part of the research team. However, when the papers were published I was acknowledged but not given any authorship. It is customary in scientific research papers to list all the members of the team by name as authors. When I asked why I was inadvertently left out, being the low man on the totem pole was the lame excuse given. I was very annoyed, didn't want to play their academic mind games, so I left.

Back home from Alaska in 1972, I was tired of academia and didn't want to work. I just wanted to have fun and run. But I did need some kind of income just to exist so I took a position in the Rye Neck school district, teaching high school physics and math, also signing on to be the assistant track and cross-country coach. Running was still a focus in my life, a main ingredient that defined who I was. I wanted to learn all I could about the art of running, as opposed to the sport of running. I took up dance to learn about movement and fluidity, to become more aware of my body and how it connects and works. I wasn't quite comfortable performing on stage, but I loved the course. It was like poetry to me, so free and unstructured. I became very aware of my body and stopped being ashamed of it, of being skinny. I actually got to like the performances, and thank God I didn't have to wear tights.

The best part of living back in New York City was resuming my daily runs in Central Park. I joined the New York Road Runners Club back in 1963 while at Hunter College and could now benefit from my membership and join all the races and club activities. The club was growing in leaps and bounds and Fred Lebow, the founder of the club, was orchestrating the first marathon that would go beyond the boundaries of Central Park. I volunteered, starting out at the bottom of the pack stuffing envelopes and moving up to become the official timekeeper.

I kept volunteering, doing more and more, and by 1978 Fred asked me to be his official assistant. I asked him what the job paid, and he responded by asking me my current salary. I was making twenty-five-thousand dollars teaching and he countered with less than half of that, twelve thousand. I didn't even negotiate, just took the job right away, crazy enough to give it a shot. My decision was based on two things: my love of running and my respect for Fred. He was so charismatic and persuasive. And finally, I knew I would have fun. This wasn't work, this was running!

One of my first assignments was flying to Honolulu with Fred to consult with their road runners club on how to improve their fledgling marathon. I knew I made the right decision to take this job! We were invited back the next two years in a row to make further improvements. In 1979, my wife and I decided to take our vacation in Hawaii and went out two weeks early. I knew the marathon course by heart and one morning decided to take a ten-mile run through the cane fields and kept a six-and-a-half-minutes per mile pace. When I got back to the hotel room, I told my wife I was going to run the marathon. She gave me that "you're crazy" look and asked why. I simply said, "Because it's there." I knew it was a nutty decision, but that's the way I do things. Besides, it was a beautiful run, I was in good shape, and it seemed a fascinating idea. I also set a goal for myself, to finish in three and a half hours. If I went beyond that, I would stop wherever I was and get a ride to the finish. I wasn't going to be stupid this time around. When I registered, by chance I received the number 66, which I thought was fate, that being the year of my ill-fated attempt at running the Boston Marathon.

At 6 A.M. on that December morning, in pitch black darkness, the Honolulu Marathon began with a wicked display of fireworks that signaled the start for seven thousand runners to begin their journey on a course that covers Waikiki Beach, Diamond Head, and Koko Head Crater. I couldn't break loose from the crowd and was running behind schedule so I had to increase my pace for a while. At mile six the climb up Diamond Head starts and proceeds for about one mile until the crest of the volcano comes into view. As I approached the top, the sun was coming up over the water, illuminating Diamond Head, a glorious scene of sparkling, incandescent light. It was magnificent and I was feeling as radiant as the sight. Then the downhill starts and the halfway point is at the Hawaii Kai Hotel, made famous from the *Hawaii Five-O* series on TV back in the seventies. There was an outcry of "Book 'em, Danno" as we passed by. The one thing that is unique to the Honolulu Marathon is the entertainment provided at the water stations. Hula girls dance and hand out leis. It is such a scene, I had to fight my way in to get water. I started to do every other water station so I wouldn't lose time.

By now I was getting hot, tired, and tiny blisters were beginning to blossom on my feet. It was getting to be that point in the race when I entertained the thought of quitting, but then I would look down at my number, remember Boston, and keep going. Then I would look up at the sky, appreciate the beautiful day and cloudless blue canvas, take a deep breath, refresh my mind, and feel good again.

I was constantly calculating my time, making sure I was on target, trying to keep to my goal of 3:30 or bust. As I started to climb the far side of Diamond Head, ten seconds after cresting my quads jammed. It felt like somebody put the brakes on and I came to a sudden stop. I was really pissed. I couldn't believe this was happening to me. I started to pound furiously on my legs with my fists, angry at them for failing me, and also trying to release the tension. I'm sure it was due to dehydration after missing half the water stops. I couldn't kick-start into a run, so started walking, then jogging, then did something resembling a run, but it felt and looked more like the character Fester, on *Gunsmoke,* who had a bum leg that he dragged along as he walked down the street, calling, "Hey, Mr. Dillon?" Well, that was me.

Finally, at twenty-five miles, my body started to relax and run at a normal gait, if you can call that normal. I kept pushing myself to finish. I could see the finish line, and saw Fred and all the race directors I had worked with lined up waiting for me. As I crossed the line, they announced my time at 3:27.

I didn't collapse, as expected, but walked through the chute and took a shower, which was hooked up for the runners for a quickie cool-down. Then all the finishers were presented with a finisher's shirt and a lei of cowry shells, draped over our necks with a kiss from one of the hula girls. I kept that necklace for years until it simply disintegrated. Then I took a shiatsu massage and went to find Fred. One of the benefits of finishing a race early is that there are no lines at the massage tent. Completing the marathon and keeping to my goal was a great feeling, very special, but I never thought of running another. Then something happened to make me change my mind.

When Fred Lebow ran the 1992 marathon in remission from cancer, with Grete Waitz at his side, and he was sixty years old, there wasn't a dry eye in Central Park. That's when I decided I would run the marathon when I turned sixty, in memory of Fred. I made that announcement with many people in attendance but I don't think they took me seriously. But mark my words, I will run my first New York City Marathon in the year 2006.

Having run one marathon and planned and orchestrated many more, and witnessing millions of people cross the finish line, I know how much a marathon impacts and changes lives. Just for the training alone, people alter their eating habits, sleeping habits, what they do, when they do it. It's a huge commitment. Part of the inspiration to run my first marathon came from Grete Waitz, who was invited to run the five- borough New York City Marathon in 1978. Grete was a great track runner, but had never gone beyond ten miles. At her first attempt, she won the race, which ultimately launched her incredible marathon career.

I have always respected the marathon. I tackled my first with sixteen years of serious running behind me, mentally tough from competition and always staying in shape. Running defines me. It is a euphoric feeling I look forward to every day. It keeps me connected to life. And every November I get to witness the outpouring of compassion and spirit that this city gives to the thousands of runners who tackle our marathon. Being in the lead car, I get to see at close range the faces of the runners, witness their fears, their anxieties, their dreams, and their determination. It's a great, great job and I wouldn't trade it for anything.

A VICTORY FOR HUMANITY

DICK TRAUM
RESIDENCE: MANHATTAN, NEW YORK
OCCUPATION: PRESIDENT, PERSONNELMETRICS, INC.;
FOUNDER, ACHILLES TRACK CLUB
FIRST MARATHON: 1976 NEW YORK CITY MARATHON
D.O.B. 11-18-40
AGE AT FIRST MARATHON: 35

Dick Traum doesn't think of himself as being disabled, despite the fact that he only has one leg. In fact, he tends to think his middle-aged paunch is more of a problem these days. His story is a wake-up call for people of all abilities. Dick isn't even trying to be inspirational, he just likes to run. He has completed eleven marathons and one ultra (sixty-two miles). His life is remarkable not only for what he has personally achieved, but for what he has achieved for others as well. He has lived up to the motto he passed under every day at the Horace Mann School in Manhattan: "Be ashamed to die unless you have achieved a victory for humanity." Dick founded the now worldwide Achilles Track Club in 1983, which trains and motivates disabled people to become athletes. Dick sums up the Achilles philosophy from his own point of view: "Reveling in the pleasure of doing it yourself, with your own body, appreciating the marvelous things the body can do rather than focusing on what it can't do—in short, just being intensely glad to be alive."

WHEN I TOOK MY ARTIFICIAL RIGHT LEG for a 26.2-mile run in 1976, I had no idea how it would change my life. I entered the New York City Marathon that year because I was a runner and that is what runners do.

It turned out that no one without the standard issue of two working legs had ever run a marathon before. It took me seven hours and twenty-four minutes to finish and the excitement generated at that race hasn't stopped yet.

I was born with two good legs that worked fine for me the first twenty-four years of life, participating at an acceptable level of high school athletics including track, wrestling, and football. During summers I had the ultimate job for a kid, selling food at Yankee Stadium. I remember watching the little kids wait every day for Mickey Mantle to sign an autograph, but he never did, not for any of them. One day a boy in a wheelchair showed up waiting for an autograph, and he received one. That angered me. Not the fact that the kid got an autograph, but that Mantle treated him differently, didn't have the guts to treat him like the rest of us. Years later, when I was in a wheelchair, I didn't want to be treated differently and I'm sure that kid didn't either.

I attended New York University, but was a poor learner and got lousy grades. I am sure I had some form of learning disability but those kinds of things were unheard of back in the fifties. I felt so badly about my grades that I insisted on paying my own tuition despite the fact that my parents could afford it. I had a part-time job working on a soda truck making deliveries and by the time I finished college I was making five hundred dollars a week on my soda route, more than some college graduates were getting at full-time jobs.

I started working on my doctorate program, a combined degree of management, human resources, and psychology. In the spring of 1965, I was almost twenty-five years old, had a good paying part-time job, had finished all the course work and written test requirements for my Ph.D. and was engaged to be married. Life was good. And then I lost my leg.

My fiancée and I were driving to Philadelphia over Memorial Day weekend to visit her parents. We stopped at a service plaza on the New Jersey Turnpike for gas. She went inside while I attended to the car. Getting out to stretch my legs, I wandered to the back of the car and took little notice of the big, old Chrysler with an old man behind the wheel pulling up behind me. As the driver leaned across the front seat to open the opposite door for a passenger, his car started rolling forward. As the driver sensed his car moving, he panicked and instead of applying the brakes, he stepped on the accelerator. The car leaped forward, smashing into my legs, crushing them between the bumpers. He hit me with such force that my parked car and I, lodged in the middle, were pushed ten feet forward. And because his foot was still on the accelerator, his car kept jamming me again and again. By the third hit, he had found the brake, but by then it was too late. His car radiator was broken from the impact and I thought my leg was also broken. I worried that I would miss my delivery route if my leg was put in a cast. Later on, I passed out in the ambulance. The first surgery was an attempt to save the leg, but they had to operate again. By this time I was in a near-death situation and could feel myself falling down a hole, out of this life. By the third operation in seven days, I knew I was going to lose my leg and signed the papers allowing the doctors to amputate. When I woke, I actually had the sensation that my leg was still attached, but when I looked under the covers all I saw was a bloody stump above the knee.

I was in the intensive care unit for twenty-four days and had a lot of time on my hands to reflect on what had happened to me. I came to the conclusion that I had accomplished a lot with my life so far. Losing a leg looked bad, but then again I'd rather lose one leg than be an alcoholic. I'd rather lose one leg than be a drug addict. It's all relative and in the grand scheme of things, my loss was not that big a deal.

I went through a wheelchair stage, then onto crutches, and finally to a prosthesis. The feeling of freedom and mobility was like the excitement I felt when I first got my driver's license. The first time I wore my new leg in public, I danced. I didn't dance well, but then again I never was a good dancer.

Life was not going to pass me by just because I lost a leg. My engagement ultimately broke off, but besides that I got right back into the swing of things, landing a job in the human resources field. This was 1967 and computers were just breaking into the corporate world. By 1970 I started my own firm and married a nurse I met while in rehabilitation. I never advertised the fact that I only had one leg, so outside of walking with a limp, life was normal. Some funny situations would arise like if I accidentally stepped on a person's foot with my prosthesis. When that happens I can't feel it, so I keep standing on the person's foot. When I finally realize what has happened, I explain my situation and apologize, but that makes the person so uncomfortable I end up getting the apology.

By 1975 my company was in full swing and things couldn't have looked healthier, especially my waistline. My one big vice is eating, that and my Type-A personality. Then a business colleague of mine about the same age died of a heart attack. I knew if I kept going at the same speed, without any exercise and continuing to gain weight, I'd be next. So I joined an exercise class at the West Side YMCA. At the beginning of the class, the instructor asked each member if they could run. Anyone who said no was thrown out. I had already paid my $250 and realized if I said no, I'd be out of class and out of $250. So I said, "Yes, I can run." When it came time to run, I did what I considered a run, although it was more of a hopping motion, similar to a person with a cast on one leg. Prostheses are built with a hydraulic system in the knee joint that controls the gait and is held on through a suction device. A below-the-knee amputee can run considerably faster than an above-the-knee amputee.

The rite of running was very progressive. At first I could only run three minutes without stopping, but after three months I had built up to a comfortable fifteen minutes. At that point I took a fitness test that required riding a stationary bicycle. When I showed up for the test I wasn't wearing my prosthesis and the technician ran out of the room, screaming, "How can I test a man on a bike when he only has one leg?" The answer was: Not very well!

I began to enjoy running and considered myself a runner. As fate would have it, Fred Lebow had just fashioned the first New York City Marathon in 1970 and needed space for his fledgling New York City Road Runners club of several hundred members, and the West Side Y became their home. I joined the club and was soon active with the organization.

Now that I was an official member of a running club, I set my sights on my first race, grandly called the Second Annual New York Road Runners YMCA of Greater New York 5-Mile Championship. The entry tag had only a number—no advertising or bar codes, a reflection of the simpler days of road racing. I finished last with a time of 72:49. A CBS camera crew caught sight of me and ran a story about running the race with only one leg. The story was picked up and I became a local hero. In August of that same year I was ready for a half marathon. It was a hot day and again, I finished last in three and a half hours. Bob Glover, our trainer at the Y, ran with me and to cool me off, he kept pouring water over my head. As the race progressed, my leg felt heavier and heavier, but I attributed that to the distance and my fatigue. After the race, when I took off my prosthesis, a quart of water poured out, the run-off of Bob's attempts to keep me cool.

Again, the story of the man with the artificial leg running races made the headlines. I was deemed an inspiration. I suppose that was nice, but I wasn't trying to be inspirational, I was being normal. Every disabled person who does more than get out of bed in the morning and brush his teeth gets a large amount of support. On one level, we are just the same as any able-bodied person who undertakes the same activity. Disabled golfers are just trying to play golf, the same as a disabled skier wants to ski or a disabled runner wants to run. I didn't want to be the official inspirator. That role tends to make the person an outsider, larger than life, and I wasn't.

My next race was a 30K (18.7 miles) in Central Park. By now I was geared up for running the New York City Marathon that fall. I was doing two two-hour runs and one three-hour run a week on the Y's track. The 30K route winds through the park on the same roads shared by cyclists. The police did their best to keep the groups apart, but I got whacked by a cyclist and my prosthesis, which is held on by suction, was knocked off and skidded along the pavement. The cyclist spent a horrible few seconds thinking he had severed my leg. As I sat there reattaching it, he apologized profusely and took off as fast as he could.

After the 30K, I was ready for the marathon. This was the first year of the five-borough route and Fred had asked Frank Shorter and Bill Rodgers to run it, along with 2,090 other runners. For safety reasons, Fred decided I should start earlier than the main pack so that I wouldn't end up late at night at a deserted finish line, since my anticipated time was somewhere around eight hours. I spent so much time preparing and anticipating that it was no longer fun, it was nerve racking. I just wanted to get it over with and started at 6:50 A.M. My support group, which included my wife and brother-in-law followed me in the car. They brought along a pair of crutches just in case I needed them. The problem with running long distance with a prosthetic leg is that, eventually, the stump starts to bleed. No matter how much you train, there are places on the stump that won't callus over, particularly on the back of the leg. The bleeding itself isn't a big deal, although it does look gruesome when the blood starts dripping down the leg. The danger is of infection setting in if the wound doesn't have time to heal.

Once I got under way, I started to have fun. I didn't have the pressure of any other goal than to finish. I couldn't fail, as no other amputee had attempted to run a marathon before. The norms of society, and of sport, dictated that it was an impossible event, but I was soon to let it be known that it was, indeed, possible.

When I arrived at the ten-mile marker, we came to an intersection with three crossways, and I chose the wrong one, going about a half mile out of my way before realizing the error. I thought about getting into the car to drive the distance back to the right roadway, but thought if someone saw me in a car I could be accused of cheating, so I ran an extra mile to ensure a valid win.

At eighteen miles the lead runners began to catch up with me, whizzing by as if I was going backward. Bill Rodgers passed me by, yelling, "Thataboy, Dick." That had to be one of the most exciting thrills of my life. Now that the entire race was in full swing, the crowds were lining the streets, something I missed by starting early. The last time I heard the roar of a crowd was at a wrestling match in college, but this was even better. I was hurting from sheer physical exhaustion, but when I heard the cheering, it carried me along. I wasn't going to stop now. The last quarter mile, when the crowds were at their peak, they roared as if I was running down a football field for the winning touchdown.

I finished in 7:24, breaking my own prediction by half an hour. I was more tired than happy when I crossed the finish line, but the excitement wasn't over yet. The Road Runners Club was holding an awards ceremony at Avery Fisher Hall and after the top runners received their medals, I was called up. After a prolonged standing ovation, my medal was hung around my neck, and the air was electric. It was something I had never felt before and never expect to feel again. It was just unbelievable. The sound of the clapping continues to echo in my ears. That day remains very special to me and if I had one day to live over in my lifetime, it would be my first marathon.

The papers went crazy with the story. It even made the *International Tribune*. One spectator summed it up best: "I was amazed to see a man running with a wooden leg. I couldn't believe a person with a handicap could work up the nerve and strength to compete. It says our troubles aren't so great. If he has enough stamina to do that, we have enough stamina to do what we have to do." The media had turned me into Rocky.

I continued to run, but not as much as I had while training for the marathon. A son was added to our family, and he would accompany me on his bike while I did a few laps around Central Park. I decided I wanted to try the granddaddy marathon of them all, Boston. But when I made inquiries, I was told I wouldn't be welcome at Boston. They told me it was a serious race for serious runners, not a three-ring circus. I was upset by their reaction, not as much by the insult as by the fact that I was being excluded. None of this really bothered me much, after all, I had New York.

Not long after my headline event, I met a woman who had lost her leg in a mountain-climbing accident and had just been fitted with a prosthesis. She asked me to give her some advice on running with it, so we spent the day in the park running the reservoir until she felt comfortable. A while later, I got a call from another amputee who also wanted advice on running with a prosthesis. Soon I was getting numerous calls from amputees all over wanting advice and I found myself coaching by phone. I also began noticing more disabled people entering road races and an idea began to germinate: helping disabled people get involved in running through the New York Road Runners Club.

With the backing of Fred Lebow, I sent out a letter to eleven hundred doctors and other medical professionals on the club's mailing list, figuring they might have disabled patients or know of some. We set a forty-dollar fee for an eight-week series of training sessions, taught by Bob Glover. Back then, I only thought of amputees as being disabled since I knew nothing of the range of the disabled community. I didn't expect much at the first meeting, but only when only two people showed up, I thought Fred would pull out of the program, but instead he said, "It's a success."

Linda Down was one of our first members, a bright young woman born with cerebral palsy. Before she started running, she couldn't do ten sit-ups, but was soon navigating the streets of Manhattan. Running was slow and painful for her. She needed crutches to navigate and would lead with her left leg, swinging her right leg in a big, awkward arc that would scrape her toes along the pavement. With each footfall, her toes were mashed inside her running shoes. But she persevered with her training and finished the 1982 marathon in eleven hours, crossing the finish line at 9:30 P.M. Her gutsy performance won her a visit to the White House with the other winners. She never did pay her forty-dollar fee, but we never asked for it and ultimately decided to make membership free.

Despite Linda's performance at the marathon and my constant mailings, membership was scant. The classes built slowly and by the end of eight weeks we had eight more or less regular members. We decided to change the weekly training sessions into a running team, dubbed "Achilles" after the Greek hero whose mother dipped him into the River Styx at birth, making his entire body invulnerable except the little spot on his heel where she held him. We were on our way.

Those first initial weeks were awkward for me because although I am disabled, I don't think of myself that way and really didn't know anything about other disabled people. I didn't know if it was proper to ask them about their disability, whether or not it was appropriate to help them or offer assistance. One woman in a wheelchair would scream at our volunteers if they so much as touched her wheelchair. She thought of her chair as an extension of herself and felt personally violated if someone touched it.

As word about the club spread, more disabled people started showing up, but not just amputees. We had blind people, stroke victims, cancer patients, people in wheelchairs, MS, cerebral palsy, and one member who was born without legs and only short stumps as arms. He had been in foster care as a child. When he got into high school, we recruited him, trained him, and he completed a marathon by propelling his wheelchair laboriously with the stumps of his arms. Even he had doubts that he would finish, but when they hung the medal around his neck, he was happier than he had ever been in his life. We have another member who is also in a wheelchair with cerebral palsy. His condition is so severe he can't use his arms to move his wheelchair so he has to push his chair backward with his feet to move. When he first came to Achilles he couldn't go a quarter mile but within eighteen months of training he completed a marathon, kicking backward the entire 26.2 miles.

Cathy Bulboca is another Achilles case in point. She came to us with a double hit—first there was the stroke on the left side of her body, then there was the liver cancer, and then a series of four ministrokes. None of her doctors advised exercise, but she had been active most of her life and a fencer in college. Every time she brought up the idea of exercise, her doctors said no. Finally she met with a psychiatrist who said, "Go for it." She showed up and told us her goal was to run a four-mile race. "When you have a chronic illness, your goals are taken away," she said. "Setting a goal of a four-mile race may not be much, but it gives you motivation. And psychologically, it gives you a break from your real life." She completed the race, and to her it might as well have been a hundred miles. It was the best feeling she ever had. Cathy has gone on to be an outspoken advocate for the benefits of exercise in disabled people.

Our training is done with a group of very dedicated volunteers, who become like family. They are assigned to a disabled person and stay with them through the marathon. In some cases that means running at a painfully slow pace, but at other times our disabled runners, such as some of the blind runners, are faster than the volunteers. These dedicated people aren't paid and come from all walks of life. They are a very noble, selfless group and there would not be a club without them.

Slowly, chapters started to develop in other states by original members who moved or by others hearing about the program and being inspired to start one. Then we started going international with our first overseas break in Poland, in 1987. We now have over 120 chapters in more than fifty-one countries. The one I am most proud of is Japan, which has a history of hiding its less-than-perfect lineage from the world. Disabled people in Japan are treated like lepers, shielded from the public eye with practically no government assistance programs. Getting a chapter of Achilles open and having their disabled people come out from hiding was a major feat for us and for their disabled population. Their Tokyo chapter now equals New York City in membership. We have fifteen chapters in the former Soviet Union, including four in Siberia, where the number one reason for having an amputated limb is severe frostbite from falling asleep in the snow after a night out at the local bar.

Our goal at Achilles has never changed. We treat our members like athletes, not objects. In the beginning, the idea was to get them out and moving. We were initially afraid of hurting them and pushing too hard. Now they get speed work and hill work. The training is based on the same principles as for all runners. Linda Down sums it up best: "I discovered I can stress my worst aspects—my legs and my body—and still be successful. And if I can take my worst aspects and be a success, then imagine what I can do with my best aspects. The focus now is what I am able to do rather then what I can't do."

We need to show them what is inside, not necessarily what is seen on the outside. Only then, can we truly drink in what life has to offer. Every time human beings realize more of their potential, whether they are disabled or able-bodied, all of society benefits.

OUTRUNNING DEMONS

JEFF BLACKWELL VLAUN
RESIDENCE: WATERFORD, CONNECTICUT
OCCUPATION: MOTIVATIONAL PUBLIC SPEAKER;
TAI CHI CROSS-TRAINER
FIRST MARATHON: 1987 EAST LYME MARATHON
D.O.B.: 8-25-58
AGE AT FIRST MARATHON: 29

Many people have said that running saved their life, but rarely in such a literal sense. Jeff Blackwell Vlaun suffered physical and mental abuse every moment he was growing up. He used running as his escape from the nightmare he was living. Jeff has managed to deal with most of the demons in his life, but it was through running that he feels he received the most therapeutic benefits. And entering his one and only marathon was a way of validating the beginning of a new era for Jeff, one that has continued to be free of the demons from the past.

MY EARLIEST MEMORY FROM CHILDHOOD BEGINS at age three. I am suffocating, I can't breathe. My throat is closing and I am struggling for air. I don't understand why no one helps me, why my parents ignore my cries. We live right across the street from the hospital, but I'm never taken to the doctor.

Years later, when I was trying to come to grips with my past, I spoke to the doctor who did my emergency tracheotomy. According to his records, my parents finally called an ambulance when I stopped breathing and the virus that infected my throat had become life threatening.

That was the beginning of the realization that my family was very dys-functional. I lived through mental and physical abuse that became part of the way I lived, normal behavior in a demented way. Ignoring the everyday needs of me and my brother and holding back any form of love or affection was a life-long behavior pattern for my parents.

Because of the turmoil and anger that surrounded my house, I tended to stay outside most of the time. My brother and I did the usual kid stuff, basketball, football, baseball, but I remember just wanting to be outside. It didn't matter if I was simply lying on my back in the grass staring up at the sky. Sometimes after being with my friends, I would go off by myself and just float. I needed to feel the open spaces and know that for a few hours I would be safe, wouldn't be screamed at, hit, or threatened for something like leaving my books on the table. The out-doors became my refuge, my protection from home. Sitting by a brook and feeling the sun's warmth was a welcome alternative to feeling the slap of a hand across my face, and wondering what I did to deserve it.

Both my parents worked, so my brother and I were on our own most of the time. When I entered high school, I signed up for just about every sport, even the band, as a diversion to going home. I enjoyed the structure and discipline of sports, something I certainly didn't receive from my parents. I would spend hours after school working on a jump shot or playing the next tune on my clarinet. Anything to keep from going home. My friends at school became my family.

As with most children in abusive situations, I accepted my plight and never hit back, although I would try to deflect some of the blows. Ironically, my father taught me not to hit women. They both came from the school of Do As I Say, Not As I Do. I became a master at read-ing their signals, knowing when the fights would escalate into violence. Screams of "I never wanted you. Why were you ever born?" would send me running out of the house. I would run as fast I could, away from the sounds of the screeching. I would run around the park, channeling all my anger into fast sprints. And in an ugly twist of truths, my parents threatened that if we ever complained to anyone or told of what went on in our house, they would have us removed into foster care. As a young child, the fear of losing everything, even a dysfunctional house-hold, was scary. The one time my brother did call the social workers, he backed down when they arrived at the house to investigate.

Running became my outlet, my way of coping. I would dream of running away, far away, but eventually I'd go home. I'd run for miles, drain every bit of emotion and anger from inside and then turn around, refreshed, to face the chaos. Running also gave me a sense of freedom I never felt anywhere else. It was an empowerment; I felt in control of myself. A feeling of peace would come over me when the anger left and a wonderful sense of being in sync with everything would prevail. I guess it could be described as a runner's high, but for me it was escaping into a world where my parents couldn't reach me. Through my runs, I learned to trust myself. I certainly didn't trust anyone else, except my brother and God.

After high school I attended Northeastern University in Boston, but I wasn't happy in the city. I kept up my running, now doing five to fifteen miles a day, but even though I was finally away from the violence, I couldn't seem to settle down. Eventually, I left college and went back home. My plan was to get a job and move out as fast as I could. I also planned to get married. Looking back, all those plans had one thing in common: moving out and proving to myself that I could take that step. I intended to finally be free.

Living at home was like getting sucked back into the hurricane all over again. Even though I was in my twenties, the abuse continued. My running escalated, now up to twenty miles a day. I also started swimming and weight training. My outlook on life was that anything I wanted to aspire to, I just had to go after it. No one was going to help me attain anything. I was very self-motivated, had done things on my own my entire life.

My marriage lasted four years, but in reality only the first year was any good. I became depressed and started overeating, developing an obsessive eating disorder. And in a pattern familiar to psychologists, I then compensated for my weight gain by running even more. The abused became the abuser. I beat up my body with exercise, training seven hours a day. At my worst point, my weight fluctuated from 265 pounds to 155 pounds. I was always either too heavy or too thin for my 6'2" frame. This cycle went on for years. My running, which was once a form of release and pleasure, became a mask for my pain. I was out of control, aimlessly searching for wholeness, happiness, and peace, but my attempt to fulfill this desire became my addiction. I was seeking a mood change and instead of turning to drugs or alcohol, I chose the path of running and eating.

I believe most people, myself included, have a deep intention within themselves to feel happy and to find peace of mind and soul. The determined ones attain it through lifelong, diligent, internal work. Any form of addiction is an attempt to control these uncontrollable feelings, and for me, this search took me through years of patterned cycles, always repeating the quest and the foreshadowed failed attempts. Finally, the wheel just stopped. I got so depressed I couldn't move, just wanted to eat. I stopped all training and running for two months and put on twenty pounds. When I got totally disgusted with myself, the wheel kicked in again and I resumed running, the familiar and comfortable patterns falling into place once again.

Eventually, I wanted out of the patterns, wanted to feel balanced and whole. I focused on my long runs, using them as a form of therapy to concentrate on what would make me happy, what would break the destructive cycle. I imagined being a writer or a teacher, fantasized about being a speaker and using my hurt to help others. I visualized about having it out with my family once and for all, imagined them apologizing and embracing me, finally accepting me and stopping the madness. Unfortunately, the family fantasy never happened.

I also focused on the beauty surrounding me, the clear white sand, the soft feel of the ocean breeze, the trees as they changed their canopy from green to gold. It helped me come to grips with my past and gave me a strong incentive to get well and stay healthy. I loved running and I wanted it to stay with me in its pure form, not the addictive, obsessive side of it.

When I was twenty-nine, I began to see the glimmer of positive change, the effects of years of counseling and dreaming of making a difference. I went out for my usual long run, planning to do about twelve miles, but I was having such a good time, I kept going, and going, and going. I was running aimlessly, with no direction or thought besides that I was having fun. Most of the time I wasn't even conscious that I was running. I had entered an altered state where I floated above the road, way out and beyond. It was kind of freaky, but so effortless. Something else took over and empowered me. When I finally stopped, I had covered thirty-three miles. I felt so powerful—tired, but so powerful. I went beyond where I ever thought I could go.

After the high of the thirty-three-mile run, I now needed to run an official marathon to validate the fact that I could do it. I didn't want a large, city marathon, so I chose a local one in East Lyme, Connecticut, for the scenic natural setting of the course and small entry numbers. I made a conscious effort to train for six months and be prepared. I had to fight off some of those obsessive behavior characteristics, but I was determined to use this marathon as an emblem of turning my life around. Every other weekend I did twenty miles.

As much as I am a loner, I was looking forward to running with others, feeling a sense of being part of a family. One of the appealing aspects of a marathon is that you are in a pack, but yet you're alone. I don't have to depend on anyone else, but yet I can interact with others if I choose.

My goal was to have fun. From the start, I noticed many differences between my thirty-three-mile solo experience and the marathon. The most noticeable was the water stops, which was a welcome relief to finding my own sources. I also enjoyed the structure of having a route already mapped out and not having to worry about where I was going, what path I'd take next. I also loved the sense of being part of a group.

Despite all my training, I started to hurt at twenty-two miles. My quads and calves were killing me. I think I was running harder than I normally did; a race will do that to you. I slowed down and ran through the pain, concentrating on my breathing. I tried to focus off the pain. I reached out and searched deep down inside and said, "God, carry me through this." That calmed me and I could feel the pain subside. Miles twenty-two to twenty-four were the most painful, so I stopped briefly to walk and stretch. That wasn't enough to recharge the body so I visualized plugging my spirit into the sun, letting the radiant warmth infuse my senses and felt a renewed sense of energy. I could finally resume my running pace.

At twenty-four miles, I knew the end was near and it made the journey easier. Crossing the finish line, I was elated. It felt good to be home and I embraced the prospect that the furies of my past were now far behind me.

My goal for the marathon was to finish and have fun, and I succeeded on both counts. My time was 3:15, placing forty-seventh out of two hundred. I had some friends there cheering for me and we all celebrated afterward.

I was now an official marathoner. For me, that was an internal validation of all my work. I needed to prove to myself that I had the confidence to do it. It also helped me in my food addictions, making me more conscious of food intake, making it work for me instead of against me. Running also helps me keep a positive outlook in my life.

I don't plan on running another, don't need to validate it again. I keep my running at a healthy distance, not obsessing, not overtraining. It's become very holistic to where I am now in my life. There was only one time I ran twenty miles, right after my vasectomy. I had done some soul searching and decided I didn't want to have children of my own. Instead, I have chosen to work with children and teach them to believe that each and every one of them are special, talented, wonderful beings. After the operation, I needed reassurance that everything was still intact, that I was strong and virile.

Presently, I am working on becoming a Tai Chi Forms Champion, which takes intense focus. I have to participate in the competitive arenas, and this year placed among the top ten at the National Championships.

Along with tai chi, running has become an expression of my emotions. They have both contributed to a cleansing of all the confusion and mental roadblocks I've endured. It saved my life and gave me back my sanity. I read somewhere that we should strive to turn our scars into stars and look toward the universe to reflect back the life we intend. By clarifying our intentions, we take one giant step in reaching them. Running does that for me.

One of my favorite things to do is run in a snowstorm. The snow makes the world seem virginal, fresh, and clean. All paths are wiped away by the wind and falling flakes. There usually aren't any cars on the roads and it's so silent I feel as if I am connected to everything in existence. It makes me feel like an old soul, like I've been here before. Still, I know there is so much more I need to learn about myself and my place in the world.

My heart and soul have suffered at the hands of the people I should have trusted the most, which has led me to be very careful with others that I meet. However, I do believe that hearts can mend, and the pain of suffering can be minimized by filling the heart instead with dreams and turning those dreams into a reality. I am totally committed to my dreams and I truly believe running has brought me a far greater distance in terms of my healing than I would have attained without it. My journey continues.

COOL CONTROLLED GRACE

GRETE WAITZ
RESIDENCE: OSLO, NORWAY
OCCUPATION: WOMEN'S SPORTS CONSULTANT
FIRST MARATHON: 1978 NEW YORK CITY MARATHON
D.O.B.: 10-1-53
AGE AT FIRST MARATHON: 25

The blonde with the pigtails stood at the front of the pack in the 1978 New York City Marathon, not knowing what to expect. She had never run a distance longer than twelve miles, but felt confident. This was to be her last race before retirement. She not only won her first marathon, but set a world record as well. Grete Waitz may have taken New York City completely by surprise, but to those who knew of her incredible track accomplishments, her feat wasn't so shocking. By the seventies, Waitz was already a name to be reckoned with on the international track and field circuit. In 1975, she ranked first in the world at 1500 and 3000 meters, and earned her first of five world cross-country titles in 1978. She set world records in the five-mile, 10K, 15K, 20K, and ten-mile events. But it was the New York City Marathon that made her a household name in the United States; she won it an unprecedented nine times, and beat her own '78 world record with another world record time of 2:25:42, in 1980. Nowadays she can be seen not at the starting line of races, but on the podium promoting the event.

THE FIRST TIME I CALLED THE NEW YORK ROAD RUNNERS Club to get an invitation to the 1978 marathon, I was turned down. I had never run a marathon before and when they asked for my records, I gave them my track and field accomplishments, but it was all in short-distance events. I wasn't terribly disappointed, but I was looking forward to a holiday in

New York with my husband. We couldn't afford the expense of such a trip and some of my Norwegian teammates had made the suggestion to contact the club. I was getting ready to retire from my ten-year track career and thought this would be a fun way to go out. After all the years of teaching full time, training twice a day, and racing almost every weekend, I was tired. The New York City Marathon was going to be my last race, but it didn't seem as if it was going to happen.

Then I received an unexpected call from Fred Lebow, the New York Road Runners Club president and race director, asking if I still wanted to come. Fred was familiar with my European records and knew that I was fast. Although he never thought I would complete the race, he needed a "rabbit," someone who would go out strong and set a fast pace for the elite women. With that as his only premise for inviting me, Jack and I found ourselves on a flight to New York City.

For us, it was a second honeymoon. I didn't think about the marathon, had no idea how to prepare for one. I thought my longest run of twelve miles would get me through. The night before the race, we treated ourselves to a nice restaurant complete with a four-course meal of shrimp cocktail, filet mignon, baked potato, red wine, and ice cream. The next morning, along with thirteen thousand other runners, I stood at the front of the line, looked around, and didn't know a soul. At the start, I went out fast and continued that pace for quite a while. In fact, I was having such a good time, I increased my speed. I was getting too comfortable and after all, this was a race.

By mile nineteen, though, I stopped feeling so great. I knew my body had reached unknown territory, never having run so far. My biggest problem was not being able to convert the miles to meters, my measurement system. And since I didn't speak English that well, I was too embarrassed to ask where the heck I was.

My quads were beginning to cramp so I decided to try and drink water, but I had never experienced this quick form of drinking before and kept spilling the water all over myself. It is definitely an acquired skill, something to be practiced beforehand.

I continued running strong, but having no idea what mile I was on or where this place called Central Park was, I began to get annoyed and frustrated. Every time I saw a patch of trees, I thought, "Oh, this must be Central Park," but no. To keep motivated, I started swearing at my husband for getting me into this mess in the first place. I started sucking on oranges for nourishment, since I had given up trying to drink anything. This was definitely harder than any track course I had run. I knew I was out of my league and hadn't trained properly. Finally, exhausted and hurting, I crossed the finish line. Immediately, I was swarmed by the media, pushing microphones and cameras in my face. I didn't understand what they were saying and tried to run away from them. All I wanted to do was find Jack and go home. I didn't like this marathon racing.

The rest is history. I had no idea that day that I had set a course and world record. In fact, I had registered so late that my entry number, 1173, wasn't listed in the prerace entries. No one knew who the blonde girl in pigtails was. To be suddenly a hero on a world basis was hard for me to understand. I was a runner. That was my job. I was uncomfortable with all the fuss Americans made over my victory. God gave me a gift and I had used it wisely since I was a little girl. By the time I was twelve, I had participated in handball, gymnastics, and track. I liked all sports, but running became my focus. My two older brothers set a wonderful example for me and since we were always in friendly sibling competition with one another and I tended to follow their training habits, other girls found me tough to beat. That's probably one of the reasons I made the 1972 Olympic team at eighteen years old. I didn't expect to set any records back then, just appreciated being there and viewed it as a learning experience. Actually it was lots of fun. I received free clothes, there was very little pressure, and it was like being at camp for three weeks with my best friends. When I returned to the Olympics in 1976, it was a different ball game. I now knew what to expect and, more seriously, knew what was expected of me. The 1984 Olympics was a highlight in my career as it was the first time women were allowed to compete in the marathon event and I brought home a silver medal for Norway.

I always took my training very seriously, getting up at five in the morning for my first workout of the day. Then it was off to my teaching job and at the end of the day, back home for my evening run. I don't like to cook and spend as little time in the kitchen as possible, so I didn't have to worry about some of the household responsibilities. Jack has always been very supportive of my running career.

I was probably the first female athlete to realize the benefits of twice-a-day training. I am a firm believer that track training is crucial to any running program. It's where you develop the speed. Distance makes you stronger, not faster. If the training isn't tough enough, it won't work. I prefer to train in the dark, cold winter months when it takes a stern attitude to get of bed before dawn and head out the door to below-freezing weather conditions. Anyone can run on a nice, warm, brisk day. That's fun, but there's no sense of sacrifice, no great accomplishment. It takes strength, courage, commitment, and many days and nights of sacrifice to win.

Looking back on my career, and thinking that I almost retired in 1978 except for that infamous New York City Marathon, I am glad I got a shot at a second distance-running career. That's where women's focus seems to be these days. I finally did retire in 1990 but only to start my third life's career, as a spokesperson for women's sports. There is so much that still needs to be learned about women in sports and, more important, getting the right information out to women. When I was running back in the seventies, and was about twenty-three years old, my period stopped. When I went to the doctor, he wasn't concerned, said don't worry, it will come back. Now we know that amenorrhea (not menstruating) is a serious condition. There are other things that affect women we are just learning about. It is very important to keep this flow of new information circulating to running clubs and women's groups. Entry numbers are on the rise in road racing, mostly due to the number of female applicants. Whether walking or running, slow or fast, women are out there competing.

When most people decide to start a running program, they start up too fast and get discouraged. It is a big step from being inactive to starting any form of exercise. I always suggest to walk first. Start at a level that is comfortable and slowly increase from a walk to a jog to a run. The first steps can be very intimidating. However, as long as you don't have any form of physical illness, your goals can be achieved. Novice runners often fail to recognize how much a part of their training is dedicated to mental energy and concentration. Those also have to be incorporated into the overall exercise program.

Two of my most memorable marathons were ones I didn't win. My 1992 run with Fred Lebow, in remission with brain cancer, was very emotional. I didn't think I could run for five hours, but he gave me the strength. It went by so quickly. My other memorable moment was in 1993, when I promised Achilles Marathon runner Zoe Koplowitz, crippled with multiple sclerosis, that I would be there for her at the finish. It took her twenty-four hours to complete the course and when she crossed the finish line at 6:30 A.M. the next morning, I was there. No one had a medal for her, so I rushed back to my hotel to get my husband's medal for her. I don't have half the struggles in life she does. It puts my own life in perspective.

My two brothers and husband have carried on the New York City Marathon tradition for me. One of my brothers has run it fourteen times. Now I enjoy being part of the scene, watching my favorite marathon be a part of running history.

A TWO-FOR-ONE VICTORY

SHAN WORTHINGTON
RESIDENCE: BARTLETT, TENNESSEE
OCCUPATION: DIRECTOR, COMMUNITY PARKS
FIRST MARATHON: 1995 TWIN CITIES MARATHON, MINNEAPOLIS, MN
D.O.B.: 2-18-56
AGE AT FIRST MARATHON: 39

As a child, Shan Worthington was on track to be an entertainer. She spent most of her youth in cities that promoted talent such as Los Angeles, Nashville, and then Memphis. She didn't even realize that sports programs existed, never having the time or the interest to pursue them. College opened up her eyes to another world, one she seemed to enjoy more than performing. Then came what could be considered one of the top ten jobs to get after college, working on a cruise ship for a year, touring the Caribbean. Later in life, completing her first marathon in a finishing time fast enough to qualify for the Boston One Hundredth was an even bigger thrill. A single mom with two young boys, it wasn't easy for Shan to fit in work, raising the boys, and training. When the alarm clock went off at 4:00 A.M., she wondered if she was crazy. But as she contemplates her third marathon, Shan seems to have found a balanced answer to that question. And fulfilling her childhood ambition, she is now a vocalist with a Memphis band and really has something to sing about.

I NEVER RAN AS A KID, NEVER participated in any kind of sport. My parents preferred to steer me in the direction of theater and drama instead of athletics, so I spent my spare time singing in the church, seeing plays, anything that had to do with cultural awareness. Even my two younger brothers were guided in that direction. I did jump hurdles in junior high school, because all my friends were doing it, but it was a short-lived stint. I knew I was fast, I always beat the boys during any type of running game, it just didn't register with me that running was something in and of itself.

When I got to the University of Tennessee in Knoxville, though, my life started to take a different direction. I took courses in exercise, weight management, nutrition, all these new areas that I found fun and exciting. I joined a sorority and played on all the intramural teams, such as water polo, football, softball; it was so much fun for me to discover these new things in life. I remember doing a one-mile race and ran it so fast I threw up afterward. I loved being good at sports, but couldn't see participating in them past those fun college days. There didn't seem to be a career in it, so I left it all behind, except for the running. I kept that up on an occasional basis.

After college, I took a job with a cruise ship line as a waitress and got to see the Caribbean. That job was such a blast, I loved it. I call it my "Julie of the Love Boat" job. I made lots of money, played, saw the islands, and had the time of my life. I also grew up on the job, seeing things I had never seen in Memphis. I was somewhat sheltered growing up and this job blew the lid off what the world had to offer. I kept up my running whenever I could on the islands, mostly as weight control because cruise ships are famous for making you fat.

Back to reality in Memphis, I took a job with the city parks and recreation department. I found a coworker who was a recreational runner like myself, and eventually he talked me into our first 5K race. I didn't think we'd finish, but we did. In fact, I was the faster runner. We had a lot of laughs at that race. Running was something I enjoyed. I wasn't consistent, didn't really train, just had fun.

I got married around that time, but my husband wasn't crazy about my running. I had to sneak it. He was the jealous type and didn't like other guys looking at my legs. We stayed married for thirteen years, and ended up divorced. He began to abuse the bottle and things got rough. We had three kids and I realized there was nothing I could do to help him since he didn't want to help himself and it was time to leave.

About the same time I was going through my divorce, to complicate my life even more, my boss was under suspicion from the city government for stealing funds. I knew he was guilty, but wanted to stay out of the mess due to my own troubles at home. Eventually, I had to blow the whistle on him as he started firing everyone. Then, mysteriously, my beautiful faithful Siberian husky was poisoned. I loved that dog. She was my running mate. When I'd go to the closet and get out my running shoes, she'd go crazy with excitement. If there ever was a time I couldn't take her with me, I would have to hide my shoes and put them on after I left the house. He not only killed her, he made sure she had a horrible death. He soaked a dog biscuit in antifreeze and threw it in our backyard. Her death darn near killed me. For quite a while, I couldn't function.

With my divorce, going through the mess with my ex-boss and losing my dog, I really needed an outlet, so I started increasing my miles and running longer and harder. At least I didn't have to sneak it anymore, but I did have to juggle my runs in between caring for my three children. I usually fit my running in at lunchtime, when the kids were in school. That was a big benefit to working close by home. Running got me through that horrible time in my life.

I joined the Memphis Runners Track Club and entered more races. I did pretty well and started wining my age division. I met a running buddy, Terry, who also had a crazy schedule, and one day during our morning run, he said, "Let's run a marathon." I replied, "No way," but he managed to talk me into it, promising to coach me, although I did question how the heck he was going to coach me since he'd never run a marathon either. One thing lead to another, and before I knew it, we settled on the 1995 Twin Cities Marathon because we heard it was scenic, it was in the fall so we could train in the summer, and most important, it was a flat course. The president of our running club, Paul Ireland, gave us Jeff Galloway's running book and a few tips of his own. We had twelve weeks to prepare, and trained religiously. The first thing I did was call my parents to make sure they could watch the kids while I was gone. Everyone I knew was very supportive, although they did think I was crazy. Terry and I set aside Tuesday evenings and Saturday mornings for long runs. I hired a baby sitter for those two times and the rest of the training was done at five in the morning, while the kids slept. By this time my oldest was thirteen, so I felt comfortable leaving him in charge for a short time.

During our training, we did everything Jeff Galloway said to do. We were fanatical about our mileage, speed workouts, you name it, if Jeff said do it, we did it. In fact, I wanted to train harder, but Terry held me back. By this time, more members of the running club joined us on our marathon quest, including Paul, whom we call Spunky. We all became very fast, very close friends. Running creates such a bond among people. It was very supportive and wonderful. We'd talk about everything under the sun.

During one training session, an ultrarunner came to join us and brought along a power drink for us to try. Well, unknown to us and him, he mixed it incorrectly. I took a drink of it before we headed out for a seventeen-miler, and took another hefty drink at twelve miles. A few minutes later, I thought I'd die. That drink gave me the worse case of stomach cramps I'd ever had. I needed a rest room badly, but there wasn't a place in site. Finally, I went up to a house, knocked on the door and asked if I could borrow their bathroom. But they said both of their bathrooms were occupied, so I was back on the street, dying. Somehow, I made it to a gas station.

The longest scheduled run was a twenty-miler, but I did one twenty-four-miler on my own. I had to see if I could go past twenty. Along the way of my marathon training, I kept hearing talk of the Boston One Hundredth scheduled for the following year. I knew that was going to be the race of the century, and I wanted to be a part of it. I started to train at a pace that would qualify me for Boston. Everyone told me I was crazy, that I should just concentrate on finishing my first marathon and then see if I wanted to try and qualify for Boston. Well, I figured, why not kill two birds with one stone? Why shouldn't I try to qualify with my first marathon? Why shouldn't I shoot for the stars? My friends weren't trying to talk me out it, they just didn't want me getting my expectations up and then be disappointed. Well heck, the only way I would be disappointed in myself was if I didn't try!

Philip, one of the runners in our group, was a strong marathoner and said he'd pace me at 8:30 miles, which should guarantee my required qualifying time of 3:50. So with that, we headed to Twin Cities. I was so nervous. A whole bunch of us rented a movie in our hotel room and ate bagels and apples all night. They tried to calm me down, but it didn't work. I did feel certain that I would finish the marathon, even if I had to crawl on my hands and knees, but I wasn't so sure of finishing in 3:50. I can hold a 6:40 pace or better for a 10K, but I never pushed beyond that. I worried about going out too fast, and I did.

Psychologically, I always like to start up at the very front of the race because I feel it's less distance I have to travel. The Twin Cities Marathon has a wonderful start. There were balloons, incredible crowds screaming and cheering and giving us high-fives as we past, and as I got caught up in the hysteria, I lost my focus. Philip kept yelling at me to stay focused and concentrate on my pace, but I was having too much fun. Philip finally said, "Well you might as well have fun now because you're going to die later."

My momentum kept up for the first thirteen miles and we were right on target with my time. Then at nineteen miles, I had a terrible drop in energy and just fell apart. Philip was right, it wasn't fun anymore and I was dying out there. He tried to encourage me but I was feeling really sick. At mile twenty, someone in the crowd was handing out Tootsie Rolls and Philip brought me one. I was disgusted at the sight of it and said, "There is no way I am putting a stinkin' Tootsie Roll in my mouth." At twenty-two miles, I saw a crowd of people sitting on a hilltop drinking Bud Light and laughing it up. I said, "Now, those people are having a heck of a lot of more fun than we are. Let's go join them."

Philip tried to get me mentally back on track as we had four more miles to go. I thought I'd never make it, couldn't take one more step much less four miles. Philip kept telling me I could still make my time if I just kept moving, just kept focused. I remember thinking this was the hardest thing I had ever tried to do, worse than childbirth. Labor contractions were easier than taking that next step, I thought about how I made it through my three deliveries, one push at a time. So, I now thought, well, take this marathon one step at a time. I started equating everything to childbirth and came to the conclusion that if childbirth was as hard as running a marathon, I wouldn't have three kids!

I kept shuffling along and finally at twenty-three miles I got a burst of sudden energy, then died again the next mile. Philip kept saying, "Pick it up, pick it up." By this time, I just wanted him and his watch to go away. I didn't think I'd make it and didn't really care anymore. I was counting the last two miles until this hell was over, but I never did see the twenty-five mile marker. We had been running over ten minutes from the last marker, and Philip finally said if we didn't get to twenty-five soon, I'd miss my qualifier. Then I heard someone yell, "It's all downhill from here." That perked me up a bit until we rounded a corner immediately after and faced a hill, not going down, but going up. I wanted to go back in the crowd and strangle that person who had filled my head with hopes, only to be disappointed. Just as I thought I'd never make it up the hill, and had missed my time, we turned another corner and right in front of us was the finish line. We were shocked. Philip yelled, "Go for it. You can make Boston if you run." Suddenly, my feet took flight and I was airborne, heading for the finish. The crowds were screaming, the balloons were floating over my head, and somewhere I heard the announcer saying, "Some of these finishers will be on their way to Boston." It was exhilarating. I was so excited, I jumped in the air and yelled, "Yes!" and then couldn't walk afterward. I hobbled from the finish line like an old lady. To make my day even better, I found out I finished in 3:48. I had two minutes to spare.

I just about had to be carried over to the blocks where they were taking pictures of the finishers. It was a dream come true. The marathon was probably the hardest goal, physically, I ever set for myself. And it's a gamble on top of everything else. Putting your body through that type of torture, well, you just don't know how it will ultimately perform. But I had done my homework, followed all the training and nutrition guides, and felt my body was well prepared for the journey. My efforts paid off, and I was rewarded.

I felt God smiled on me that day. All the stress of the last few years lifted off my shoulders like a cloud passing by. The sky was now going to be blue forever. I called my children right away and they were real happy for me. When I got back home, they had made signs saying, YOU'RE THE GREATEST AND THE FASTEST, MOM. My friends at work gave me a party with flowers on my desk, I was interviewed by the local paper, who did a major article on how I managed as a single mom to train and still be with my kids. The headline read, BARTLETT MOM RUNS TO MARATHON VICTORY. Heck, I was a celebrity.

I started training for Boston the next month. I got up at four in the morning in order to do the long runs and stay on schedule with everything else in my life. There were days I fell asleep at my desk at work.

I did have to train in the winter, which for Memphis isn't too bad, but that winter, we got hit bad. It was freezing. On the day I had put aside to do a seventeen-miler, it was thirty below with wind chill. The news stations were warning people to stay inside, but I bundled up and did my seventeen miles. When I finished, I had icicles on my eyelashes. It was a stupid thing to do, but it was the only day I could do it. It couldn't be put aside for another time.

Being part of the Boston Hundredth was very exciting and not half the stress of my first marathon. I just wanted to enjoy Boston, I didn't care what my time was. I finished in 3:52, four minutes slower than Twin Cities. I now have a theory about running for speed: The faster you go, the longer it takes. After I finished Boston, I took a two-hour tub, drank champagne with my brother, and we danced till two in the morning.

I am not the same person I was when I started to run. I now know I have the stamina and the perseverance to do whatever I have to in life. It gave me the relief I needed to know that my life would turn out fine. When I run, I block out the world and everything I am feeling is centered in that moment in time. It's a different level of consciousness, I can become anything I want to be, I become one with myself. It made me a stronger person. I believe in me now and have a new formula for life: Be fit, have a sense of humor, love what you're doing and who you do it with.

50 AND D.C

SANDY ZANCHI
RESIDENCE: LOUISVILLE, KENTUCKY
OCCUPATION: CASE MANAGEMENT REPRESENTATIVE,
BLUECROSS BLUESHIELD
FIRST MARATHON: 1994 COLUMBUS MARATHON
D.O.B.: 1-8-51
AGE AT FIRST MARATHON: 43

Sandy was a self-proclaimed couch potato through the first forty years of her life. Although there was her obsession with softball, four nights a week, Sandy would never describe herself as an athlete. She and her husband, both heavy smokers, finally decided to lose some weight. The first few weeks, her husband, Dale, had to pull her kicking and screaming out the door. Eventually, she started to enjoy it, especially when she noticed her dress size moving down from a fifteen to a seven. Completing her first marathon three years later was a thrill, but she said, "Never again." Finishing her second marathon, she said, "Never again." Finishing her third, fourth, and fifth marathons she still said, "Never again." So after her fifteenth marathon in three years, she had to change her recurring statement to, "I think I'll slow down for awhile." Sandy and Dale don't sit on the couch anymore. There isn't time since they started their new goal of running a marathon in all fifty states, plus Washington, D.C.

I NEVER RAN. I GREW UP IN KENTUCKY with four siblings but sports wasn't a big thing in our family. I did play volleyball and softball in high school, but it wasn't a big deal. I attended a vocational high school for business, since college was not going to be in my future. Financially, my parents couldn't afford to put all of us through college and said if any of us went, it would be our brother. Ironically, he didn't go either.

I did get hooked on softball. That became an obsession with me. I do tend to be compulsive about things I like, as you'll see later on. I got married right out of high school, found a job, and settled down to raising our two boys. Life went on very uneventful in the Zanchi household. Dale and I were long-time smokers and as we comfortably settled into midlife, so did our waistlines. As I approached forty, I decided to lose some weight and stop smoking, but it was really hard to get off that couch. In fact, Dale had to drag me out the door. I didn't want to run; maybe take a short walk, but run? No way.

Dale had already started a walking program during his lunch at work, so he was already getting fit. He was becoming a convert and wanted me to feel his enthusiasm. I didn't. The first few nights I could barely walk a few telephone poles. Ever-so-slowly, I built up some endurance and managed to run a few poles, walk a few poles until I could get a pace going and actually run two miles. Now that I knew there was no going back, since Dale was committed to keeping me fit, I decided to buy the most expensive pair of running shoes I could find and splurged seventeen dollars at the local Kmart.

Four months later we entered our first 5K race to see how well we were doing. Dale thought it would spark some interest for me, as I was still complaining about this new health kick he had me on. Well, I still had to walk part of the way, and I wasn't having fun, but I will admit there was a strong sense of accomplishment when I finished. I also noticed how friendly all the people were and what a great time they seemed to be having. Maybe there was something to this running thing after all. To further spark my interest, my younger son, Danny, participated on the track team at his high school, making first string on a very competitive team. He encouraged me with my running and later on would enter races with us. I began to like running, especially in the winter months when the weather is cool and crisp.

Our neighbor across the street noticed our running and joined us. Now we had our own little group, but she and Dale were faster and I was always lagging behind them. That bothered me. Another friend of mine, Mike, knew about training and took me to the local track for speed work. Now that was tough. Can't say I enjoyed it, but it did make me faster and eventually I caught up to Dale. Then, with my new speedy form, I started winning my age division at the 5Ks. That was wonderful. I actually started to look forward to my birthdays so I could be in another age division.

Louisville is the home of the Kentucky Derby, and around Derby time, the last Saturday in April, everyone goes Derby crazy. There's a Triple Crown Run, which is a series of three races: a 10K, 15K, and half marathon. This is a big deal in the running community and everyone starts training in the winter at Iroquois Park, where the races start. So, Dale and I figured, why not enter? We'd been running four months now, so we thought we could tackle a half marathon. As were training in Iroquois Park, we met another runner named Eugene. He starts talking to us about his running club, the Iroquois Hill Runners, and convinces us to join. That was the best thing we ever did. The club of three hundred members meets every Saturday morning in Iroquois Park to train and then have breakfast. Being novice runners, Dale and I were thrilled to meet so many runners who were so knowledgeable about our newfound sport. They taught us everything we ever needed or wanted to know abut running. There was always someone to run with, whether you wanted to go fast, slow, or just keep a steady pace. I can't say enough about the benefits of joining such a club. It changed our entire lives.

We completed the Triple Crown, which was a huge accomplishment. Eugene ran it with us and acted as our personal coach. Afterward, he started talking to us about a marathon and we said, "Never will we run a marathon. I can't imagine having to run that half-marathon distance twice." But Eugene was relentless. He had a group of runners from the club already signed up for the 1994 Columbus Marathon and kept saying, "There's room in the van." This was spring of 1993 and the idea of a marathon was nonexistent in my mind. But every Saturday morning in the park, Eugene would say, "There's still room in the van."

One Saturday morning, he took me on a distance run, but wouldn't tell me exactly how long. We ran together and had a wonderful time. I never felt tired, never thought about how far I was going. I knew it was longer than thirteen miles, but I didn't even care. Finally, Eugene stopped; we had gone seventeen miles, and I was thrilled. I wanted to continue, but Eugene, always the coach, insisted I stop because he didn't want me to injure myself. He just wanted to plant the seeds in my mind that I could, in fact, complete a marathon.

His scheme worked and the next time he said, "There's still room in the van," I put my name on that seat. I had three years of running under my belt, lots of local races, a half marathon, I was injury-free, so I thought, "Why not? I can do this." I had come along way from that first day in the park when I met Eugene and didn't even know what a marathon was. I was so excited about my new obsession, my husband couldn't shut me up, so he decided to run it also!

Eugene gave me a copy of Jeff Galloway's training book and we followed it religiously. I had so much fun training for that marathon. I still believe that training for one is more fun than actually running it. I made new friends and learned so much about the art of running. Eugene, our president, has run about 150 marathons. Another member ran his first marathon at age seventy and I have trouble keeping up with him. There were always great conversations, lots of laughs, sharing, and bonding. There was a wealth of knowledge and experience that I gladly tapped into. Aches and pains? Someone there has had it, and knows how to treat. Need a doctor? Someone will know a specialist for anything.

Running helped me in all aspects of my life. I was now truly goal oriented, I could focus better, and it helped get me through the hair-raising years of teenage boys. There were many days I just needed to get out of the house and calm down. And it was great having Dale train with me. It was a comfort having him share the same aches and pains, not asking me where dinner was after I'd come in from a long run, always supportive and by my side. But the reaction from other family members wasn't so supportive. My mother just about died. She was horrified. "It's not feminine to sweat. You're getting too skinny. There's nasty snot dripping from your nose. How can your husband let you run around in those skimpy halter tops?" If I heard it once, I heard it a thousand times. On the other hand, my dad was great. I'll never forget coming close to the finish line at that Derby Triple Crown half marathon, and suddenly hearing my name. I looked up and saw my dad, yelling out to me, cheering me as he ran along the sidewalk, following me. To this day, it makes me tear up to think of him out there for me. Mom was there also, but not cheering. That's not ladylike.

Eventually, I won everyone over and the support followed. I remember the Mother's Day when my oldest son bought me a halter top and running shorts. It was a lot of money for him to spend as he was working his way through college at the time and I admonished him. He replied, "Mom, you're worth it. I am so proud of you for staying in shape and taking care of yourself." He brought me to tears.

The day before the marathon, we hopped in that van Eugene kept talking about and drove four hours to Columbus, Ohio. We were warned not to start out too fast, but I couldn't help it. The adrenaline just carried me. The first thirteen miles I ran with Dale and we talked the entire time, but eventually he slowed down, but I was still charged up so took off. Right about thirteen miles, the course loops through downtown Columbus and the crowds were unbelievable. It was such a boost. I fed off the crowd's energy and felt as if they were cheering just for me. From then on, I ran by myself, picking up people along the way and having fun. Eugene ran with me for a while, but eventually passed me. Up through twenty miles, I was pain-free and having the time of my life. Then I fell apart. That's when I knew I had indeed started too fast. The aches and pains finally kicked in and haunted me the rest of the way.

The remaining six miles was hell. I was tired, it hurt, my pace kept getting slower and slower. It was a struggle to keep going. I concentrated on how many miles were left, and broke it down into one 10K. I knew I could run that. Now I actually break that down even farther, into two 5Ks. Mentally, that works better for me.

I never thought of quitting, never walked. In the last mile, I actually picked up my pace and flew across the finish. The crowds were amazing. There's nothing better in the whole world than crossing that finish line It's the best feeling in the world. Nothing hurts more, but is so rewarding at the same time.

When I finished, they wrapped me in one of those silver blankets, and I asked one of the volunteers how to get back to my hotel. I almost started to cry when he told me I had to walk half a mile. Heck, I couldn't even lift my leg to cross the curb, no less walk another half mile. The volunteer just laughed at me, saying, "Honey, you just ran 26.2 miles. Surely you can walk half a mile!"

On the four-hour drive home, Eugene told me I could probably qualify for Boston if I trained just a little harder. I was tempted to say, "Never again," but held my tongue. The next day back home, Dale and I could hardly walk. In fact, our washer and dryer are in the basement of the house and we got into some pretty strong arguments about who was going to do the laundry.

Well, the following year, thanks to Eugene's constant nagging, I was back at Columbus running the same marathon and did, in fact, qualify for the Boston One Hundred, in 1996. That was a thrilling experience and I am so thankful Eugene kept at me to do it. Again, I thought I was ready to quit my marathons and just go back to a nice, quiet run in the park.

After Boston, which was my third marathon in three years, I said, "That's it for a while." But Eugene had other plans. He started to tell us about a club called 50 and D.C. and how much fun it is to travel around the states running marathons. It takes twenty states to get into the club and then you get the first T-shirt, which says, 50 AND D.C. Then, when you complete all the states plus Marine Corps in D.C., you get a shirt that says the same thing, plus FINISHER. I have to admit, it did sound like fun, so we decided to join Eugene and his gang of other crazies in this adventure. He made it sound so sane. According to him, Kentucky is centrally located so we can drive to most of the marathons on the East Coast and in southern states. There's always at least four to six of us traveling together so we share expenses. For the states out West, we turn the traveling time into a vacation and hit two or three in a row. For instance, next year Dale and I will fly to Washington state, do that marathon, and then drive to Idaho since that marathon is a week later. When we finally do Hawaii, we'll take a nice long vacation and stay a while. So far, we've completed fifteen states and with two months left in the year, we're scheduled for four more, Nebraska, Oklahoma, West Virginia, and Florida. We started out only planning one a month, but sometimes the schedule works out so that we'll find another one that's just too convenient to pass up. And if there's an airline fare war going on, we'll take advantage of that and squeeze some more into the schedule.

Two weeks ago we drove sixteen hours to South Dakota and back for a marathon. That was a special marathon, as it was so beautiful but cold! Coming from Kentucky, I knew it would be somewhat colder out there, so I packed a long-sleeved T-shirt along with my standard halter top and shorts. The morning of the race, we took the marathon bus to the top of the mountain for the start, and I thought I would die. It was twenty-two degrees with seventy-five-mile-an-hour wind gusts. My long-sleeved shirt didn't help do much to keep me warm. As I got off the bus, the wind nearly knocked me over. Somehow, though, I ran my best time out there, 3:50. The only problem with driving such long distances is cramping up in the car on the way home.

I have managed to stay injury-free throughout all this and credit that to my weight training and aerobics classes. The best part of running marathons every week is that I don't have to train. I am always ready for the next one.

This may seem like a crazy thing to do, but I'm at a point in my life where the kids are twenty-four and eighteen years, old enough to take care of themselves, and Dale takes courses three nights out of the week, so it keeps me busy and off the couch. I know that seems extreme and this pace probably isn't for everyone, but we love it and are having the time of our lives. This weekend, we get our first official T-shirt and I can't wait to wear it. The shirts spark a lot of conversation at races. The next time you're at a race and see one, remember to say "Hey!"

Running has been wonderful for me. It got me to stop smoking, lose weight, and get into a healthy lifestyle. I've always been disciplined, but running has brought that to a higher level. Compulsive is the word, I guess. It is my life, what I do. It's how we socialize with our friends. I wear a gold chain around my neck with the numbers 26.2. That about sums it up. I also have a quote framed on my desk at work, HELL AND BACK: 26.2 MILES. I really don't think I'm doing anything amazing. It's just fun.

ADVICE
FROM
TOP COACHES

JEFF GALLOWAY
1972 UNITED STATES OLYMPIAN;
FORMER AMERICAN RECORD HOLDER IN THE TEN-MILE,
BESTSELLING AUTHOR OF *GALLOWAY'S BOOK ON RUNNING*

I SPENT THE FIRST TWENTY YEARS OF MY RUNNING career trying to run as many miles as I could as fast as I could. Then I spent the next twenty years trying to figure out how to run the least amount of miles needed to finish a marathon. And I've come to the conclusion the second way is much more enjoyable and less prone to injury. The new generation of marathoners are having more fun than I ever did in my first fast twenty years. They fit training into their lives with a healthy balance the runners back in the eighties never experienced. My new training program is based on this premise, which promotes low weekly mileage, no more than three days a week, and stresses walk breaks in the marathon from the very start.

The biggest problem of overtraining is the risk of entering the marathon with fatigued leg muscles. No matter how well you've trained, if you've done too many miles too fast you won't be fresh at the start. Most runners hit the wall at the distance of their longest run, three to four weeks prior to the marathon. You can manipulate this and perhaps avoid the wall altogether by running two to three miles slower than your normal pace and using walk breaks from the beginning. Walk breaks have become the miracle ingredient to running a best-time marathon. For first-timers, I recommend walk three minutes, run one all the way through the marathon. Advanced beginners work their way up to walk two, run two, and veteran marathoners will walk one, run five. We have an over 99 percent success rate with this plan. Even runners attempting to break three hours will use this plan, revised to ten- to fifteen-second walk breaks for every mile from the beginning.

The walk-run plan fits any level of experience and any anticipated time goal. The average improvement among veterans (ten marathons or more) inserting at least a one-minute walk break every mile is thirteen minutes. Basically, the plan forces us to walk before we get the running muscles too fatigued. It also allows the runner to enjoy the experience. It's a kindlier, gentler marathon program.

DON KARDONG
SENIOR WRITER, *RUNNER'S WORLD;*
PRESIDENT, ROAD RUNNERS CLUB OF AMERICA;
1976 OLYMPIC MARATHONER, FOURTH PLACE

THE KEY TO RUNNING A GOOD MARATHON is to not listen to anyone's advice the last week before the race. That's when people tend to do stupid things that disrupt all the input and training of the previous months. They're looking for some magical food or special tip to improve their performance and it's just not going to happen that way. If someone tells you to eat a plate of kelp and drink a quart of eggnog to cut minutes off your time, just say no. Stay cool. I've known more people who say after the marathon, "That the race went well, but gee, I shouldn't have cut my toenails at the last minute like my friend suggested, because they bled the whole time." Or, "Gee, I shouldn't have worn those new shorts that looked so great at the expo last night, because they cut into my thighs for twenty miles."

Also, remember to pace yourself throughout the entire race. Don't go out too fast and think that will give you time in reserve. It won't. Have a pretty good idea at the start of what your per-mile pace should be and hold to it. Hold back the first ten miles. You can't put time in the bank. If you push too hard, you may find out the last five or six miles that the bank is bankrupt.

And one more thing. In these days of hydration frenzy, I'll go against the grain and suggest that you don't drink too much the day of the race. Hydrate the day before; that's when it counts, when you are fueling the reserve tanks. I've started to see people overhydrate the day of the race and then spend more time behind trees or bushes than on the course. You wouldn't fill your car's gas tank over the top, so don't do it to yourself by drinking too many fluids.

BOB GLOVER
DIRECTOR OF RUNNING CLASSES FOR THE N.Y. ROAD RUNNERS CLUB
COACH OF THE GREATER NEW YORK RACING TEAM;
AUTHOR, *THE RUNNER'S HANDBOOK* AND
THE COMPETITIVE RUNNER'S HANDBOOK

THE BEST PIECE OF ADVICE I CAN GIVE is to start training early. Whether you chose a four-month or a six-month schedule, develop a fifteen- to twenty-mile-a-week base for at least a month prior to the marathon build-up.

Do not attempt to do your long runs (eighteen to twenty-two miles) on consecutive weekends or you'll risk injury. Schedule them well in advance so you can fit them in every other weekend. It can be intimidating for beginners to even think of running eighteen miles, so make sure you clear the calendar ahead of time so there aren't any excuses for getting out the door.

Transition runs of eight, ten, twelve, and fifteen miles should be incorporated along the way prior to the long runs. I suggest you get in at least three runs of eighteen to twenty miles before the marathon. You have to get your body and mind used to going the distance.

BILL DELLINGER
TRACK COACH, UNIVERSITY OF OREGON;
1964 OLYMPIC BRONZE MEDALIST, 5,000 METERS;
COACHED STEVE PREFONTAINE, ALBERTO SALAZAR,
MARY SLANEY, JULIE BROWN

MY FIRST PIECE OF ADVICE IS *DON'T DO IT*. For the average person to go out and run 26.2 miles is nuts. I think they're crazy. You can get the same enjoyment by running thirty minutes on the beaches or in the woods, or wherever you can find some peace of mind.

But if you are headstrong to run a marathon, here's what I told Salazar and all the other runners I've coached: Train to run the best 10K you can. At the marathon, run a steady, strong pace for eighteen to twenty miles, then kick in and run the fastest 10K you know how. There's nothing magical about it. In the fifties and sixties, the best marathoners were track runners who weren't good enough to win the medals so they turned to distance instead of speed but kept to their track training.

Also, avoid too many miles per week or you risk injury. The days of the 120-mile weeks are over. It's not necessary, especially if you're not getting paid. And I never advise running the full 26.2 miles during training. If you've trained consistently and with a strong pace, the endurance will be there when you need it. Ask yourself the following question: If you had to run across a hot bed of coals a hundred feet long, would you train for it over and over again? Are you having fun yet?

PETE SQUIRES
TRACK COACH, FAIRLEIGH DICKINSON UNIVERSITY
AND NORTH JERSEY MASTERS RUNNING CLUB;
THREE-TIME WINNER OF THE YONKERS MARATHON; WINNER OF
FINLANDIA MARATHON (1979) AND JERSEY SHORE MARATHON (1977)

DON'T FALL INTO THE MIND-SET OF RUNNING FOR MILES. Instead, run for time. The body has a better memory for the amount of time it's been running than the miles logged. Instead of planning to run ten miles, run for an hour. Then make a mental note of what you did during that hour: Did you run faster than your normal pace? Was it steady? Was it your race pace or a training pace? Don't waste your energy on junk miles just to log in a diary. Concentrate on how you've run the miles. The old saying of quality, not quantity, really comes into focus for marathon training.

Also, be consistent with your schedule. Stick with it and don't make excuses. You'll risk injury if you stack up too many miles because you've missed a few days. It's like taking a prescription: Missing one day doesn't mean taking twice the amount the next day. Remain focused on your goal and it will be easier to maintain the routine.

JAN MERRILL-MORIN
ASST. COACH, UNITED STATES COAST GUARD ACADEMY;
GIRL'S TRACK COACH, WATERFORD HIGH SCHOOL;
FORMER AMERICAN RECORD HOLDER IN 1500, 3000 AND 5000 METERS

I HAVE THREE WORDS OF ADVICE for marathon runners: *recover, recover, recover.* Let your body recover and repair itself at least forty-eight hours (longer if you are getting up there in the age division) before continuing your training routine or it won't derive the benefits of the next training session. It will be too tired and eventually you'll be too fatigued to continue any type of consistency in your routine. The body needs rest before it can work itself again. And I don't recommend the marathon event to anyone under twenty-five years of age. It's too hard on the body, especially when the muscle and bone structure may not be fully developed.

Strengthening and stretching is also important to maintaining peak performance and avoiding injury. Most people don't have time to go to a gym but there are simple exercises you can do at home and get the same results. I use a four pound medicine ball instead of weights and get great results.

FAVORITE SONGS TO RUN BY

Beethoven's Ninth Symphony	Matt Shafner
Hello Dolly Rogers and Hammerstein	Erich Segal
Theme from "Superfly" Curtis Mayfield	Ted Corbitt
"Running On Empty" Jackson Browne	Gail W. Kislevitz
"My Favorite Things" Rogers and Hammerstein	Donna Isaacson
"One Too Many Mornings" and "Positively Fourth Street" Bob Dylan and anything by George Thorogood	John J. Kelley
"Every Breath You Take" The Police	Heidi Butts
Theme from *Chariots of Fire* Vangelis and "When the Saints Come Marching In"	Larry Smith
"It's A Long and Dusty Road" Tom Paxton	Allan Steinfeld
"Born To Run" Springsteen	Allan Steinfeld
"Runaway" Del Shannon	Allan Steinfeld
"Into The Mystic" Van Morrison	Bill Rodgers
"Groovin'" The Rascals and anything by The Rolling Stones	Bill Rodgers

GLOSSARY
OF SOME BASIC RUNNING TERMS

ACHILLES TENDON: The body's most vulnerable spot, named after the mythical Greek hero whose mother dipped him in the river Styx at his birth, making his entire body invulnerable except for the small spot on his heel where she held him. The Achilles tendon connects the lower leg muscle to the heel. An injury to this area is painful and long-lasting, requiring rest. Stretching of the tendon is the most common cure and should be incorporated into a daily stretch routine.

AEROBIC/ANAEROBIC: Aerobic refers to the presence of oxygen available in the blood stream. Aerobic running is done at a comfortable pace, not exceeding the speed or distance set at training. Anaerobic refers to exceeding the speed or limit of training, thereby making one's muscles use more oxygen than the body can provide. After an anaerobic workout, rest is required to build up the oxygen in the blood stream.

AMENORRHEA: The absence of menstrual periods due to extreme low body fat levels. Consequently, estrogen production diminishes. This condition increases the risk of osteoporosis.

CARBOHYDRATES: A source of calories derived from sugars and starches that fuel the muscles and brain. It is recommended that 60 percent of daily calories come from the carbohydrates found in fruits, vegetables, and grains.

CARBOHYDRATE-LOADING: Prior to an endurance event that will last longer than ninety minutes, an increased carbohydrate intake over several days prevents glycogen depletion. The extra fuel, known as "carbo-loading," allows the body to compete at its best.

CROSS-TRAINING: A complete exercise regime that involves all areas of the body, not just isolated areas such as the legs or upper body. It also allows for proper rest of muscle areas that may be getting too much of a work-out. Biking, swimming and weight training are ideal cross-training sports for runners.

DEHYDRATION: Not having enough fluids in the body. Dehydration causes impaired performance, cramps, chills, nausea, severe headaches and in extreme conditions, such as a marathon, can cause hallucination, dizziness and heat stroke.

ELECTROLYTES: Minerals such as potassium and sodium that help the body function normally. During exercise, electrolytes are lost through sweat and must be replaced through foods and fluids.

ENDORPHINS: Natural chemicals inside the brain that are released during exercise and give a pleasurable feeling, sometimes referred to as the runner's high. Endorphin levels in the blood rise during prolonged exercise.

FARTLEK: Swedish for *speed play*. An unstructured training method using repeated short bursts of speed over various distances followed by a slower pace. Some runners use telephone poles or street corners to define their fast/slow targets. Fartlek teaches the body to cope with race-like conditions of discomfort and anxiety.

FAST TWITCH: see muscle fiber

GLYCOGEN: The principle form in which carbohydrates are stored in the muscle and liver. When glycogen stores get too low, it adversely affects how long you can exercise. Depleted muscle glycogen causes athletes to feel fatigued and hit the wall. Depleted liver glycogen causes light-headedness and inability to concentrate. For the first ten minutes of exercise, the body uses muscle glycogen almost exclusively. After that, the body starts a transition to fat as a fuel source.

HAMSTRINGS: The large tendons in the back of the knee and thigh, and colloquially, the associated muscle. Distance runners develop strong hamstrings.

HYDRATION: Maintaining and restoring the proper amounts of fluid in the body. The easiest source of fluids is water, an important nutrient in a well-balanced sports diet. Water transports glucose, oxygen and fats to working muscles and carries away by-products such as lactic acid. Drinking too little water or losing too much through sweat inhibits the body's ability to perform at its maximum potential.

HYPERTHERMIA: A condition when the body temperature rises above normal. This is a problem when running in heat. During exercise, the body usually produces more heat than it can get rid of through sweat. If the runner isn't properly hydrated, the body heat will rise to a dangerous level, causing heatstroke.

HYPOTHERMIA: A condition when the core body temperature drops below normal A potential problem for winter runners who wear insufficient clothing. Also, runners tend to forget to drink fluids in the cold, which can also contribute to hypothermia, as drinking helps to keep the body warm.

ILIOTIBIAL BAND: A thick, strong tendon that extends from the hip across the outside of the knee, inserting into the shinbone below the knee joint. It can become inflamed and irritated if the foot rolls too far to the outside, putting pressure on the band. This can be caused by worn-out shoes, too much mileage, or sudden increase in mileage.

INTERVAL TRAINING: The most stressful form of speed training, more structured than fartlek. Runs are broken up into a series of hard, fast segments and the period between them is purposefully short so that the heart rate does not drop too low before the surge commences. Excellent for building cardiovascular strength.

LACTIC ACID: When muscles are pushed beyond their normal limit, they can no longer process oxygen and fuel efficiently (see "anaerobic"). The result is a buildup of waste products in the muscle, primarily lactic acid. This is "the burn," and the source of muscle soreness after a hard workout or a race.

MASTERS CATEGORY: Most races allow for age-division categories, with the master's division beginning at age forty.

MIXING MILES: Running different distances throughout the week without increasing mileage. Instead of doing 5 miles every day for a total of 35, mix up the distance and run a different pattern without increasing the overall mileage. Or run a fast day, followed by an easy day.

MUSCLE FIBER: Recent studies on muscle fiber composition show a pattern of either a high concentration of FT (fast twitch) or ST (slow twitch) according to sports. In good distance runners, the percentage of ST fibers is high, as opposed to high FT fibers found in sprinters and jumpers. Cyclists, swimmers and middle-distance runners have an equal proportion of ST/FT fibers.

NEGATIVE OR REVERSE SPLITS: Running the second half of the race faster than the first.

PEAKING: A careful scheduling of workouts and races designed to deliver the runner to a particular event in his or her best possible fitness level.

P.R.: Personal record. A term that refers to a runner's best time for a particular distance.

PRONATION: The normal movement of the foot, as runners land on the heel and the foot rolls forward and inward with body weight on the center of the forefoot. Over-pronation is when the foot rolls excessively to the inside, particularly in the forefoot. The knees and the inside of the shins become stressed. Supination is when the foot rolls to the outside of the foot, causing strained ligaments, tendons and bones. Frequent check-ing for unbalanced heel wear on the shoe will disclose any indication of proration or suppination.

QUADRICEPS: The front thigh muscle. Tears and pulls-in the "quads" are common in runners, especially during downhill running when the force through the muscle can equal three times the body weight. A strong quadriceps supports the body's weight and absorbs the shock of landing. It also keeps the knee cap in track.

REPEATS: A training workout that involves running at a very fast pace for a short distance, followed by a relatively long period of time to recov-er by walking or doing a slow jog. The hard run is referred to as the "rep." The recovery time is critical to the rep, so that maximum speed can be attained again, without injury.

RICE: A regimen for inflammation or swelling of muscles consisting of: Rest, Ice, Compress, Elevate.

ROAD RUNNERS CLUB OF AMERICA: A national organization for local running clubs throughout the United States. For information contact: RRCA National Offfce, 1150 S. Washington St., Suite 250, Alexandria, VA 22314.

SINGLET: A sleeveless, loosely worn top, formerly known as the tank top.

SLOW TWITCH: see "Muscle Fiber."

SPEED WORK: Any workout with segments run faster than normal training pace. Speedwork isn't for everyone and can increase the chances for injury if not done correctly. If you aren't running for time, you proba-bly don't need it. If you do try it, work into it slowly. See "Fartlek," "Interval training," and "Repeats" for types of speedwork.

RECOMMENDED BOOKS

Anderson, Bob. *Stretching*. Bolinas, California: Shelter Publications., 1987.

Bakoulis, Gordon. *How to Train for and Run Your Best Marathon*. New York: Fireside, 1993.

Burfoot, Amby, editor. *Runner's World Complete Book of Running: Everything You Need to Know to Run for Fun, Fitness, and Competition*. Emmaus, Pennsylvania: Rodale Press, 1997.

Clark, Nancy. *Nancy Clark's Sports Nutrition Guide*. Champaign, Illinois: Human Kinetics, 1997.

Chodes, John. *Corbitt*. Los Altos, California: TAF News Press, 1974.

Craythorn, Dennis, and Rich Hanna. *The Ultimate Guide to Marathons*. Sacramento, California: Marathon Publishers, Inc., 1996.

Derderian, Tom. *Boston Marathon*. Champaign, Ill.: Human Kinetics, 1994.

Galloway, Jeff. *Galloway's Book On Running*. Bolinas, California: Shelter Publications, 1984.

Glover, Bob, and Jack Shepard. *The Runner's Handbook*. New York, New York: Penguin Books, 1977.

Higdon, Hal. *Marathon: The Ultimate Training and Racing Guide*. Emmaus, Pennsylvania: Rodale Press, 1993.

Jerome, John. *Staying Supple: The Bountiful Pleasures of Stretching*. New York: Breakaway Books, 1998.

Noakes, Tim. *The Lore Of Running*. 3rd edition. Champaign, Illinois: Leisure Press, 1985.

Sheehan, George. *Personal Best*. Emmaus, Pennsylvania: Rodale Press

Traum, Dick, and Mike Celizic. *A Victory For Humanity*. Waco, Texas: WRS Publishers, 1993

Waitz, Grete and Averbuch, Gloria. *On the Run: Fitness for Busy People*. Emmaus, PA: Rodale Press, 1997.

Will-Weber, Mark. *The Quotable Runner: Great Moments of Wisdom, Inspiration, Wrongheadedness, and Humor*. New York: Breakaway Books, 1995.

SOME USEFUL WEB SITES

Runner's World Online: http://www.runnersworld.com
Road Runner's Clubs of America: http://www.rrca.org
Cool Running: http://www.coolrunning.com
Running Network Online: http://www.runningnetwork.com
The Penguin Brigade: http://www.thepenguin.com
Masters Track & Field: http://members.aol.com/trackceo/index.html

LESSONS LEARNED

THOUGH THEY'RE ALL AS DIFFERENT as the people telling them, the pre-
ceeding stories have some glue that holds them together. Certainly, they
all followed the same marathon formula: a strong dose of determination,
unshaken courage, and depths of faith. These are a runner's secret
weapons, amidst an arsenal that also includes daily workouts, a balanced
diet, and rest.

When I asked these runners to cast their memories back to their first
marathon experience, I had no idea the responses would be so epochal.
In most cases, the thought process that led to the idea of a marathon
started out many years before the event. Not many people wake up one
morning with a burning desire to run a marathon.

Certain background factors do help. Coming from a family that promotes exercise and a healthy lifestyle makes it easier to step up to the
task, but is no guarantee. On the other hand, obstacles in life such as
low self-esteem, unyielding grief, weight problems, or a smoking habit,
can be even stronger motivations for taking on the challenge.

Reasons, and results, are effected by sex and age. Women in their forties and fifties who run marathons have attained a level of sports fitness
and achievement they never dreamed possible. These are the women
who grew up without the benefit of high school sports programs. For
many of them, their first run was around the block in an old pair of
sneakers to get a few minutes of private time away from the kids, the
housework, the drudgery. It took them longer to get to the marathon
finish line because they always put something or someone else's needs
before their own.

The younger female runners who had the advantage of sports programs entered the arena with tested skills, a knowledge base of training
techniques and a competitor's mind-set.

For men who came out of high school and college sports, running a
marathon was a way to get back in shape, to find the one-time athlete
who disappeared behind a corporate desk and a sagging waist line.
Whether it's labeled a midlife crisis, the battle of the bulge, or reliving
the glory days, running a marathon is an awesome way to attain the
goal. For those that never were the high school jock, the marathon offers
indisputable proof of entry into the athletic class.

The marathon has no prerequisites; it doesn't matter how tall you are, how strong you are or how fast you are. Everyone is a contender.

The media tells us there is a new running boom with perhaps twice as many runners now as in the first boom back in the 1970s. U.S. Track and Field reports there were 400,000 marathon finishers in 1997, a sixteen-fold increase from the 25,000 finishers in 1976.

The marathon has become accessible to the weekend warrior, the plodder, the increasing population of consistently slow but dedicated runners.

A little-known fact that should soothe the soul and lighten the feet of many first-time marathoners is that legendary runners John A. Kelley, John J. Kelley, and Bill Rodgers all *dropped out* of their first marathon attempts. They may have been born runners, but they weren't born marathoners.

Records will continue to fall and the elite will always test themselves in the marathon, but the average marathon runner—profiled as a thirty-eight-year-old male and a thirty-five-year-old female with respective median finishing times of 3:54 and 4:15—are taking over the field. An estimated seventy percent of all marathon finishers are first-timers.

For some, once is enough. However, for many, it seems they can't get enough of that special feeling crossing the finish line brings to their lives. No matter how painful it gets, a few months, sometimes weeks, down the road when the euphoria is losing its golden glow the need to experience it again comes back with a whole new list of questions. No longer is it, "Will I finish?" but, "How can I improve my time?"

No matter what your foibles or follies are in life, and we all have them, the marathon somehow makes them less pronounced. It's the day you can always look back on when you need a lift.

If you want it, go for it and be true to your dream. The only thing preventing you from running a marathon is your own list of excuses. Don't give up. Anyone can run a marathon. As Grete Waitz is fond of saying, everyone must learn how to walk before they can run. Be patient. It's demanding, it's not always fun, it will punish you but ultimately reward you with a gift of the purest and most enduring form of satisfaction attainable. You can become your own hero.